A PLUME BOOK

HOW TO RETIRE OVERSEAS

KATHLEEN PEDDICORD has written about living and retiring overseas for more than thirty years, first working as publisher and editor of *International Living* before starting her own company, LiveandInvestOverseas.com, a website offering its members advice on living abroad. She has lived in Ireland, Panama, and France, and currently divides her time between Panama City and Paris.

HOW TO RETIRE OVERSEAS

Everything You Need
to Know to Live Well
(for Less) Abroad

(Revised Edition)

Kathleen Peddicord

A Plume Book

PLUME
An imprint of Penguin Random House LLC
375 Hudson Street
New York, New York 10014

Originally published in hardcover by Hudson Street Press, 2010
First Plume printing, April 2011

LIBRARY OF CONGRESS CATALOGING-IN-PUBLICATION DATA

Names: Peddicord, Kathleen, author.
Title: How to retire overseas : everything you need to know to live well (for less)
abroad / Kathleen Peddicord.
Description: 2 Edition. | New York : Plume, Penguin Random House, [2018] |
Revised edition of the author's How to retire overseas, c2010. | Includes index.
Identifiers: LCCN 2017040654 (print) | LCCN 2017041614 (ebook) |
ISBN 9781101186046 (ebook) | ISBN 9780452296848 (trade pbk.)
Subjects: LCSH: Retirement, Places of—Foreign countries. | Americans—Foreign
countries. | Retirees—Life skills guides.
Classification: LCC HQ1063 (ebook) | LCC HQ1063 .P43 2017 (print) | DDC 306.3
/8—dc23
LC record available at https://lccn.loc.gov/2017040654

ISBN 9780525538462 (revised edition)

Printed in the United States of America
9th Printing

Set in ITC New Baskerville
Original hardcover book design by Eve L. Kirch

For Lief, Kaitlin, and Jackson.
Wherever we wander, you make it home.

ACKNOWLEDGMENTS

After more than thirty years living and investing around the globe, my best friends are attorneys, tax advisers, immigration experts, real estate agents, property developers, architects, contractors, and fellow expats based in all the places where I enjoy spending time. Good thing, too, because I never would have been able to put together the pages that follow without a lot of on-the-ground help from experts who call the places featured in these pages home. Thank you, all, for your quick responses to my endless questions and, especially, for your friendship all these years.

In particular, I want to thank Lee Harrison; Paul Terhorst; my husband, Lief Simon; and my daughter, Kaitlin Kalashian; without whose help certain sections of this book would be nowhere near as complete and comprehensive as they are.

Thank you to my Live and Invest Overseas team in Panama City, Panama, who provided hugely appreciated research and fact-checking support.

And thank you to my expert editor at Penguin, Nina Shield, whose guidance and enthusiasm have helped to make this project much more fun and much less work than it otherwise could have been.

CONTENTS

PART III.
THE WORLD'S EIGHTEEN BEST PLACES TO REINVENT YOUR LIFE AND CHASE ADVENTURE OVERSEAS　　　　　　　　　129

PART IV.
SETTLING IN　　　　　　　　　　　　　　227

As I write, my husband, Lief, and I have just completed our fourth international move. After nine years in Panama City, Panama, we have returned to Paris, where we lived with our two children for four years before swapping the City of Light for the Hub of the Americas. For this move, we packed two suitcases apiece with clothes and books and hopped a direct flight from Panama's Tocumen International to Paris's Charles de Gaulle. Hard to imagine an easier relocation from one continent to another.

The simple logistics of this most recent migration both ignore the significance of this transition and leverage the two decades of living and investing overseas experience that we have invested in to get us to this point.

When we showed up in Paris early one Monday morning about a month ago, we slotted immediately back into the life we've worked for years to create for ourselves in this city. We moved back into the apartment we purchased a decade and a half ago (the most recent renters having vacated two weeks before our return to the scene). Our first afternoon we walked down the street to the grocer and the baker, who greeted us by name, stopped in at our neighborhood wine shop, bought two carnets (discounted packets) of Métro tickets, and texted local friends. That evening we went for a long walk and chose a café along the river for dinner, just as we have done so many times before. For us, this repositioning from Panama City to Paris has been very much like coming home.

How can you engineer a similarly comfortable, welcoming situation in the place where you decide you'd like to chase adventure overseas? A little patience, please. We'll get to that. My point in showing you a snapshot of the lives we've returned to in Paris is to assure you that the dream you have of living wherever you're dreaming of living can be realized. This is a daydream, not a pipe dream.

Before we begin looking at your options for where and how to reinvent your life overseas, though, I'd like to highlight an important difference between this new edition and the original *How to Retire Overseas*. Ten years have passed since I wrote that first book. In those ten years, this retire-overseas idea has come of age.

Today we're not talking about retiring overseas. At least we're not talking *only* about retiring overseas. Today we're talking about living a borderless lifestyle at any age. When I began covering this beat in the mid-1980s (yikes), nobody but rock stars thought much about the benefits of moving around the globe. When I first suggested that retirees consider relocating to Costa Rica or Mexico rather than Arizona or Florida, most of them thought both me and my suggestion loony. Today millions of American retirees have chosen to up sticks and make the most of their post-work phase by enjoying it somewhere sunny, exotic, adventure-filled, and affordable . . . beyond U.S. borders.

For many, the decision begins with a concern that their retirement nest eggs may not be big enough to carry them through. No matter why they first considered the idea, though, every retiree I've known who has taken the bold, brave leap and moved to a foreign country at this later stage of life eventually comes to realize that the real benefit isn't the reduced cost of living but the enhanced quality of life.

And that gets to the point. This is about living better, and why should living better be the monopoly agenda of us oldsters? I mean, who doesn't want to live better?

I've spent the past nine years building a business in Panama City. In that time, my Live and Invest Overseas operation has employed dozens of expats ages twenty-one to thirty-five. These millennial wanderers have made their way to Panama from the United States, Canada, and across Europe. They are "retired" overseas well ahead of retirement age. They aren't in Panama to try to stretch their nest eggs. They're in Panama to see what being in Panama is like. They're moving around the world as curiosity and wanderlust dictate and figuring out how to generate incomes as they go to fund their fun. I happened to connect with them in Panama.

Thirty-plus years ago, when I first suggested folks think about going overseas, this phenomenon wouldn't have been possible. Then came the Internet. It and twenty-first-century technology from iThings to WhatsApp mean that anyone of any age and under any circumstances can be anywhere he or she wants to be and, by bringing to bear a little imagination and industry, find ways to make enough money to enjoy a comfortable lifestyle while in residence.

Retire overseas has been my beat since the mid-1980s, but until this recent relocation from Panama City to Paris, it was never my personal agenda. I've been moving around the world—from Baltimore, Maryland, to Waterford, Ireland, then Paris and Panama—chasing not a relaxing lifestyle, a lower cost of living, or better weather (as retirees often do) but business and investment opportunity.

Now, though, two decades later, Lief and I find ourselves at the stage when we can begin thinking about slowing down. The past nine years in Panama City, we were noses to the grindstone building a business and raising our son. Last month we launched Jackson into his post-lycée life (he graduated from the French high school in Panama City) and began looking ahead to a lifestyle of more travel, more discovery, and greater flexibility.

Hold down the fort, we said to our now trained and proven team in Panama City. Thanks to all that twenty-first-century technology I mentioned, Lief and I know from experience that we can stay in day-to-day touch from Paris or wherever, and we'll work Panama into the schedule at least every eight weeks or so, allowing regular time in the office. Thus we launch what I'd say is the most significant turning point in our lives since we decided to take them global twenty years ago.

Our long-term plan has long been to follow the seasons, moving around among four or five or more spots where we enjoy spending time and where we have established both a home base and a community connection, as we have done in Paris and Panama City. In addition, we have invested in the infrastructure of a life in Medellín, Colombia; Algarve, Portugal; Istria, Croatia; and Waterford, Ireland, where it all began.

Maybe your daydream is nothing nearly as complicated. Whatever form your dreaming takes, I'm here to tell you, based on two decades of personal experience and three decades of focused attention, that it's not only possible to make that dream come true but easier right now than it's ever been before in history and easier all the time.

If you could live anywhere, where would you most like to live?

Don't have an answer for that question yet? Start here: If you could have any view from your bedroom window each morning, what would you most like it to be?

You fill in that blank, and I'll do my best to help with the rest.

—KATHLEEN PEDDICORD, Paris, France, July 2017

I made my first overseas move about a dozen years ago. With the help of the international publishing company where I'd been working for more than thirteen years, I relocated with my family from Baltimore, Maryland, to Waterford, Ireland. The morning we were to fly to Dublin to launch this grand adventure, my then nine-year-old daughter lay crying on her bed, holding her grandmother's hand and begging to be left behind. Between sobs she'd mumble, "I'm an American. I belong in America."

Ignoring her pleas, we loaded her into the SUV along with the ten oversized suitcases we'd packed with all the worldly possessions we wanted to have with us upon our arrival on the Emerald Isle.

I'd always wanted to live in Europe. So when the publishing company I was working for decided it wanted to open an office in Ireland, it was kismet. We were off for a new life in the Auld Sod.

Fast-forward seven years, and we were packing again, this time for a move from Waterford to Paris, where my daughter had decided she wanted to spend a year studying abroad.

Most recently, we moved from Paris to Panama, this time, again, for business.

But I'm getting ahead of my story. I simply want to show that there are many good reasons to think about living or retiring in another country—reasons to do with a reduced (sometimes significantly) cost of living, with better weather, with a healthier lifestyle, with a lower tax bill, and with an enhanced quality of life. In some places around the world that I'll introduce you to in this book, in fact, you could dramatically reduce your cost of living while elevating your standard of living, affording little luxuries that are probably not possible to manage back home—a full-time maid, for example, a cook, a gardener, even a driver.

The challenge as you begin preparing to launch a new life in a new country is to make sure that you're moving for your own reasons and that you understand what those reasons are in your own mind. At this early stage of your overseas retirement adventure, the most important thing is to be honest with yourself and, very important, with your significant other. There is no one-country-fits-all overseas retirement paradise. It's a question of priorities. I've told you my reasons for my initial move overseas a dozen years ago and for the three international moves I've made since. Your reasons for thinking about residing elsewhere at this stage of your life might be very different.

Retirees in the States right now face a serious dilemma. Many have lost much of their retirement savings as a result of recent market downturns, and it's increasingly difficult to live on Social Security alone. The cost of quality retirement living choices in the United States is escalating rapidly. Most retirees can't afford a retirement home, and a lot of people currently working can't afford to retire at all. But the truth is, the situation is not as desperate as some fear. There are good options—which is my fundamental reason for writing this book.

Economies collapse and then recover; values—of real estate, of stocks—fall and then rise again; financial meltdowns come and go. The circumstances of life change. When living becomes intolerably difficult in one place, move to another. I'm not being flippant. I'm sharing what I believe is the secret to realizing a dream retirement. The first move is the hardest, so as you embark on this overseas retirement adventure, you need help and options. My book will deliver both.

Let's start with this: You do not have to resign yourself to reducing your standard of living during this important phase of life. You do not have to plan for two or three decades of scraping by and making do. All you have to do is to think outside the box and beyond your own borders. Do that, and you discover opportunities for a completely new and improved life available for a bargain price.

In places like Las Tablas, Panama; Mendoza, Argentina; and Languedoc, France, the concerns and struggles in the United States about the costs of living, housing, and health care seem far away. These and the many other beautiful, safe, and often super-affordable places I'll introduce you to in these pages offer alternatives, viable, appealing options for Americans at and nearing retirement age trying to figure out how in the world they're going to make it in this phase of life.

My friend Paul Terhorst began his overseas adventures over thirty years ago, when the accounting firm he was working for decided to pull him out of Argentina. Paul and his wife, Vicki, had grown to like Buenos Aires. When his superiors told him that his posting there was over, Paul told them that his retirement had begun. Paul and Vicki have spent the many years since then discovering the world as their wanderlust inspires them and their budget allows. They lived in Paris when the U.S. dollar was strong and Buenos Aires when Argentina was a bargain. Today they're at home in Chiang Mai, Thailand, one of the cheapest places on earth to live well right now. Paul made a brave leap, walking away from a good-paying job with a big international firm. But he and Vicki haven't regretted a minute of their adventures since.

Another friend, Lee, also took early retirement, about seven years ago, when the engineering firm he was working for was bought out by a larger one. He saw the corporate restructuring as a chance for a bigger change. Instead of moving up the company ladder, he and his wife, Julie, moved down south, to Cuenca, Ecuador. As Lee explains, Cuenca was a great first move outside the States. It's a safe, friendly, comfortable city. But it wasn't his and Julie's dream. What Lee and Julie really wanted was a home at the beach. So, from their new base in Cuenca, they launched a search up and down the coasts of Central and South America. Two sun-filled years of beach-scouting led them to Uruguay's Gold Coast, which today they are delighted to call home.

I could cite business, financial, and tax reasons for why my husband and I decided to move abroad, first to Ireland, then to Paris, now to Panama, and then back to Paris. And, indeed, we've enjoyed serious financial advantages living in these places. But these aren't the real reasons we've pursued a life overseas. The truth is, we savor the adventure. We look forward to finding out where it leads us next. And we're not alone.

Our last evening in Paris, the night before our move to Panama City, I went to dinner with a group of local women friends. Around the table in that restaurant at Odéon sat an Italian, a

Spaniard, an Aussie, a Brit, a Croat, four Parisians, and me, the American. They chatted in a crazy mix of French, Spanish, Italian, and English, and I did my best to keep up. What did they talk about? A desire for change. This eclectic mix of forty- and fiftysomethings shared a common yearning for something new at this stage of their lives. Again and again, my friends brought the conversation around to their longing for more, for new, for different, for adventure.

The Croatian woman and her husband were considering moving to Australia to start a business. The Spaniard and her husband were looking ahead to when their children would be in university so they could spend part of each year in Paris and part of each year elsewhere in Europe. The Brit was thinking about Asia. The Parisian women and their significant others had no idea where they wanted to go or what they wanted to do, but they had an itch to travel. All of us recognized that it's a big, interesting world, and we simply wanted to see a little more of it.

The reasons for packing up and starting a new life in a new country are many. Some are urgent—a need to reduce the cost of living, for example. But retiring overseas isn't only about the money. This is about an opportunity to enrich your life and to reinvent yourself.

The payoffs of a retirement overseas can be myriad, but so, in truth, are the challenges. This book will prepare you for the hurdles and frustrations involved in realizing your dream retirement in a foreign country, helping you minimize the hassles and maximize the adventure and the fun.

The big question, of course, is where. Where should you think about spending your golden years? In the pages that follow, I'll walk you through the critical thinking you need to do to make that decision. More than a country, you're choosing a way of life. To make that choice successfully, you want to understand all the options you're choosing among. The truth is, there is no "best place in the world to retire." But there is a best place in the world for *you* to retire. Let's go find it. . . .

—KATHLEEN PEDDICORD, Panama City, Panama, July 2009

HOW TO RETIRE OVERSEAS

PART I

TEN STEPS YOU CAN TAKE NOW AT HOME

How do you get from the life you're living now to the new, better, cheaper life you're dreaming of for your retirement overseas?

You break the adventure down into steps.

Step 1: Know Yourself

This will be a piece of cake, I told myself as we prepared for our move from Baltimore to Waterford what now seems like a lifetime ago. How different can Ireland be from the United States? My husband, my daughter, and I, we'll slide right into Irish life. I discovered quickly, though, that I'd been overly optimistic. The Irish speak English (sort of), but they operate differently from Americans. In truth, adjusting to life in Ireland was more difficult than we ever could have predicted. We discovered that launching a new life on the Emerald Isle was in some ways more challenging than it would have been in Ajijic, Mexico, say, or Boquete, Panama. Ajijic and Boquete are established expat communities, home to thousands of foreign retirees who speak the same language, share the same interests, and approach life in the same way. There are no expat communities in Ireland. In Waterford, we settled in among the locals and embraced Irish country living. We had no choice.

Our Irish neighbors were friendly and welcoming, but sometimes we longed for American company. For fellow Yanks who'd appreciate our offhanded cultural references, understand our slang, and laugh at our jokes.

In Paris, we had a different experience. While you won't find established expatriate communities in the French capital, you will find lots of expats. Living in Paris, we made new friends who were Italian, Spanish, Portuguese, Argentine, and yes, to our relief, American. We made many French friends in Paris as well, but we had no trouble finding American company when we wanted it.

In Panama City, where we've called home for nearly a decade, again, we're living among the locals. We're not the only gringos on the block, as we were in Waterford (our next-door neighbor hails from Arizona), but we're not living in a gated community of fellow foreigners, either.

One of the fundamental choices you must make as you survey the world map in search of the overseas retirement haven with your name on it is this: Would you be more comfortable retiring to an established expatriate community, a place where you'll have no trouble slipping into the local social scene and finding English speakers who share your interests? Or do you want to go local, immersing yourself in a new culture completely?

This important early decision may never have occurred to you. But I encourage you to consider the question directly and as early as possible in your "where and how should I reinvent my life overseas?" thinking, for the answer sets you on one track or another, and they lead to very different places.

It can be easier, frankly, to seek out a place like Ajijic, where your neighbors would be fellow North Americans, where you'd hear more English on the street than Spanish, and where you'd have like-minded compatriots to commiserate with over the trials and tribulations of daily life in a foreign country. Ajijic, for example, could as easily sit north of the Rio Grande as south. It can seem like a transplanted U.S. suburb. This can make it a terrific first step for some, a chance to dip your toe in the overseas retirement waters rather than diving in headfirst. In Ajijic, you'd be living abroad and enjoying many of the benefits (great weather, affordable cost of living), but the surroundings and the neighbors would feel familiar in many ways. You could shop at Walmart, meet up with fellow Americanos for bridge on Thursday evenings, and never have to travel far to find English-language conversation.

On the other hand, life in Mexico would be a very different experience if you were residing in a little fishing village or a small colonial city in the mountains where you were the only foreigner in town. Settling among the locals means you must learn to live like a local.

Is that thought appealing, exciting, and invigorating? Or is it terrifying? Be honest with yourself as you consider your response.

In addition to that fundamental question, in my experience fourteen other factors are important to take into account when you're shopping for a new country to call home. The key is to consider each of these things within the context of your personal circumstances. I list these considerations according to a general order of priority. Your personal priorities may be very different. You must determine for yourself what's most and least important to you. On which points are you happy to be flexible? I'll walk you through some exercises to help prompt your thinking, but here's the list for reference:

➤ Cost of living

➤ Cost of housing (renting or buying)

➤ Climate

➤ Health care, both the quality and the cost

➤ Infrastructure

➤ Accessibility to the United States

➤ Language

➤ Culture, recreation, and entertainment

➤ Residency (if you want to be able to stay indefinitely in the country you choose)

➤ Environment (things like pollution levels)

➤ Taxes

➤ Special benefits for foreign retirees

➤ Education and schools (if you're making the move with children, in which case this becomes one of your top priorities)

➤ Safety

I include safety last on the list not because it's the least important but because you can take for granted that every place I introduce in these pages is safe. In some, you won't even have to worry about locking your doors at night. Everything else on the list of factors to consider is a matter of priorities and perspective, but unsafe is unacceptable.

One of the most important issues for anyone considering a move to another country is cost of living. In some cases a reduced cost of living is the primary and driving agenda. It's also the issue most affected by your answer to the "go local/don't go local" question. Living among the locals can decrease your cost of living significantly, certainly compared with the cost of trying to export your U.S. lifestyle to another country.

Climate is probably the next most common reason (after cost of living and cost of real estate) for thinking about moving to another country and could be your main motivation for considering the idea. Some places around the world boast springlike temperatures year-round. For many, this is reason enough to relocate at least part of the year.

Issues such as taxation and special benefits for retirees, on the other hand, are important but probably not key factors. You don't want to organize your life around tax codes or senior discounts. These are secondary factors that may help later when you have narrowed down your choices and are torn between two or three destinations.

If you have an ongoing health concern or if you're moving with children, your priorities are set for you. If health care is your key issue, then your Dream Havens list can include only places with first-class and first-world health facilities. If you're moving with children, the determining factor is the availability of international (preferably bilingual) schools. If you're considering starting a business to help support your adventures overseas, then tax and other government incentives targeting entrepreneurs and foreign investors can tip the scales for you.

Culture, recreation, and entertainment are not key but important considerations. How do you like to spend your time? What diversions would you miss most if they disappeared from your life?

Considering the issues on this list is perhaps the most important part of planning a new life abroad. Every decision should be made based on your preferences and circumstances, which I will help you to think through. I encourage you to get out a pen and pad of paper now and work through these exercises with me. You can use these notes for reference as you read through Parts II and III, where we'll consider current top overseas lifestyle options, country by country, region by region. I'll help you connect the dots between your priorities and preferences and the pluses and minuses of each destination of interest.

First, though, we need to clarify your priorities and preferences. To that end, consider the questions that follow honestly and fully.

Cost of Living

➤ What is your total monthly income, not including your current paycheck? Tally up all your income beyond any salary that will disappear with the move. If you're moving in retirement, maybe you have Social Security, pension, 401(k), or IRA funds. Whatever your age, maybe you have investment income.

➤ If your total monthly income as you project it beyond the end of your current working life isn't enough to support the lifestyle you want in the overseas destination that has your attention, what are your options for supplementing it? You could:

- **Invest for income.** If you have available investment capital, consider using it to create an ongoing monthly cash flow. The easiest option for this is a rental property, perhaps in the location where you're considering moving, meaning you'd be generating cash flow in the local currency to supplement your local living costs.

- **Start a laptop business.** In today's world this is easy, common, and possible anywhere you have a good Internet connection. You could become a travel writer, a travel photographer, a consultant in a field of expertise, or an online teacher, to suggest just a few of the possibilities. As I write, I know expats making good incomes plying all those online trades and many others.

- **Start a bricks-and-mortar business.** This is usually a more ambitious undertaking than a laptop enterprise, but the options are nearly unlimited and can allow you to leverage past professional experience or to pursue a long-set-aside hobby. Obvious business ideas for an expat most anywhere in the world include opening a restaurant, a bar, a bed-and-breakfast, or a hostel. Less typical but very realistic possibilities include auto repair, pool cleaning, landscaping, and hospitality training services. (That last item is desperately needed in many developing-world destinations trying to cater to growing expat communities but unable to find local help with any sense of real-world service.)

➤ When thinking through the cost of moving to a new country, remember what I refer to as the "capital budget" of the initial move. This can be as controlled as gas and tolls if you're moving part-time from Arizona to Mazatlán, Mexico, for example, which would constitute one of the easiest possible international adventures. If, at the other end of the spectrum, you want to move full time to Panama and bring your entire household of belongings and two dogs with you, you'll need to allow for a capital budget that includes plane tickets (including for the pets), shipping, and residency visas. If your savings don't stretch to cover the capital budget you face, the quickest way to raise cash to cover the deficit can be to sell some of those household belongings you're otherwise thinking about paying to relocate with you.

Cost of Housing (to Buy or to Rent)

➤ First, decide whether you intend to buy or to rent your new home. I strongly encourage you to rent, at least at first, for six months or longer. Renting long-term as an expat or retiree overseas has serious advantages, too. We'll discuss these in a minute.

➤ Whether you own or rent your new home abroad makes a big difference in your budget. If you invest in a home of your own, you have no rent, but perhaps you have a mortgage. If you have a mortgage, you have a life insurance expense, as this is required when financing property almost everywhere in the world. In addition, as a property owner you have the cost of repairs, maintenance, property insurance, and (sometimes) taxes.

➤ On the other hand, owning your home overseas gives you an asset that you can rent out for income while you're away. I know many people who've chosen not to limit their adventures abroad to a single new country but move between or among two or even three. Invest in a home in each place, rent it out while you're elsewhere, and the rental income can offset your carrying costs and maybe even provide income in the local currency to cover living expenses when you're in town.

➤ If your intention is to divide your time between the United States and another country, you may want to keep your home stateside. In this case, renting while abroad can make even more sense.

➤ If you are more interested in owning than renting, this position has a lot to do with which countries you should consider for your list of dream havens. Determine your property purchase budget. Is it contingent on the price you realize from the sale of real estate back home? Once you know how much you can spend on your new home overseas, you can focus your list on those countries where that budget will allow you to afford your dream home.

Climate

➤ Do you enjoy a change of seasons?

➤ Do you need regular sunshine?

➤ Do you mind rain?

➤ Can you handle heat? Humidity?

➤ Do you prefer a varying length of day?

➤ Are you okay living in a place that is at risk for hurricanes?

Health Care

➤ Do you have preexisting conditions? How old are you? These are the two most important factors when it comes to qualifying for international health insurance. It is possible to get health insurance to cover you anywhere in the world at any age . . . if you're willing to pay for it. Affordable options, however, become limited after age seventy-four.

➤ If you have an ongoing health concern, this is your primary consideration, the issue around which you must organize your plan. Focus on countries where the cost of health care is affordable, and restrict your search within those countries to places with top-tier health facilities. That is, choose a place near an international-standard hospital (this typically means a big city, probably a capital) where, ideally, at least some of the staff speak English.

➤ Would you be uncomfortable seeing a physician whose first language is not English?

Infrastructure

➤ Do you lose your cool if you can't send an email the first time every time you try? Do you plan to start an online business? If the answer to either of these questions is yes, limit your search for where to chase adventure overseas to places with first-world infrastructure, including and especially reliable high-speed Internet.

➤ Would you mind living on a dirt road?

➤ Would you mind your road access being temporarily cut off during the rainy season?

➤ Do you need American television? Would you be unhappy without football on Sunday afternoons?

➤ Are you afraid of the dark? In much of the world, electricity isn't 100 percent reliable.

➤ Would you be comfortable owning a car and driving yourself around in a new country? If not, think about places where you could afford a full-time driver or where a car is unnecessary.

➤ Would you want to travel outside the country often, either to visit family back home or generally? If so, consider how far it is to the nearest international airport.

➤ Would you be unhappy without your favorite comfort foods? If so, consider places with access to international-standard grocery stores.

Accessibility to the United States

➤ Do you have children or grandchildren you want to see regularly?

➤ Are you hoping family and friends from back home will come to visit often? This goes both ways. If you want visitors from back home, move someplace that can be reached easily. If you don't, move wherever you want.

➤ Are you going to be keeping a home in the States?

➤ Will you have some ongoing business concerns back home?

➤ Do you have a health condition that could necessitate a quick return stateside?

Language

➤ Do you speak a second language?

➤ Are you terrified at the idea of learning one?

Culture, Recreation, and Entertainment

➤ What's your favorite thing to do on a Friday night?

➤ How would you rather spend a free Sunday afternoon—in a museum or taking a long walk in the woods?

➤ How regularly do you want to be able to dine out? To watch a first-run movie in English? To visit an art gallery or attend the theater?

➤ What would you like to see from your bedroom window? The ocean? A mountainside covered with wildflowers? A vineyard? A busy street scene?

Residency

➤ Would you like to be able to live full time and to stick around indefinitely in the country you have your eye on? If so, you need to understand the options available in that country for establishing legal residency. You can avoid the hassle and expense of establishing residency by coming and going within the window of time allowed a tourist.

➤ Are you interested in the idea of citizenship and a second passport in the country where you move? In this case, your choices are more limited, though in today's world, you have many good and straightforward options for obtaining a second passport, either through residency or investment.

Environment

➤ Do you have any respiratory concerns? If so, take cities with high or rising pollution levels off your list.

➤ Would you be okay seeing litter and poor children every day? Garbage and poverty can be two of the toughest things to take about life in any third-world country. Some visit a developing country and see unrealized potential; others see struggle. If you don't want to live with these things as part of your day-to-day life, you have two choices. You can live in an expat community in Latin America, the Caribbean, or Asia . . . or you can focus on the developed world.

Taxes

➤ From where will you be deriving your income while living overseas?

➤ Will you have earned pension, dividend, interest, rental, or capital gains income to account for? The source of your income has a lot to do with your ultimate tax liability, both in the United States and in your new jurisdiction.

➤ Will you be starting a business? In this case, you need to understand the local tax implications, both for filings and tax potentially owed.

➤ If your only income will be from Social Security or a retirement pension, moving overseas should be a tax-neutral experience for you. Most countries don't tax retirement pension income (though you should confirm this jurisdiction by jurisdiction).

Special Benefits for Foreign Retirees

➤ What's your age? This is the key question. Some countries offer special benefits, such as tax breaks and shopping discounts, for resident seniors. In Panama, for example, all seniors over a certain age (midfifties) are eligible for savings on in-country transportation, on museum entrances, and even on prescription medicines or closing costs on a home.

Education and Schools

➤ If you're not moving with children, this is not an issue. If you are, your priorities are clearly set, and your options, frankly, more limited. Unless you intend to homeschool your child, you can consider a move only to a place with suitable schooling choices. I would not recommend enrolling your child in a local school anywhere in Central America or the Caribbean, for example. In those regions, focus on cities with bilingual international school options. In some places in Europe, on the other hand, the local public schools can be better quality than most private schools elsewhere in the world. This is the case in France, for example. The question in this case is whether you'll be able to enroll your child.

Safety

➤ Are you a woman moving alone?

➤ Are you moving with children?

➤ Do protests bother you? The French, for example, seem to assemble to make a point at the drop of a beret.

➤ Do you speak the local language? If you do, situations that might otherwise seem frightening won't bother you. If you don't, you may sometimes feel uncomfortable even if there's really no cause for worry.

➤ Have you spent much time outside the United States? If yes, again, you're probably better prepared for what otherwise might seem worrisome situations.

No place abroad is the United States. You must assume (and accept) that everything—from the health care system to the property purchase process, from the foods they eat for breakfast to the way they celebrate Christmas—will be different from what you've known until now.

But that's the point, isn't it? New and different. Exciting and exotic.

One more thing: As I've mentioned, if you're planning to make this move with someone else (a spouse, a partner, a sibling, etc.), work through these ten steps and address all the points I'm suggesting together. Be honest with each other. It's better to identify and address differing priorities or interests early, rather than after you've sold your U.S. home or settled into a new one in a different country.

In the more than three decades I've been covering this beat, I've yet to meet a single person who regretted making the move overseas (no kidding). I have, though, known couples who've struggled because they wanted different things out of the move and didn't address the competing agendas early enough in their planning. Maybe one of you isn't up for learning a new language or for being a twelve-hour plane ride away from the grandkids.

Years ago, while a friend of mine and I were walking down the street in Paris, he remarked to me, out of the blue, "You and Lief [my husband] sure are lucky. You both seem to have the same ideas about how you want to live and where you want to spend your time.

"My wife and I are struggling with this," my friend continued. "I've been trying for years to persuade her to move here to Paris. This is where I'd like to spend our retirement. I've dreamed of it for decades. But she'll have no part of it. She doesn't want to leave the grandchildren. I can't even get her to agree to spend part of the year here. Do you have any suggestions?" he asked.

I didn't at the time, and I don't even now. Making a success of a new life overseas requires energy, commitment, and a positive attitude. You don't want to force someone into it. My best advice is what I've already explained: Address all of your concerns directly, during the initial thinking phase, to try to reconcile your individual priorities as early as possible.

(My friend has chosen to stay home with his wife, by the way. He dreams of Paris still.)

Step 2: Budget Your New Life Overseas

How much money do you need to move to a new country? That's not the question to ask. The question to ask is this: How much money do you have to live on?

In Part III, I'll introduce you to places where you could live comfortably on $1,200 or $1,300 a month, maybe less. That's not a big nut . . . about equal to the average monthly Social Security check.

But maybe a monthly Social Security check is a far distant

possibility. If you have no other income to count on, what options do you have?

Here are two, one taking a conventional retirement-planning approach, the second providing a blueprint for a new life overseas at any age.

Funding Your New Life Overseas Strategy #1— The Retiree's Plan

One strategy would be to sell everything you own. Seriously.

Think about it this way. If you were to liquidate every asset you have, where would that leave you? What lump sum of capital would you net? Then, next step, with that capital invested, what level of yields and dividends might it throw off on a monthly basis? That's how much money you have to retire.

A great example for how to approach this strategy for budgeting your new life overseas comes from my longtime friends Vicki and Paul. This happy couple "retired" abroad in 1984. They were thirty-five years old.

The couple made the move with $500,000. That was their total net worth, including the sale of their house, cars, investments, pension funds, and so on. If we take inflation into consideration, Paul and Vicki's $500,000 in 1984 would be the equivalent of $1 million today.

Now, you don't need a million dollars to make a move to a new country, but your expectations about the life you'll live abroad should be in line with the size of your budget.

As Paul explains it, back in the mid-1980s, he and Vicki had it easy. At that time, CDs paid 16 percent interest. Paul and Vicki cut their money into chunks and put it into one-year CDs, with a couple of CDs maturing every month or two. They lived well on $40,000 a year, which was 50 percent of their interest income of $80,000 (a 16 percent return on their $500,000). Reagan was president, inflation was low, the dollar was strong. More important, Paul and Vicki had arranged their lives so that they had virtually no fixed costs. They had downsized completely, meaning no house, so no property repair or upkeep costs; no car, so no vehicle maintenance or insurance costs; generally, no hard assets that came with carrying costs; and no debt.

A decade later, interest rates fell, and Vicki and Paul had to diversify their portfolio into stocks and bonds, foreign currencies, and natural resources (like oil and gas). As Paul explains, "Though we cried a lot along the way—especially beginning in March 2000, when the stock market tanked—our investments have performed well, providing us with a much larger stash. However, that stash shrank again during the 2007 to 2008 bear market, one of the worst ever."

But Paul is not worried. As he puts it, "You quickly catch on that, to succeed at this, you're going to have to assume some risk. You're going to have to withstand market ups and downs." In other words, as you work through your own financial planning for your retirement overseas, remember that markets fluctuate and cycles turn. One key to success in your new life overseas, both financial and otherwise, is flexibility.

Once you've put together your nest egg, the next step is to project how long that lump sum of capital will carry you. Here's one of the most useful retirement-planning tools I've found for that purpose. It's a retirement calculator called FIRECalc, available free on the website Firecalc.com. FIRECalc can help you answer this most fundamental of all retirement-planning questions: Will you have enough money at the end of your life? It uses a database of stock and bond returns over the past century to find an answer. You plug in how much money you have, how long you expect to live, and how much you'll be spending every year.

The calculator assumes your spending will increase by inflation, and then it gives you the result—that is, whether or not, based on your given circumstances, your money will run out. Say you've saved up the $1 million nest egg I mentioned before. You're fifty years old. And you expect to live until age ninety (so you plug forty years into the calculator). Your budget is $30,000 a year, adjusted for inflation over forty years.

That's probably less than you're spending now but more than you'd need to live on in many of the places I'm going to introduce you to in these pages. The key, again, is not to load up on fixed assets with carrying costs. (This is one good reason not to invest in owning your retirement home overseas.) With a million-dollar nest egg, FIRECalc says that you have a 100 percent chance of making your overseas retirement work. Of course, I understand that not everyone can put together $1 million worth of assets. If you have less, you'll have to plan to live on less, which is very possible.

A minimum amount for a comfortable retirement in a number of beautiful, safe, and appealing places (Cuenca, Ecuador, and Chiang Mai, Thailand, are two good examples) would be $1,300 a month (coincidentally, only slightly less than the average Social Security payment). In some places you could live on less, and, anywhere in the world, you could certainly spend more if you wanted to. But $1,300 a month is a good benchmark. That's $15,600 a year, about half the $30,000 I used in my first FIRECalc example.

Assuming the other variables are unchanged (you're fifty years old, projecting your retirement to age ninety), FIRECalc projects that, spending $15,600 a year, you've got a 91.6 percent chance of not outliving your retirement nest egg.

How much total capital would you need to generate interest and dividend income of $15,600 a year? About $400,000.

In fact, you could make this work with a bit less. I'm assuming that you're fifty years old right now. Perhaps you're older. If you run the calculations using sixty-five as your current age, using the same $400,000 nest egg, then you'll have a 99.2 percent chance of making those retirement funds last through the entirety of your retirement. Furthermore, regardless of your current age, at some point in the future, Social Security should kick in, taking the pressure off your monthly interest and dividend requirements.

Until the month when you do begin to collect Social Security income (and assuming you don't have some other regular monthly pension income to rely on), aim to keep at least six months' worth of living expenses in cash at all times. This will help guard against the risk of having to sell an asset (a stock, for example) in a down market to pay your rent.

Funding Your New Life Overseas Strategy #2— The Millennial's Plan

I call this the millennial's plan, but in truth, anyone of any age could use this strategy to realize a life of reinvention, discovery, adventure, and opportunity almost anywhere in the world.

Simply put, if you don't have a nest egg or a trust fund to

count on, your option is to generate the income you need. You probably aren't going to be able to get a job in your new country of residence. In most places it's hard or impossible to obtain a work permit as a foreign resident. (Panama is one important exception to this rule; more on this in Part II.)

But who wants a job anyway? The point of taking off for some beautiful, exotic overseas haven is to escape workaday life, not to reproduce it. The good news is that while it's difficult to get a job as a foreigner in most of the world, it's easier than it's been at any other time in history to start a business.

As an American abroad, you have an advantage. You come from a sophisticated, competitive marketplace. You understand the idea of identifying a niche and then filling it. In many countries around the world, the marketplaces are much less developed. When you arrive, you'll notice straightaway opportunities for small businesses and services that you've watched mature and become successful in the States but that here, in this developing environment, don't exist at all.

Years ago, a friend moved to San Juan del Sur, Nicaragua, where he decided to build a house and a small hotel by the beach. Jim began importing building materials and furniture and then realized that he had nowhere to store the things while construction was under way. He looked around the area, even in Managua, for a self-storage facility. No such thing existed. So, along with his house and his small hotel, Jim decided to build self-storage units as well. The first units were contracted for before he'd finished erecting them.

Perhaps the easiest way, though, to earn money living overseas is to set yourself up with a laptop-based business. Thanks to twenty-first-century technology, it's easy to generate a small stream of income to supplement whatever nest egg or other income you have or even to support yourself 100 percent. My friend Christian, who took early retirement at age forty-nine to move with his wife to Cuenca, Ecuador, decided that, as part of his overseas reinvention plan, he would take up travel writing. Christian supplements his pension income by selling articles on living, traveling, and investing in real estate in Latin America to magazines in the States. He travels continuously, and some months earns more now from his writing than from his pension.

Budgeting Your New Life

Once you've figured out how much money you'll have to live on in retirement, you can begin to consider what kind of retirement that budget could buy you. The bulk of any budget is given over to housing—rent or a mortgage—so start there. Are you going to rent or to buy? As I've mentioned, I strongly recommend that you rent at least at first, for six to twelve months, to give yourself a chance to try the place on for size before committing.

Housing affects your cost of living in a big way. Buy a home in a country where you can arrange financing as a foreigner, and your mortgage may be no more than your rent would be. On the other hand, if you own a home, you'll have to allow for the costs of maintenance and repairs. Maybe you'll have groundskeeping costs. In some places, you'll pay property taxes. You'll probably want homeowner's insurance. As a renter, you have none of these liabilities.

The other key housing consideration has to do with where in a country you want to settle. In Panama, for example, your rent could be $1,500 a month for a two-bedroom apartment in a nice building in Panama City with a doorman and a pool . . . or it could be $500 a month, if you choose instead to settle in a little house near the beach in Las Tablas, on the coast of the Azuero Peninsula, a beautiful, welcoming, more remote, and therefore much more affordable, region of this country.

Because housing is such a major and variable cost, the best way to approach a budget for wherever you're thinking about relocating can be to itemize all other expenses you'll incur, then address housing separately. Following is a list of the items to include in your budget. This gives you an overview of the expenses you'll need to plan for, not including housing, which we'll consider separately, as well as ideas for how to control and mitigate each cost.

Condo/Building/Homeowners' Association Fee

The monthly condo or homeowners' association (HOA) fee is your contribution to the costs of maintaining and managing the apartment building or private development community where you're living. It covers your part of shared expenses, including security, groundskeeping, internal roads, maintenance of the swimming pool and other amenities, and sometimes a concierge in an apartment building (in Paris, Panama, Medellín, or Buenos Aires, for example). You may incur this expense as an owner or a renter. It's called different things in different places. In Paris, for example, the building fee is called the syndic fee, and it covers the costs of maintaining the courtyard, the lobby, the elevator, the building facade, and so forth. In Panama, it is referred to as the PH (*propiedad horizontal*) fee, and again, it's to pay for the cost of maintaining and improving public areas, the elevators, and— important in Panama City—the building's *área social* (social area), which typically includes a pool, a game room, sometimes a gym, a children's play area, and a barbecue. Apartment buildings in Panama City compete on social areas.

This fee is the expense of the owner of the property, but typically it's bundled into the rent you pay as a tenant. And in some parts of the world you, as the tenant, are responsible for making the payment to the HOA management group directly— that is, you could be asked to write two "rent" checks, one to your landlord and a second to the building association to cover the monthly fee.

The HOA fee is more for newer buildings than for older ones and more for bigger residential communities with many shared amenities than for smaller ones with simply, say, a little clubhouse and pool.

Don't be scared off by a bigger-than-you'd-like HOA expense. You should be more concerned about an HOA fee that's not big enough. If the HOA doesn't have funds enough to maintain and repair the property and amenities, you, as the owner or the tenant, are the one who suffers.

Property Taxes

You won't be liable for any property taxes in Croatia, for example, or in Buenos Aires (though you will pay annual tax on property you own elsewhere in Argentina). That is to say, not every country imposes property tax, and for those that do, the cost to you will likely be considerably less than you may be paying for property tax now, because the percentage is less, the value of the real estate is less, or both.

If you intend only to rent, of course, property tax won't be an expense for you anywhere.

Transportation

Will you need a car where you're thinking of relocating? If so, this likely will be your greatest expense after housing. In some places, in fact, the cost of owning a vehicle can be greater than the cost of your rent. In the friendly mountain town of Santa Fe, Panama, for example, you could rent a two-bedroom house for $400 a month. However, unless you're comfortable with the idea of using your own two feet or a taxi to get around town and the national bus service to travel the rest of the country, you'll need to invest in a vehicle. In a remote mountain region like this one, where roads can flood during the rainy season, maintaining your vehicle won't be easy. It might seem as though you're repairing tires and replacing shock absorbers almost as often as you're filling the gas tank. If you're not up for the expense or the hassle of car ownership, consider less remote options and cities with good public transportation. If you live without a car in many of the places I discuss in these pages, the cost of transportation could go from being one of your biggest expenses to a negligible line item in your monthly budget.

Gas

Often used for cooking, gas is typically a negligible expense— a few dollars a month—except in places (France, for example) where homes are heated with gas. If you're using gas for heat, the cost varies according to the size of your residence, of course. In Paris, we pay the equivalent of $90 per month on average to heat our three-bedroom apartment.

Electricity

We spent more for electricity living in Panama (where we ran the air-conditioning day and night) than we did for both gas and electricity in Paris (where we needed it for both heating and cooling, depending on the season). The truly budget conscious should think about places like Cuenca, Ecuador; Medellín, Colombia; and Boquete, Panama, where the weather is springlike twelve months a year and you can get by most of the time without either heating or air-conditioning.

Telephone

A local cell phone and Skype are probably all you need. Depending on the country, a pay-as-you-go cell phone can make more sense than investing in a contract with a local cell phone service provider. In Panama, a $10 calling card for my pay-as-you-go cell phone lasts me all month.

You can call from Skype to a telephone for a few cents per minute, and Skype-to-Skype calls, including video calls, are free.

If you'll be operating a business, a voice over Internet phone (VoIP) system can be the most cost-efficient choice. Nowhere in the world is a landline phone any longer a necessary expense.

That said, some landline options bring benefits. In France, for example, you can buy a phone package from Orange for less than 40 euros a month that includes unlimited free calling to the United States and Canada, much of Latin America and the Caribbean, and all of Europe. Hard to beat that anywhere else in the world.

Internet

The cost of Internet service can be a significant part of your budget if you need uninterrupted access 24/7 and aren't relocating to a city. In Panama City, for example, you can have wireless Internet for as little as $30 or $40 a month. But for reliable service in the interior of the country, at the beach, or in the mountains, you'd have to invest in satellite Internet. This would cost you several hundred dollars in hardware and setup and then $150 a month or more.

Cable TV

I'd say skip the hassle and expense of cable unless you want to use it as a means for staying connected with the local culture and community (by watching local news, talk shows, and commercials, for example). You can access U.S. and international television shows and movies through Netflix, iTunes, Amazon Prime, and other streaming services. Nearly all American sports leagues offer comprehensive international streaming services for less than the cost of cable or satellite packages. Netflix's offerings depend on the country and are more limited outside the States. A virtual private network (VPN) or proxy service can help you access the U.S. options of some streaming apps but not Netflix.

Household Help

One of the big benefits of living overseas can be the opportunity to indulge in little luxuries you never could have afforded back home, including full-time help around the house for as little as $150 a month in Nicaragua or Uruguay. The going rate for a good maid who'll also cook for you and do your laundry in Panama City is $400 a month, half as much in the interior of the country. A gardener can cost as little as $300 a month (in Uruguay, for example). In Panama, you'll spend $600 a month for a full-time driver/man Friday.

Food

Anywhere you live in the world, including the States, groceries are a hugely variable expense. Your monthly food spend depends on how you want to live and eat. In Panama, a couple could spend less than $400 a month on groceries. On that budget, you could eat well, but you'd be eating like the locals.

Or you could shop at the Riba Smith superstore every week and load your cart with imported cheeses, specialty hams, wine, and prepared foods, in which case a couple's monthly grocery spend could be as much as, say, $800.

Grocery costs also vary according to region. In Paris, we live in the seventh arrondissement, in the historic heart of the city. Prices in the grocery stores in our neighborhood can be 25 percent more than prices for the same items in grocery stores in the fifteenth arrondissement, for example, a more working-class district. The longer you live in a place, the lower many expenses, especially grocery costs, can become as you get to know the least expensive places to shop for particular items.

Entertainment

This is another big variable that you control. If we stick with Panama City as an example, you could budget $150 a month for entertainment. That'd allow you two or three dinners out at modestly priced restaurants (Panama's capital boasts many good ones) and a couple of nights out at the cinema each month (a ticket for a first-run movie in English costs as little as $4, depending on the day of the week). On the other hand, you could spend $100 on a single dinner for two at Gaucho's, one of Panama City's best steak houses. You get the idea.

One way to keep your entertainment budget small is to locate yourself in a place where there's not much to do and little to spend money on. Beachcombing is free.

That . . . or choose a big city like Paris offering loads of fun stuff at no cost. Every museum in Paris offers at least one free admission day per month. Photo exhibits, gallery openings, and designer sample shows are regular occurrences and, again, sometimes at no cost . . . as are book clubs, expat happy hours, and conversation groups. Living in a city like Paris, you might have a monthly entertainment budget of thousands of euros or next to nothing.

Miscellaneous (Dry Cleaning, Haircuts, Household Bits and Pieces, Etc.)

In the places I recommend to you in the pages to come, these little everyday expenses can cost a fraction of what they're costing you now. In Granada, Nicaragua, whenever we visit, my husband has his hair cut at the barbershop on the main square for $3 (and no, I'm not embarrassed to be seen with him). Dry cleaning costs in Panama City average $2 per item (compared with 12 euros per item in Paris, for example).

Travel (Within Your New Country of Residence and for Visits Home)

How often will you want to return home? Your biggest related expense will be airfare. Allow for it in your budget, as well as for in-country travel. You're taking a big step and making a big effort to relocate somewhere new and exotic. Once you're there, you'll want to get out and see the place.

In Part III, I provide detailed monthly budgets for each country on my list of the world's best places to think about reinventing your life overseas. In every case, your cost of living depends on how and also where exactly in the country you choose to live. I'll walk you through the choices you'll need to make as we consider each destination in turn.

Step 3: Take Out a Map

Once you've taken inventory of your personal priorities and agendas and figured the budget for your move, you're ready to consider the geographic possibilities. Here's where this gets fun.

There are about two hundred countries in the world. Some are cheap, many are beautiful. Some have sandy coastlines; others boast interesting histories, lively cities, and great weather year-round. If you could live in any one of them, which one would you choose?

Start there. Below is a list of fifteen countries that bring a lot to the table whatever your reasons for considering a new life overseas:

➤ Argentina

➤ Belize

➤ Colombia

➤ Dominican Republic

➤ Ecuador

➤ France

➤ Italy

➤ Malaysia

➤ Mexico

➤ Nicaragua

➤ Panama

➤ Portugal

➤ Spain

➤ Thailand

➤ Uruguay

Which of these countries might make sense for you? Here's a pop quiz to jump-start your thinking:

Question 1: Which country offers year-round springlike temperatures in some regions?
A. Ecuador
B. Panama
C. Mexico
D. Colombia

Question 2: Which country offers exemptions from import duties (the tax you're charged when importing personal items, household goods, or a car, for example, into the country) for foreign residents, depending on the residency visa program you qualify for?
A. Panama
B. Uruguay
C. Malaysia
D. Belize

Question 3: In which country can you reduce your annual tax liability as a foreign resident, depending on the sources of your income?
A. Uruguay
B. Panama
C. Belize
D. Malaysia

Question 4: In which country can you find Joint Commission International (JCI)–accredited health care?
A. Panama
B. Colombia
C. Malaysia
D. Italy

Question 5: In which country could you live comfortably on $1,300 a month or less?
A. Thailand
B. Ecuador
C. Nicaragua
D. Portugal

If you chose A in each case, you're correct.

If you chose B in each case, you're also correct.

And yes, if you chose C or D in each case, again, you guessed right. My point is to show you that this isn't a straightforward A + B = C or D exercise.

Once you understand what you're looking for—a reduced cost of living, great weather, tax breaks, etc.—your plan isn't made. Deciding that you'd like to live in a land of eternal springtime, for example, doesn't point you in the direction of one country and one country only. Many countries offer some of the same advantages and benefits, but each has its disadvantages, too. The key is to understand not only the pluses but also the minuses in each case, so you can compare and contrast your options in that context. It's as important to understand the reasons *not* to move to a country as it is to appreciate the charms and attractions of any place that catches your attention.

Each of the fifteen countries on my list is appealing for many good but differing reasons. Start with these benefits. Allow your imagination to roam free. Let yourself get a little drunk on the possibilities of a new and better life someplace beautiful, sunny, cheap, and adventure-filled. Then sober up. You want a place that still measures up the morning after.

You've made a list of what's important to you, the reasons you're interested in starting a new life in a new country in the first place, and you've figured out how much you'll have available to spend to support your adventures overseas on a monthly basis. The next step is to connect the dots and to consider how each country on my list might—or might not—meet your needs, interests, expectations, and budget.

First I must admit that, in truth, my list is almost useless. You aren't going to retire to Uruguay or to Thailand or to any other country. You're going to retire to a neighborhood or a community or a region or a seaside town.

Once you begin thinking seriously about the idea of relocating overseas, you realize quickly that you've got to focus your search. I call it thin-slicing your options. You can't plan to retire to Panama or Spain any more than you could plan to retire to the United States. Think about that for a second. What would that mean, to retire to the United States? It's a silly question, impossible to answer. I could tell you what the weather would be like in Scottsdale, Arizona, what the cost for groceries for a couple would be in San Diego, California, and what the view from your balcony might be like living on the coast of Naples, Florida; but no one could answer those questions for the United States considered as a whole.

Neither does that kind of broad thinking make sense when you are pondering your options beyond U.S. borders. When thinking about your new life in Mexico, say, or France, you have to consider what it might be like to live in the Mexican colonial coastal town of Mazatlán or perhaps in the French countryside around Languedoc. Your life in these places would bear little resemblance to a life in the Yucatán around Cancún, for example, or in central Paris. As we consider each country on my list in Part III, I'll make particular regional recommendations to help you thin-slice your thinking.

This is one place where the Internet provides great support. As you consider and compare different overseas choices, go to a search engine like Google or Yahoo! and enter phrases like "expat groups" or "resources for expats" combined with the name of the country or region you're interested in. You will undoubtedly be presented with a list of local organizations of people just like you who've already done what you're planning to do. These folks are established in the place you're dreaming about, and they're standing by to lend a helping hand to others thinking about following in their footsteps.

Take them up on the offer. Join online chat groups and read expat bulletin boards specific to the countries on your short list. Expats are a friendly, welcoming bunch. They enjoy nothing so much as sharing their collective wisdom earned at the global retiree school of hard knocks and telling tales of the good, the bad, and the ugly of their personal adventures. After reading this book for general advice, check out the message boards and directories for answers to specific questions related to specific countries. Expats know better than anyone what it costs to rent a home in a particular neighborhood . . . the best local options for health insurance . . . the ins and outs of bringing your dog or cat into the country with you . . . the best place to bank . . . the peculiarities of the residency process . . . the best place to look for a maid . . . and on and on. The more current on-the-scene intelligence you're able to gather as you prepare for your move overseas, the more successful your relocation will be.

Step 4: Research Residency Options

You could move around the world, traveling from one country to another every few months as your curiosity and wanderlust dictate. You could divide your time among three or four countries each year. You could avoid the cold, escaping for a few months somewhere sunny and sandy every winter . . .

Each of these "live overseas" strategies is ever more common and easier all the time to organize at any age. If you don't have the nest egg or investment income to support the lifestyle you're imagining for yourself, earn the money you need along the way through a business you carry around the world with you in your laptop.

You could do all those things and never have to worry about or invest in the time or expense of formalizing your residency status anywhere. Don't overstay the time in country allowed a tourist, and you avoid the question of residency altogether.

However, if you'd like to be able to live full time and to stick around indefinitely in a particular country, then you need, early on in your planning process, to consider the options that country offers for becoming a legal resident.

In the 1980s, Costa Rica realized it could make a business of foreign, especially American, retirees and promoted the world's first formal *pensionado* (retired) visa program. You qualified by showing a minimum amount of retirement income. In return, Costa Rica granted you the right to live indefinitely in the country and to benefit from tax and other incentives. In the decades since, Panama, Ecuador, Nicaragua, Uruguay, Belize, Colombia, the Dominican Republic, and others have conceived and put into action similar programs. U.S. retirees have become a hot commodity. Countries compete for your attention.

If you're not a retiree but want to settle indefinitely in a particular country, you also have many good options today and more all the time, most predicated on an investment in the country, typically in a piece of real estate. It's also possible in many places to qualify for residency by starting a business.

A local attorney can detail all the potentially suitable possibilities available in the countries on your list, and in most cases I recommend you use a local attorney to process the associated paperwork for the visa you choose to apply for. It's worth the minimal expense, and it saves you the effort of trying to wade through the related red tape in a foreign language.

The most important thing about residency visa options for any country is to understand the rules before you get too far into your relocation plans. You don't want to begin house hunting in a country only to find that you don't qualify for any visa option and won't in fact be able to take up full-time residence as you'd hoped.

Here's some relevant terminology to keep in mind as you research the particular visa options for the countries that have your attention:

A visa is a document that allows you to remain within a country's borders for a specified period, sometimes with specified restrictions, limitations, and/or benefits. A tourist visa is the easiest form of entry into a country. This is all you'll need for your initial scouting visits, and maybe all you'll ever need if yours is a plan of perpetual wandering. Most Western passport holders (including Americans) aren't required to apply for tourist visas to most countries. You need only show up. When you arrive at the entry point into the country (typically the international airport), you show your passport, and you're automatically granted a tourist visa and allowed to enter the country. Sometimes you'll be required to fill out a form, and sometimes you'll be asked to pay a fee.

A tourist visa allows you to stay in a country for 30 to 90 or even as many as 180 days (in the case of Mexico), depending on the country and the passport you carry. To stay in a country beyond the number of days allowed for by the tourist visa, you'll need a residency visa.

When you hold a residency visa or permit for a country, you're a legal resident. You're not a citizen. This is an important distinction, especially for tax purposes. You're not a citizen, and you don't necessarily have the right to work. A work permit is a separate thing.

Residency visas come in different forms—temporary and permanent, for example. A temporary visa, as you might guess, gives you the right to remain in the country for a limited time, typically one year. After that time, you must renew your status. The reapplication is usually a formality, but you may be asked to prove again that you meet whatever requirements you were required to meet to obtain the visa in the first place.

Depending on the country, after you've renewed your temporary residency visa a certain number of times (three or maybe five, for example), you can be eligible then for permanent residency. It depends on the type of temporary residency visa you started with.

In addition, some countries offer programs that grant permanent residency from the start. This is the case with the Fast Track program in the Dominican Republic and Panama's Friendly Nations program (more on this below).

Once you've obtained permanent resident status, you're done. You're free to live in the country as long as you like and to come and go as you please.

Residency visa requirements aren't onerous, but the paperwork can be a hassle and the process can require several trips to the local immigration office (where the bureaucrats behind the counter aren't going to speak English). This is why I recommend that, for most countries, even if it's not required, you engage an in-country attorney experienced at helping foreigners obtain residency. The cost is typically modest (maybe up to $2,000, though residency costs in Panama, for example, have risen in recent years and can add up to several thousand by the end of the process), and you save yourself time, headaches, and missteps.

I've heard stories from people over the years who've tried to apply for foreign residency status in various countries on their own, spent sometimes months battling with the local bureaucrats, resubmitting forms, refiling applications, collecting more and other documents, only ultimately to have their applications denied for reasons they didn't understand. In the cases where the would-be applicant then enlisted the help of a local attorney to restart the process, the attorney was able to identify quickly where the mistake had been made the first time around.

This isn't rocket science. But it is a process. And it takes place in another language and in another country, where they do things the way they do things. The systems and protocols don't have to make sense to you, and sometimes they won't. I've found that it's a waste of time and energy to try to understand. You don't need to understand how the residency visa application process works in France. You need only qualify for a visa to remain in the country (if that's your objective). Why drive yourself crazy (and waste your time and money) trying to make heads or tails of French immigration law when you could easily hire a French attorney who has spent years interpreting it?

Generally, to apply for a residency visa, you'll need an FBI report (one that, hopefully, shows there's nothing to report). You may also be required to undergo a physical exam and to show proof of health insurance that covers you locally.

Most of the countries on my list offer a "retiree" visa (typically called a *pensionado* visa in Spanish-speaking countries). The minimum monthly financial requirements vary by country but range from $600 to $2,500, sometimes more. In many cases, your Social Security income alone is enough to qualify. Typically, a retiree visa comes with tax-exemption benefits, including the ability to bring your household goods, personal belongings, and a car into the country duty-free.

Pensionado visa programs can come with age restrictions and require that the minimum monthly income is retirement income specifically (from a pension or Social Security, for example). This is not the case for a *rentista* visa available from some countries.

You can generally apply for *rentista* residency status at any age. You qualify by showing minimum monthly income (the amount differs country to country), but this income can come from any reliable source.

Without a minimum amount of provable monthly income, your options for qualifying for residency include making an investment in the country, typically in a piece of real estate or an operating business. If you intend to start a business anyway, obviously that'd be the residency strategy to pursue. Otherwise, an investment in a piece of property is certainly a less onerous requirement than starting and operating a business. Some countries also allow you to qualify for an investor visa by putting funds in a local bank CD.

Another option available in some countries is a "person of means" visa. You qualify by showing that you have sufficient assets to support yourself while residing in the country (and therefore will not be a burden on the state). The cost of living in a country is usually a guide to the level of assets you'll have to show to qualify for a person of means visa. Typically, you'll be required to put a minimum of $100,000 in a local bank (in an interest-bearing account).

In 2012, the then president of Panama, Ricardo Martinelli, launched a unique residency option that has come to be known as the Friendly Nations program. If you hold a passport to one of the fifty countries on the list, you can qualify for Panama residency and a work permit by purchasing a piece of property, opening a Panama corporation, or showing an offer of employment in the country and depositing $5,000 in a Panama bank account.

Martinelli launched this one-of-a-kind program to attract educated, English-speaking labor from around the world to fill the thousands of jobs being created by the hundreds of foreign companies setting up shop in his country. He knew that if he didn't import enough workers to keep the foreign enterprises staffed, the foreign investors would go elsewhere. The program is one reason Panama City is the fast-growing boomtown that it is.

If you're nowhere near retirement age, need an income, but aren't up for starting a business of your own, put Panama at the top of your list. This is one place in the world where an English-speaking college graduate will find it relatively easy to land a job.

Your final residency visa option can be to marry a local. I'll leave you to sort out the details of this on your own.

How do you find an in-country attorney to handle your visa paperwork? I suggest you seek referrals from expats already retired in the country. An attorney is one resource you don't want to choose randomly over the Internet. Try to get at least two referrals from expats who've gone through the residency process, then follow up to interview each referred attorney informally over the phone or perhaps during your first country visit.

Two final notes on the topic of residency. First, some but not all residency programs can lead to citizenship and a second passport. If this is an agenda for you, be sure you confirm that the residency program you choose qualifies you for eventual naturalization.

Second, visa rules change, and visa programs come and go. When you identify an option that works for you, act on it even if you're not planning an immediate move. Put your residency visa in your back pocket when you're able and keep it current. Then you're assured the right to take up residence in your chosen Shangri-la whenever it suits you.

Step 5: Get Good Tax Advice

We didn't move from the United States to Ireland all those years ago to save on taxes. Neither did we make our third international move in 2008, from Paris to Panama, for the tax benefits. However, the tax advantages of both these moves were not lost on us.

Controlling your tax liability can make a big difference in your standard of living. Reduce your tax bill from 40 percent to 20 percent a year, and it's like giving yourself a raise and supercharging your investment portfolio. You're earning no more, but you've got a whole lot more disposable income.

So, again, we've never made a move to reduce our tax burden, and neither should you. I don't recommend trying to organize your life according to tax codes. But you don't want to ignore them, either. We Americans have it double tough. No matter where we go, our obligations to Uncle Sam follow. When we take up residence in a foreign jurisdiction, therefore, we've got double the tax masters. We're beholden to both the IRS and the local tax collector.

We must understand the tax requirements on both sides, and we must file annual tax returns in both jurisdictions (the only exception is if you earn less than the annual reporting requirement amount in income), but that is not to say we owe double the taxes. On the contrary, as an American abroad, you can reduce your annual tax burden, even significantly, from what you were paying when you were residing full time within U.S. borders. This is where things can get complicated.

Which leads to my first and probably most important piece of advice on the subject of taxes for the overseas retiree: Don't try to become a global tax authority. Hire one.

In fact, you need the advice of two attorneys: one who works in the jurisdiction where you're planning to live or invest and one in the United States (or your home country, wherever that is). During one of our scouting trips to Ireland before our move, we met with Ernst & Young in Dublin. We didn't know what we didn't know, but we knew enough to ask for help.

At the time, Ireland taxed its foreign residents on a remittance basis. That is, living in Ireland as a foreigner, you paid tax on only whatever money you earned in or brought into the country. You could earn hundreds of thousands of dollars a year, but if you brought (remitted) only $50,000 per year into the Emerald Isle, the Irish tax authorities expected their cut of that $50,000 only. Maybe you owed other tax authorities in other countries tax on other pieces of your total income, but Ireland cared about only the piece of your income that flowed into Ireland.

In addition, as Americans residing abroad, Lief and I both were able to take advantage of the IRS's foreign earned income exclusion (FEIE), meaning that our first $80,000 to $85,000 of income each year apiece (the amount of the exemption has increased over the past two decades and stands today at $102,100) was free from U.S. tax. Plus, Ireland and the United States have a double-taxation agreement, meaning we received tax credit in the States for income taxed in Ireland.

Bottom line, by organizing ourselves carefully, as Irish residents, we were able to reduce our total overall tax rate to less than 20 percent per year. Unfortunately, the tax laws in the Emerald Isle have changed significantly since, and Ireland no longer taxes its residents on a remittance basis. Today, Ireland taxes its residents on their worldwide income, just as the United States does (with some complicated exceptions). In other words, an American today couldn't live in Ireland as tax-efficiently as we did.

For tax-efficiency today, look at Panama, Belize, Uruguay, or Malaysia. The position of these countries on taxing their foreign residents is about as good as it gets. In these four countries, you pay tax on only the money you earn in the country. Earn no income within the country, and you pay no tax in the country.

If you become a full-time resident of one of these countries, you could be 100 percent exempt from income tax in the United States as well, meaning that as an American residing full time in one of these countries, you could live tax-free. This is completely legal. And, depending on your situation, it can also be a relatively straightforward exercise to organize your financial affairs to keep you both compliant and tax-exempt.

It comes down to how much income you earn and where it comes from. But it's possible and legal. You need counsel you can trust to help you consider the options and make a plan.

Don't type "foreign tax specialist" or "international tax adviser" into a Web search engine—you'll find lots of resources that way, but none you'll know you can trust. The Internet is awash in people who'll set you up with offshore structures for a fee and who'll be glad to help you put one over on the Internal Revenue Service. You don't want to put one over on the IRS. You just don't want to pay that U.S. government agency a dollar more of your income than you absolutely have to each year.

And you don't necessarily want offshore structures, either.

I have no idea what you do want or need. And probably neither do you. But I can tell you this: Take the advice of some offshore expert you find with the help of Google, and your chances of ending up someplace you don't want to be (engaged in a one-on-one conversation with a representative of the IRS, for example) are probably increased.

I also don't recommend sending a request to your U.S. accountant or attorney asking for help managing the tax consequences of your new life or investments abroad. He won't have answers for you, and your questions will make him nervous.

My U.S. attorney at the time we were planning our first international move, to Ireland, told me not to mess around with the foreign earned income exclusion for Americans living abroad. "It's too risky," he counseled me. "Better just to pay what you owe and not to try to get away with anything." I understood almost nothing about any of this at the time, but I knew enough to know he didn't know enough.

I didn't replace that attorney immediately or easily, though not for lack of trying. I began looking for a competent, experienced, and open-minded U.S. tax adviser as soon as I realized my attorney of many years was none of those things when it came to the issues faced by Americans living abroad.

I've met many fellows over the years who called themselves offshore tax experts. Finally, a few years ago, I found a guy whom I'd call an offshore tax expert. His name is Vincenzo. He knows his way around the offshore world. He knows what's allowed and what's not, and he respects the rules. Vincenzo also knows how to solve problems and how to get things done. This is the kind of tax adviser you want helping you to manage this part of your life overseas.

As I told you, though, you need not one, but two global tax authorities, one to manage tax, reporting, and structure issues for you in the States and one to manage those things in your jurisdiction of residency. Again, you don't want to find this second tax counsel on the Internet. I recommend you employ the same strategy I suggested for finding an attorney to help you with your residency visa work: Ask for referrals from expats already living in the country you're considering. Get two or three recommendations and interview each in person.

Fundamentally, the most important tool in the U.S. expat's tax toolbox is the foreign earned income exclusion (FEIE). If you qualify, the FEIE allows you to exclude from U.S. federal income tax up to $102,100 (in 2017) of foreign-earned income.

Like all U.S. citizens and residents who earn more than a certain amount—$10,350 (single) or $20,700 (married filing a joint return) in 2017, for people under age sixty-five—you must file a U.S. personal income tax return no matter where you reside. You must file, but that does not mean you must pay tax. One of the many benefits for an American living or retiring abroad is that once you're a foreign resident, you're eligible to take advantage of the FEIE.

The exclusion applies to foreign-earned income only—that is, wages or self-employment income (independent contractor earnings, for example, or payments for travel articles or photographs) you receive for services you perform while living outside the United States. Wages can come from a U.S. corporation or a foreign corporation, including an offshore corporation, and it does not matter if you are also a shareholder or owner of that foreign corporation.

The important thing to understand is that earned income does not include interest, dividends, or other investment or passive income.

The key is to qualify. You do this in one of two ways:

1. The 330-Day Test. To qualify for the FEIE using the 330-day test, you must be in another country for 330 days out of any 365-day period. It does not matter if the 330 days run over two calendar years (between November 1, 2017, and October 31, 2018, for example), and you can avail yourself of a special extension to file your tax return to give you time to meet this requirement.

2. The Bona Fide Residency Test. In this case, you achieve foreign residency by moving to another country and making it "home." You can intend to return to the States in the future, but you must move to the foreign country for an "indefinite" or "extended" period of time that must include one full calendar year.

The 330-day test is fact based, while the residency test hinges on your intentions and is therefore more difficult to use and to prove.

The bona fide residency test is one of the most misunderstood and misused sections of the U.S. tax code. You are a bona fide resident of another country if you move there and make it your home. You show this, typically, by filing and paying taxes in that country.

Bottom line, and in layman's terms, the following is what you need to know about filing and paying taxes as an overseas retiree. These are six things I wish someone had told me about international tax planning before I made my first international move.

1. Maybe you don't need to do anything. Asset protection isn't an issue until you've got assets enough to warrant the investment of time and money to figure out how to protect them. In some jurisdictions, yes, you're wise to hold property in a local or an offshore corporation, but not all. Before you do anything, make sure you understand why you're doing it and what the real benefit will be.

2. Whatever you do, it shouldn't cost you tens of thousands of dollars. Okay, maybe if you're Bill Gates or Warren Buffett, a big investment in managing your tax and asset issues is warranted. But for average Joes, it's not.

3. The foreign earned income exclusion may be the beginning and the end of the tax planning you require. It alone can allow you to live and work overseas tax-free.

4. When it comes to purchasing and holding real estate overseas, remember these two things. First, the jurisdiction is the key. Second, as a result, no attorney in your home country is going to be able to help you figure out what to do. You need a local attorney, experienced at working with foreign buyers, to help you determine how to purchase and how to hold (in a local corporation, in a foreign corporation, in your own name, in a trust, etc.).

5. When it comes to dealing with the tax issues in any new jurisdiction where you take up residence, the key is to research, plan, and take action *before* taking up residence. Certain options for mitigating your local tax bill can come off the table once you've taken a local address. Again, you need local legal advice.

6. You can avoid any local tax issues by being only a part-time resident. The particulars differ from jurisdiction to jurisdiction, but even if you're a legal resident, generally, if you spend fewer than six months in a place, you won't be considered a resident for tax purposes. There are exceptions, so, again, get advice.

Step 6: Shop for Health Insurance

In some places around the world, the cost of medical care can be so low that it can make more sense to pay for it out of pocket rather than insuring against it. Further, in some places worldwide, under certain circumstances, health care can be free. Almost anywhere in the world, medical care is more affordable than in the United States. These realities all speak to what can be one of the biggest upsides of spending time in another country.

How you decide to plan for health care and health insurance is one of the most personal aspects of a move overseas. Start your planning by understanding that with few exceptions (some military policies, for example), your U.S. health insurance, whatever it is, probably won't cover you outside the United States. Medicare definitely won't work overseas. However, Medicare can be an important part of your total strategy if supplemented with a local or an international policy that excludes coverage in the United States.

Big picture, when preparing for medical costs in your new life overseas, you're choosing among four options. You could purchase a "local" or "domestic" insurance policy; you could purchase an international insurance policy; you could opt not for health insurance but a travel insurance policy; or you could go naked, as I refer to it, opting out of insurance altogether. All can be good options, with pluses and minuses. Which you choose depends on your circumstances.

In Panama, for example, a local health insurance policy can cost as little as $170 a month, and it can be all the coverage you need. The trouble with local agencies in this country (and in most countries) is that they'll write a policy for you as a new client only up to a certain age (typically early sixties or midsixties).

Most international insurance groups, on the other hand, will insure you as a new client up to the age of seventy-four. One company, Cigna, has an international policy you can qualify for up to age eighty. Of course, the cost is more than $170 a month, but the point is, you can get insurance as a new resident in a foreign country up until age eighty. And once you're insured, the coverage continues for the rest of your life, as long as you pay the premiums.

Of all the international options, I recommend Cigna. It's the best-quality coverage for the best price. Moreover, Cigna is a big and solid operation. When it comes to health insurance, you want to buy from someone who's going to be around in ten or twenty years . . . when you need them.

A Cigna policy might be more expensive than a local insurer (typically, it will be), but a Cigna policy is also usable anywhere in the world. And unlike with a regional plan, the risk that Cigna is going to leave you holding the bag just when you need them most is small. And even the most expensive international policy from Cigna (rates vary, depending on the country where you base the policy, your age, and your general state of health) can be far, far less expensive than comparable U.S. health insurance.

Here, then, is the thinking you should entertain as you consider your options for health insurance overseas:

First, do you want a local policy or an international one from a company like Cigna? Second, if you intend to be only part-time retired to another country, spending only a limited time abroad each year, perhaps a travel insurance policy would be the most cost-effective choice.

Finally, as I mentioned at the start of this section, depending on where you're thinking about taking up residence overseas, you could consider the option of going without insurance, period.

The most important thing in making this decision is that you can sleep at night. If the thought of going naked, as it were, sounds horrifying, don't consider it.

However, I know a number of expats who do just that. Since these folks spend most of their time in places where the cost of medical care is extraordinarily low, they don't worry about insuring against it. Thailand would be a good example.

What's more, in some countries, once you become a permanent legal resident, you're eligible for free health care. During our years living full time in Ireland, for example, we enjoyed medical care at no cost, including coverage for the delivery of our son, Jack.

Which option is right for you? In short:

Local insurance is cheap but limited in its coverage. International insurance is more expensive (though less expensive than comparable coverage in the United States, for example) and should cover you anywhere you travel. What you decide to do depends on your age, your current health status, and your ultimate retirement plan. Lief and I carry an international insurance policy with a high deductible for our family. We're still relatively young and healthy, and we move around a lot, typically in countries where health costs are low, so the high annual deductible isn't a concern for us. We've decided that we don't mind paying as we go for ordinary medical care. However, we want to be covered in the event of a medical catastrophe anywhere in the world. That's what our high-deductible international policy allows for.

Most countries have both public and private health care facilities. Public health care systems (called social security systems in many countries), especially in developing nations, typically offer a lesser standard of care than you are probably accustomed to. If you are traveling to (or living in) a country that does offer private health care, I recommend that as your number one option for medical and emergency treatment.

If you determine that you're not comfortable with (and/or not eligible for) the public health care system in the country where you intend to live or retire, following are your other, paid options.

1. A Hospital Insurance Plan

In many countries you can arrange medical insurance through specific private hospitals. These hospital insurance plans are not general health insurance, and *they cover your treatment in that hospital only* (in some cases, you can also be treated at an affiliated facility). If you travel outside the country or even within the country but far from the hospital through which you've organized your coverage, and you find yourself in need of medical care, you could be in trouble. You'll either have to pay all medical costs out of pocket or find your way back to the hospital where you're insured (covering the related costs yourself). Traveling back to the hospital may not be a viable option in an emergency.

Furthermore, the care you receive with a hospital insurance plan is sometimes not as good as it should be. Say you have a serious health crisis and are admitted to the hospital for an extended period. You mount a hospital bill upward of, say, $10,000, yet you have paid only a total of $5,000 in premiums to your hospital plan. In this case, the hospital may take steps to cut costs. It is not unheard of for hospitals to withhold tests or treatments if they feel the patient has become too expensive.

Also, hospital plans generally do not have long life-spans. The hospitals tend to lose money on these programs, and when any business is losing money, the easiest solution can be to pull the plug. You do not want to have paid your insurance premiums for a number of years, assuming you will be covered for life, and then discover suddenly that the hospital will no longer honor your policy. By this time, your circumstances could have changed. You could have passed a certain age or you could have developed some condition, making it more difficult now to obtain alternative coverage.

On the other hand, in-country hospital policies can be very affordable and can include extra benefits that make them very appealing. The Hospital Santa Fe in Panama City, Panama, for example, offers an insurance program through the hospital that accepts new policyholders of any age. A sixty-year-old man might pay $130 per month for coverage; a male ninety years old or older might pay $210.

A private hospital membership plan in Uruguay is called a *mutualista*; membership is about $100 a month, depending on your age. The British Hospital in Montevideo has its own hospital plan called the Hospital Scheme. This offers premium plans but can be twice as expensive as the *mutualista* plans.

Hospital insurance policies are risky but can be a good option if you live close to the hospital offering the coverage and do not plan to travel much throughout the country or, especially, abroad.

2. Travel Medical Insurance

A travel medical insurance policy can be a good option because these are low cost and guaranteed issue. You don't have to file a lengthy health history, and coverage can be put into effect within minutes. Further, you can opt for a $0 deductible, 100 percent coverage beyond a deductible (rather than any copay requirement), and you can be accepted as a new policyholder long after you can typically qualify for local or international insurance.

In many ways, a travel medical policy can be the most flexible possible insurance. It's not intended to be long-term insurance but can work longer term than you might imagine given the name. Definitely, a travel medical insurance policy is a good choice for coverage during your scouting stage, when you're trying a place on for size, and if you're beyond the age cutoff for a local or an international policy.

The best resource for more information on a travel medical insurance policy is Insurance Services of America (www.insurancefortrips.com).

3. Local (Domestic) Medical Insurance Policies

Paid hospital insurance plans and travel medical insurance can make sense under certain circumstances, as I've explained. However, if you plan to live or retire overseas, either full time or part-time, and certainly if you plan to travel regularly, your two top options are an in-country medical insurance policy or an international medical insurance policy.

A local medical insurance policy can be ideal for you if you have no preexisting conditions and are younger than sixty-three. These insurance providers typically are connected with hospital networks and doctors throughout the country, meaning you are not limited to one health care facility, as you are with a hospital plan. Typically, your coverage follows you anywhere you might travel in the country. It does not, however (and this is the critical thing to understand), follow you outside that country.

Again, if you'll be traveling internationally on a regular basis or spending part of each year somewhere else, an in-country policy probably doesn't make sense for you. However, if you plan to be based in one country most of the time, a local medical insurance policy can be less expensive (in some cases, much less expensive) than a comparable international medical insurance policy.

On the other hand, the coverage is usually more basic. And as I've explained, the cutoff age for coverage can be a serious limitation. For instance, in Panama, most local insurance companies will not enter into a new policy agreement if you are over the age of sixty-three. As well, local insurance companies have smaller client bases than big international insurance agencies, so they are much more affected by the claims you make. If they believe you are costing them too much money, they could terminate their contract with you. Local insurance companies may be ideal if you are moving to a country where medical care is inexpensive. If you need minor treatment, and it is affordable, you can choose to pay out of pocket rather than making a claim to your local insurance company, saving that for catastrophic coverage.

When shopping for in-country insurance providers, don't be confused by their names. A number of countries, for example, have franchises of well-known U.S. insurance companies, such as Blue Cross and Blue Shield (which has branches in 170 countries). You must understand, however, that these international branches of Blue Cross and Blue Shield are franchises only. Foreign policies are not the same as the coverage you may know from the United States or Canada. The international franchises work with locally owned insurance companies. *Your Blue Cross and Blue Shield policy from the United States or Canada generally will not follow you if you move overseas.*

4. International Medical Insurance Policies

Frankly, the safest, most secure, and most reliable option for international health insurance, certainly if your plan is to be living overseas for an extended or indefinite period of time, is an international health insurance policy with a big international insurance agency that has a long track record. In most cases, international insurance policies provide the most comprehensive and most appropriate level of medical coverage.

You do not have to rely on one hospital or even facilities in one country. International insurance companies have networks of doctors and hospitals around the globe where you can receive excellent treatment. An international medical policy should cover you nearly anywhere you choose to travel and for whatever period you choose to stay there. Note, however, that some international medical insurance policies do not cover you for travel within the United States. Health care costs are so high in the States that some international policies specifically omit it from their areas of coverage. If you plan to travel in the States, check with your insurance provider to see if you will be covered. If not, the option can be to purchase a more expensive policy.

International medical insurance premiums are based on your age and the amount and type of coverage you want. Most policies are guaranteed for life once you have been accepted for coverage. That is to say, the insurer cannot discontinue your policy as you get older or if you become ill. Furthermore, if you're moving to a country where you do not speak the local language, international medical insurance providers will give you access to physicians who speak your native language or provide a translator. The larger international insurance companies have networks of providers around the globe so they can settle bills directly with hospitals and ensure that you are receiving the appropriate care. Other benefits of international insurance policies are that they often cover medical evacuation and repatriation.

International insurance may not be ideal for everyone, but you should take a good look at it before making any other choice. I recommend it as the top option for globe-trotting expats.

Cigna, Bupa, and HTH Worldwide are three top international insurance companies (for Americans; HTH Worldwide is not available to non-Americans). HTH offers annual plans for global living, short-term travel medical insurance, and trip cancellation coverage. All things considered, Cigna can be the best option in the majority of situations. If you are living or working abroad, Cigna's international health plans offer choice and flexibility with optional add-ons. Cigna also runs a twenty-four-hour multilingual help line and online access to your policy and account. Cigna is often not the cheapest option, but I feel it's typically the best one. And a policy with a high deductible can be very affordable.

Perhaps the most important piece of advice on this subject is to decide as early on as possible in your planning which strategy you want to pursue for health care and insurance. Then if you decide you want to invest in health insurance, proceed with the process of obtaining it, even if your move isn't until some time in the future. The longer you wait to apply, the older you are on the date of application. The older you are, the more difficult and more expensive it can be to qualify for coverage. I met a gentleman at a conference in Panama recently who approached me and said, "I'm sixty-three years old. What are my options for health insurance?"

"When's your birthday?" I asked. "In four months," he replied.

"Your option is to arrange a policy in the next four months," I advised.

Step 7: Understand the Local Real Estate Market (for Both Sales and Rentals)

Here's the first and most important thing to understand about most real estate markets beyond North American borders: They don't come with multiple listing services.

In the United States, if you want to shop for a house, you can walk into any real estate agency, sit down with an agent, dictate your criteria for purchase (neighborhood, number of bedrooms, number of bathrooms, total square footage, range for the purchase price, etc.), watch as the agent types those details into the multiple listing service (MLS) system, then review, immediately, with the agent, the matches. Within a matter of minutes, you're presented with every piece of property currently listed for sale that matches your purchase parameters. Piece of cake. Model of efficiency.

And impossible in most of the rest of the world. With a handful of localized exceptions (for example, you can access pseudo multiple listings for particular regions of Mexico, for the island of Roatán, in Honduras, and for Buenos Aires, though not for the rest of Argentina), in most of the world, to get a full picture of what's available for sale or for rent (in most countries, agents handle both sales and rentals), you're going to have to meet with every agent in town. This is true not just in emerging markets in Latin America and the Caribbean, but in Europe as well. Outside North America, real estate listings are proprietary, not shared. Agents do not cooperate and will look at you as though you've lost your mind if you suggest to them the idea that they might split commissions with one another and all make more money in the long run.

The U.S. real estate industry is developed and competitive. Real estate industries elsewhere are a study in inefficiency. Outside North America, it's common to find the same property listed with more than one agent—not because the agents are sharing the listing (what a notion), but because the seller gave the listing to each agent individually, sometimes at different prices. Between the lack of an MLS and the possibility that the same property is listed with different agents at different prices, it's nigh on impossible to get a read on comparables. What *should* a particular size and type of property cost? Who could say?

When we moved to Ireland two decades ago, I'd been covering the "retire overseas" beat for more than thirteen years already. I was well familiar with how the real estate industries work in the emerging, unregulated markets of Latin America and the Caribbean. But I thought Europe would be different. Naively, I expected the real estate industry in Ireland to operate like the real estate industry in the United States. When we arrived in Waterford, therefore, my husband and I went to the offices of the biggest real estate agency in town. We explained what kind of house we were interested in buying (Georgian and old). The agent took us to see two houses.

"Neither of these suits us," I explained. "What else is available?"

"That's it," the agent replied. "That's all I have."

Could there really be only two old Georgian houses for sale in all of County Waterford? In fact, no, there were others. But the agent we were speaking with had only two on his books. Then it struck us. The Irish property market doesn't operate like the one in the United States. It operates more like the emerging markets of Latin America. We reconciled ourselves to the consequences of this and made appointments to sit down with every agent in Waterford City to review the listings each carried. In the course of these meetings, we encountered more than one case of the same property being listed with different agencies at different prices.

Here's the second thing to understand about many real estate markets outside the United States, especially the unregulated ones south of the Rio Grande: The real estate agent you meet with doesn't work for you, and he doesn't really work for the seller, either. He works for the commission, which he wants to be as big as possible. In some markets, this can lead to what's called net pricing, whereby the agent will promise the seller a fixed amount for his property. The agent then sells for whatever he can sell for and pockets the difference. Maybe he walks away with a reasonable commission, or maybe he makes 20 percent, 30 percent, or more on the deal. You, as the buyer, never know. I make this point not to alarm but to prepare you. Don't take for granted that "your" real estate agent works for you (as you might in the States), and you'll be fine.

When you meet initially with local property agents, you're trying to get the lay of the land and a read on the market, to find out what's available at what price. You're not necessarily preparing to buy. You're not ready to make that commitment yet. First you want to take your chosen haven for a test spin.

Once you've narrowed your list of dream havens to one, and you're thinking you've found your ideal match, plan to spend at least six months living in the place. During that period, rent. Maybe your chosen haven won't turn out to be all you imagined it to be. Or maybe you'll find that the country suits you fine, but the neighborhood where you've settled for your trial living experience doesn't. As I've mentioned, I've yet to meet a single expat who regrets having made the move overseas. However, I have known some who weren't happy with their initial location choices. That's no problem—as long as you haven't invested in the purchase of a home, which is why I strongly recommend renting first.

In both Ireland two decades ago and then, seven years later, when we began spending time in Paris, we rented for nearly a year before buying, and in both cases we were glad we did. In Ireland, at first we thought that we wanted to be in Waterford City center. We rented a small house on the river within walking distance of our daughter's school. Ideal . . . on paper. In fact, we realized quickly that Waterford City living wasn't for us, and we began looking for a place in the country. When our lease in town ran out, we were ready to take up more permanent residence in the old Georgian farmhouse we'd found twenty minutes outside the city, with fields of sheep and cows and low stone walls all around. Lahardan House, as the place is known, was our comfortable and cozy Irish country home for more than six years.

Likewise, in Paris, we'd always thought we wanted to settle in the fifth arrondissement, in the heart of the city. A few months in a rental apartment across the Seine from Notre-Dame cured us of that idea. We realized that in fact we wanted something a little quieter and more removed from the tourist throngs. We found and purchased an early eighteenth-century apartment on a narrow street in the seventh arrondissement that few tourists ever find. Our place in Paris is tucked away from the beaten path, yet only one block back from the river and five minutes' walk from the Louvre.

In some cases, you may want not only to rent first but to rent, period. For my money, property, especially land, is the most sensible place to put your investment capital. On the other hand, property as a place to live, especially in the context of a move overseas, might best be rented rather than acquired. Certainly, as I've said, you want to rent first. But renting rather than owning your dream home overseas also has long-term advantages.

First, renting keeps you mobile. When you're ready for your next adventure, you need wait only until the term of your lease is up. You don't have to find a buyer for your immovable asset, and you don't have to relocate your movable ones (that is, your furniture and other household goods, assuming you're renting furnished and don't need to bring your own furniture with you). As a renter, your options are eternally open.

Second, renting means you have no maintenance worries or expense, no property upkeep, and no property taxes.

In addition, there's another reason why you might want to rent rather than buy: You may have no choice. In some of the places on my list, financing isn't an option. Nicaragua, Uruguay, Ecuador, Colombia . . . these are cash economies. No local bank is going to lend you, as a foreigner, money to buy a house. You can borrow locally to buy in some overseas jurisdictions—including Panama, for example, and most of Europe—but qualifying can be difficult unless you're able to show sufficient local income, and the terms likely won't be what you're accustomed to. Fixed rates of interest are uncommon. Also, to qualify for a local mortgage in any country outside the United States, you'll be required to obtain local life insurance for the entire term of the loan. In the United States, you can buy a life insurance policy that will cover you through age one hundred. That's not true anywhere else. Typically, in the rest of the world, you won't be able to obtain a policy to cover you beyond age seventy or seventy-five. If you're sixty-five years old at the time you apply for financing, therefore, you'll be offered, at best, a ten-year loan. Better than no loan at all, but perhaps not good enough to make the idea of borrowing sensible.

Your best option for a noncash purchase in a market where bank financing is not an option can be seller financing. In Latin American and Caribbean markets, this is a viable strategy. When you've identified a piece of property you're interested in buying, approach the seller—either directly or through your attorney or real estate agent—to ask if he'd be open to carrying back some portion of the purchase price. You aren't likely to find someone willing to carry a twenty-year loan for you, but three, five, or seven years, say, can be possible.

Before 2008, another option was to pull equity out of real estate assets "back home." But that's not so easy post the global property crisis. Maybe your place back home isn't worth what it was worth a few years ago. And maybe it's not so easy right now for you to get a second mortgage. So what? You don't have to own your home overseas to enjoy the retirement of your dreams. You only have to find it.

It's important to note, though, that even renting abroad can come with complications you may not expect. Below are twelve important things to know before you sign a lease in a foreign country.

1. What's included in your monthly rent? Make sure the lease establishes clearly what's included in your rent and what's not—building or homeowners' association fees, water, utilities, phone, Internet, etc.

2. If you're liable for utilities, find out the previous renter's average costs. Sometimes these can be a shock.

3. Understand what's included with "furnished" versus "unfurnished." In some places, unfurnished means no refrigerator, no stove, maybe even no lighting fixtures. Does furnished include air-conditioning units? Years ago, when we were shopping for a house to rent in Waterford, Ireland, I was confused by ads that indicated "all mod cons" (that is, "all modern conveniences"). Finally, I came to understand that this meant the house had central heating. Many in Ireland at the time still didn't.

4. Understand how, where, and to whom you pay which bills each month. Maybe you deposit the rent directly into the owner's bank account. Maybe you pay a rental manager. Maybe you have to hand-deliver the check to your landlord. In Europe, rent is often paid by direct debit from your local bank account, which means you need a local bank account. And often building and HOA fees are paid to a different person or organization and by a separate check, not as part of the rent.

5. Check for a sales clause in your lease. What protection do you have against the owner selling the apartment and giving you limited notice that you have to move out? The lease should include a compensation allowance in case the place is sold while you're renting.

6. Understand who is responsible for setting up the utilities. Will they remain in the landlord's name or will they be switched to your name? There are pluses and minuses either way. For example, what is your liability if the electric bill is transferred into your name?

7. Ask what documentation you'll have to produce to be able to rent. In France, you need to satisfy the landlord that you can afford to become his tenant, and because it's France, you do this by creating a thick dossier of financial documents, bank statements, pay stubs, reference letters, bank letters, guarantor letters, etc. It's a serious effort that you can't undertake lightly.

8. What repairs and maintenance are you responsible for? In some countries, as the renter, you can be responsible for structural repairs (cracks in the facade, for example, or a leaky roof).

9. Document any existing damage and the current condition of used fixtures or appliances. Take photos.

10. Understand when the rental period begins. The start date of your rental (that is, the date from which you're paying rent) doesn't always coincide with the date when you take up occupancy. Our first year in Panama City, for example, we paid rent for two weeks in advance of our moving in. The market was so competitive at the time that we had to agree to pay half a month's rent in advance of the first of the month we moved in.

11. Don't sign anything until your lawyer reviews it first.

12. Don't be surprised if you're not asked to sign anything at all. Outside the main cities in countries like Panama and Nicaragua, for example, the protocol for renting a person's house from him might be a handshake, not a written agreement. This shouldn't necessarily make you nervous.

If you do decide you want to invest in owning your home overseas, clarify your expectations and your objectives. Are you buying 100 percent for personal use? Or are you buying for personal use with the hope of an investment upside?

The best case is when you find a piece of real estate in your chosen locale that catches your fancy and that also holds out the potential for an investment return in the form of capital appreciation and/or a yield from rental. So by all means, shop the world with that agenda in mind, but be prepared to put it aside. Be ready to invest in a home, period. Don't look, necessarily, to make an investment at the same time. If your investment portfolio and budget allow for it, you can do both things, of course, but don't set your heart on finding a place to live that you can also bank on for big returns.

If you're buying straight up for profit, every decision is based on the numbers. If you're buying for personal use, you'll want to make your choice based on many things, including some that can't be quantified in a spreadsheet. When you buy for investment, one important consideration from the get-go is your exit strategy—when you'll sell and to whom. If, on the other hand, you're buying a home base for your overseas adventures, then your highest priority isn't the potential for market appreciation or the likelihood for finding a buyer when you want to sell. It is the potential for good living. You're buying a new life, not an addition to your investment portfolio.

If you decide you do want to own your own home overseas, here are questions to know the answers to before you sign a contract. (Some of the general questions are important considerations when renting as well.)

In General

1. What is the drive time from the nearest airport?

2. What is your access and right-of-way? That is, how do you get to your house or property? Must you cross another person's property? If so, are you certain your neighbor can't ever restrict your access?

3. Is the property accessible year-round, including in the rainy (sometimes called the winter) season?

4. How far away is the nearest medical care facility? How far is the hospital?

5. Is there enough water and water pressure? Is there hot water?

6. What distance are you from day-to-day services (grocery stores, dry cleaners, pharmacies, banks, etc.)?

7. Will you need a car living in this place? Does your budget allow for a car?

8. What's included with the property? In many places in the Americas, for example, when you buy a home, you buy bare, stripped walls and empty rooms—no lighting fixtures, no appliances.

If You're Buying into a Private Development

1. How will security be provided?

2. Is there a building requirement? What is it? Does it fit with your time frame and plan?

3. What construction and design standards are in place? Zoning is almost nonexistent in Latin America, the Caribbean, and Asia. If you're buying into a private development, you want building covenants.

4. What is the current existing infrastructure? Understand what's planned, but understand as well that you're buying only what you see. Promised infrastructure doesn't always materialize.

5. Likewise, understand which amenities exist and which are promised, but recognize that you're buying only what exists. If there's no marina when you buy, there may never be a marina, no matter what the developer's nice brochures and pretty drawings indicate. Will you be happy with your purchase if it's never anything more than what it is at the time you buy?

6. What are the plans for a homeowners' association? What will the monthly fees be? Are these enough to cover the developer's responsibilities? You don't want to pay high HOA fees, of course, but neither do you want to invest in a development where the developer has so underestimated his costs that the HOA fees don't cover them. The result can be that essential maintenance and services (for example, security) are reduced.

7. Is the development company financially sound? Does it have a track record? What else has it built?

If You're Buying Land with the Intention of Building Your Own Home

1. Will you be in the country during construction? If not, how will you build from thousands of miles away? Who will oversee the work for you?

2. What's your timeline and budget? What are your contingency plans if the project takes longer and costs more than you're planning? (It will; take my word for it.)

If Your Plan Is to Live in the Place Only Part of the Year

1. Who will look after the property while you're away? At what expense?

2. Will you be able to rent the place out while you're elsewhere? If so, you could earn enough in rental income during the months you're living somewhere else to cover the property's annual carrying costs.

If you're thinking you'd like to become a foreign property owner, here's something else you should know before you start shopping: The markets of Latin America, the Caribbean, and

Asia are unregulated. Anyone can be a real estate agent, and sometimes it will seem as though everyone is.

In places like Nicaragua, Panama, Ecuador, and the Dominican Republic, every guy you meet in a bar is going to try to sell you a piece of property. Assume that he's not a licensed agent. And don't take for granted that he owns or legally represents the piece of property in question. When it comes to real estate purchases, these countries can be Wild West markets. Don't be scared off by this fact; simply accept it. Make no assumptions and take nothing on faith. You don't have the safety nets that you have when buying real estate in the States, nor the process checks and balances.

Your best defense and most important ally is your attorney. Engage one who speaks fluent English and who is experienced in helping foreign buyers navigate the local property purchase process. Don't use the attorney of the seller or of the developer you're buying from. That attorney is paid by the seller or the developer and works for him. You want to find an independent attorney who works for you. The best way to accomplish this is through expat referrals. Ask every expat you meet in any country where you're considering a real estate purchase if he has bought himself. If he has, who was his attorney? How did he find his attorney? And was he happy with his attorney's work?

Step 8: Figure Out What to Do with All Your Stuff

Early one sunny April Saturday morning, as nine-year-old Jackson and his cousins manned their lemonade stand at the foot of their grandmother's driveway, behind them, Jackson's older sister, Kaitlin, offered for sale all the household bits and pieces she'd managed to collect during her first two years at college in Annapolis.

Kaitlin was coming to spend the summer with us in Panama. She had decided not to return to Annapolis the following year to continue her higher education, but was moving to New York. Meantime, she'd join us for a couple of months in the tropics. But what should she do with all the stuff from her Annapolis apartment?

The things she'd want in New York come September went into

paid storage. We decided that at the end of the summer, Lief and I would return to Annapolis with Kaitlin from Panama, rent a truck, and drive her and her necessities north to Manhattan.

The extra furniture was sold on Craigslist. Keepsakes were stored in Kaitlin's grandmother's basement in Baltimore. Most everything else was sold at the yard sale that April weekend, and the leftovers we gave to Goodwill. Setting up for the sale that April morning, I asked Kaitlin if she remembered the first time we'd prepared for an adventure abroad. "Do you remember the yard sale we staged before we left for Ireland?" I asked. "You were nine. It was the eve of our first international move, from Baltimore to Waterford . . ."

Back then, I was figuring things out as we went along. My first mistake was shipping my houseful of Baltimore antiques to Ireland with us. I later discovered that I could have bought nicer antiques in Ireland for half as much as I'd paid to ship the lesser-quality pieces across the Atlantic. It would have been easier, cheaper, and more fun to buy all new old furniture in Waterford.

My second mistake was overestimating what we'd "need" upon arrival. I wanted to make our rented house in Waterford as homey as possible, right from the start, so I arranged for Mail Boxes Etc. (now the UPS Store) to collect, pack, and deliver Kaitlin's favorite games and toys, our everyday kitchen gear, photos, knickknacks, and keepsakes, as well as four boxes of books.

In all, we shipped a dozen boxes with Mail Boxes Etc. On the one hand, these essential items were waiting for us when we arrived at the little house on the river that would be our home our first year in Ireland. On the other hand, it was a great deal of money spent, frankly, for little reason. I could have replaced most of the stuff locally, easily, and affordably.

To find an international shipper back then, I pulled out the Yellow Pages, sat down at the counter in my kitchen, and picked up the phone. I called at least a dozen firms out of the phone book. Some never returned my calls; some didn't ship to Ireland. After days of back-and-forth, I arranged for representatives of three companies to visit my Baltimore home and give me estimates for packing, shipping, and delivering to Waterford and then unpacking in our new home. Two weeks later, I had cost quotes. More phone calls, more follow-up, and finally I settled on a group headquartered in the UK. A lot of hassle to ship a bunch of stuff that, believe me, we could have lived without. I swore I'd never do it again.

Seven years later, I was back on the phone, this time shopping for an international shipper who'd take my Waterford household stuff to Paris. I rationalized this exercise to Lief by explaining that we'd never be able to afford to replace my Irish antiques with French ones. (I happened to be right about this.) "But I promise, dear," I told him then, "this will be the last time we'll mess with this."

Then, four years later, as we prepared for our move from France to Panama, I wondered again how we'd furnish our new home in this new country. Over the years, we'd bought, renovated, and furnished an old building in Panama City's old town, Casco Viejo, as well as a preconstruction apartment downtown. Those experiences had taught me that while you can buy antique furniture and good-quality reproductions in Panama, the supply is limited and the prices are high. How could I head off the inevitable budget and overspending discussions with Lief?

Living in Waterford, I'd gotten to know the local antiques dealer. The month before our move to Panama, we visited Ireland. I stopped in to see my friend Rody at his Waterford City Auction Rooms. I was greeted at the door by a sign proclaiming that Rody was planning an auction that very evening. Serendipity.

I'd buy furniture for the new place in Panama from Rody in Ireland! We'd come out ahead, even allowing for international shipping. Our Paris apartment furniture stayed in our Paris apartment, which we rented out to a nice Japanese banker and his wife. Keepsakes and things we didn't want to risk the renters breaking went into paid storage. When we walked out the door of our apartment on the rue de Verneuil bound for Panama, we carried only two suitcases full of clothes each and a couple of duffel bags of toys and books. The furniture from Rody arrived in Panama, without incident, a month later. We paid no Panama import duty, thanks to our residency status.

When Kaitlin called a few months later to explain she'd like to spend the summer in Panama with us and then return, in September, not to Annapolis but to New York . . . "Okay, here we go again," I thought. The good news is that by this time, in 2008, it had become far easier to manage an international move than it had been a dozen years earlier when we'd struggled through our first transatlantic relocation. It's even easier today.

The first step is thinking through (more objectively than I did for our first move) what you need to take with you, what you want to ship for immediate delivery, and whether you want to invest in shipping a full container load of stuff. For some people, this process is no more than another item on their Move Overseas checklist. For others, it's a serious psychological stumbling block.

My friend Lucy really struggled with the question of what to do with all her family's things. As she explained, "When we first decided to pack up our home in Spain and take a working 'sabbatical,' journeying through Mexico, Central America, the United States, and Europe, my biggest mental block was what to do with our houseful of belongings. At first I resisted selling anything but defunct objects and dusty, unused baby equipment. Then we took the time to figure out the costs of storage and transportation for things like china, kitchen equipment, and furniture. It was going to be cheaper to replace most things than to ship everything and have it waiting for us in an expensive storage facility. Besides, when we set out, we didn't know where we were going to settle!

"I thought it would be impossible to choose what was important," Lucy continued, "but then I came up with some 'benchmarks.' First, did an item have lasting memories? The kind of memories that make your hair stand on end or bring a smile to your face? Second, could I replace it without having to travel around the world again to a remote island? Finally, did it have thick dust on it? You and your partner may have different ideas about what is important. For instance, our beautiful blue Andalusian bowls were not on my husband's list, but they were on mine. And it wasn't only because they're pretty. It was also because when I look at them, I see clearly the ceramics workshop where I bought them. I remember the smell of the mountains of the Alpujarras in southern Spain. And I recall how, during the negotiations for their acquisition, the old man I bought them from turned mid-haggle to relieve himself in the most beautiful bowl in his courtyard! That's a memory worth keeping."

Lucy used her system of benchmarks to determine that all of her everyday china could be sold, with the exception of the blue bowls from Andalusia, the antique jugs from England, and the handblown glasses from an anniversary trip to Napa. "Out went our off-the-rack mountain bikes, but I held on tight to my custom-made road bike," Lucy explained. "The children sold their toys that had dust on them or were no longer trendy, but they kept the currently in-use and much-loved ones. We sold virtually all our furniture. Not a big deal for us because we didn't have any antiques. We sold nearly all the kitchen gadgets, but I kept my grandmother's potato masher. Rugs that were bought in a chain store . . . sold. Rug from a swap with a Sarawakian indigenous Indian . . . very definitely kept and stored. And so on. Now that we have settled in our new home and unpacked the treasures, do I miss anything? No.

"Well, okay, occasionally I think that it would be handy to have such and such a utensil, but I've yet to have any gut-wrenching moments of regret about not keeping anything in particular. That's because I stuck to my 'benchmarks,' even when I was being cajoled into loosening my grip on a few things. I stuck to them, because I didn't want any regrets in my new life."

Like me, Lucy also realized that sometimes you can buy better locally in your new home. After settling in France, she bought a new and improved mountain bike for only $70 more than she'd sold her previous American one for—much less than the cost of storage or shipping.

On the other hand, perpetual-traveler friends Paul and Vicki have downsized completely. For more than thirty years, since the age of thirty-five, they have been traveling the world continually with but a few suitcases and a couple of laptops. They worry not about shipping furniture or storing heirlooms. I envy their freedom in this regard, but I can't bring myself to follow their lead. Lief and I have designated Paris as a kind of home base. Packed away there in paid storage are family photo albums and our children's christening outfits, my son's first-grade report card and my daughter's high school art portfolio, my grandmother's recipe files and the bedspread my mother embroidered for Lief and me when we were married. I can't let these things go. So as we move around the world, we have to factor in the cost of storing them. Unless you're ready to part with all your worldly possessions, you will, too. Paid storage is available in much of the world, even in remote regions of Nicaragua and Panama, for example.

Furthermore, fortunately, as I've mentioned, international shipping is far more easily accomplished today than it was two decades ago when we arranged for our first transatlantic container. Go to the International Movers website (www.intlmovers.com). Type in the details of what you'd like to have shipped from where to where, then sit back and wait for estimates from international shipping firms interested in the gig. This online brokerage service is how I found the company that delivered our container load of furniture from Ireland to Panama, and I heartily recommend it.

But I'm getting ahead of myself. Maybe you don't want or need to ship an entire container load of furniture and belongings to your new home. In some cases it doesn't make sense to undertake that investment. Start by thinking through (as objectively as possible, using a system of benchmarks, as Lucy described) what you need to take with you (on the plane), what you want to ship for immediate delivery, and then whether it makes sense in fact to invest in shipping a full container load of stuff. One key to making these decisions is knowing what you'll be able to replace easily in your new country of residence and at what cost. The UPS Store is probably still the best choice for shipping things you want waiting for you upon your arrival.

Here are other things we've learned:

1. Depending on where you're moving from and to, you may not want to ship appliances or electronics. Models are more or less common in different parts of the world, and some models are not available some places, meaning you'll have trouble finding qualified repairmen and replacement parts.

2. On the other hand, if you're moving from the States to Central America, you may find it much cheaper to buy big U.S.-standard appliances and take them with you. A Maytag washing machine will cost considerably more in Nicaragua than in Florida.

3. Beds are complicated. In Ireland, for example, they don't have twin or queen-sized beds. They have three-foot-, five-foot-, and six-foot-wide beds. In France, you find 90-, 140-, and 160-centimeter beds. American twin-sized sheets don't quite fit an Irish three-foot bed. A five-foot Irish mattress will not fit in an American queen-sized bed (trust me on this). The safest thing is to buy beds and bedding when you arrive in your new country of residence.

4. If you ship a container, buy the insurance. The mirror-fronted door of our two-hundred-year-old armoire slid from the unpacker's hands smack onto the cobblestones of the courtyard upon delivery in Paris; then that same unpacker banged one table into another, chipping away the carved rosewood edge. Luckily, the repairs to both pieces were covered by the insurance we'd opted for.

5. Your exemption from import duty (a benefit of most permanent residency visas) is most easily processed if you ship everything in one go. In Panama, for example, it's possible to take your exemption over a series of maybe two deliveries, but it's more complicated.

6. Note that, thanks to ever more restrictive airline luggage restrictions, it's more challenging today than ever to carry much more than clothing with you on the plane.

7. Research what you *won't* be able to replace in your new locale. If you want to wear haute couture in Cuenca, Ecuador, you'll have to bring it with you. Lief can't shop for clothes of any description in most of Central America. He's too tall.

8. Finally, think long and hard before shipping your car to your new home. Import duties vary country to country but can be absurdly high. As with appliances, if the car you import isn't common in the place where you move, you'll struggle to find competent mechanics and will have to have replacement parts shipped to you from outside the country, which is costly and can take weeks or months. Finally, your luxury sedan does not belong on the dirt roads of Cayo, Belize, or even the mean streets of Panama City. In any rural region of Latin America and the Caribbean, you need an SUV, preferably one with four-wheel drive. On the narrow cobblestoned lanes of a European country town, an SUV is the last thing you want. You get the picture. Your best bet is almost always to buy local.

Step 9: Set Up a Virtual Home Office

When I began writing about the idea of living and retiring abroad more than three decades ago, the would-be expat and entrepreneur had his work cut out for him when it came to paying bills, receiving mail, managing investments, moving money around, and staying in touch with the folks back home. Today, these things are ever easier.

Your goal should be to go as paperless as possible. Organize your administrative life so that you can access everything online and tell your credit card companies, banks, and investment account managers that you want to receive electronic statements only. If you need a paper copy of something, you can print one yourself from your electronic files. You can even opt to receive most subscription services digitally these days, eliminating the need to figure out how to have your favorite magazines delivered to wherever you're living each month.

Thinking more specifically, here's a checklist for what you need, technologically speaking, to support your new life overseas.

An Email Address

I'd bet you've already got one, but if you don't, go set one up right now. You can create an email address for yourself free at a service like Gmail or Yahoo!

This amounts to your first and most important practical step as you begin planning for your overseas adventures. Your email address will be your main point of connection with the life and the world you're leaving behind "back home," and it will be the easiest way for you to operate as you begin moving around the globe. Some days, your email address will seem like your lifeline.

Your next step is to sign yourself up to begin receiving free email newsletters on the subjects of living and retiring abroad. I write one daily. You can read past issues at Live and Invest Overseas (www.liveandinvestoverseas.com) and sign up to receive each day's new dispatch as it's published. It's free.

A U.S. Address

I recommend that even after you've moved beyond U.S. borders, you keep a U.S. address.

A U.S. address can make it easier to deal with U.S. banks, credit card companies, and brokerage firms. The thing is . . . how can you have a U.S. address when you're not living in the United States? Many people use the address of a friend or family member who is still living in the United States. This works as long as the person is happy to receive mail and forward it to you at regular intervals. Other options include private mailbox services such as the UPS Store or Pak Mail. These offer a real street address, which is important. More and more financial institutions recognize the not-real addresses provided by some mailbox services and refuse them. More on this in the "Online Brokerage Account" section on the next page.

Online Banking Access

You probably already have this set up, too. If you don't, you want to arrange for online banking as soon as possible. If your current bank doesn't support it (nearly every bank does nowadays), change banks.

You want the ability to pay bills online, and you want a bank that allows you to initiate international wire transfers online. You aren't going to be able to go into the branch in person to sign wire instructions once you're off enjoying your new life at the beach.

The easiest and most cost-efficient way to access your money anywhere in the world is through an ATM. Check the fees you'll be charged for using an ATM that isn't part of your bank's network. Most banks now charge a fee for this on top of the fee the ATM machine may charge you. Some U.S. banks charge an extra or higher fee when you use an ATM outside the country. Outside North America, ATMs generally don't charge a fee for taking out cash. Panama is one glaring exception. Banks in Panama charge between $4 and $5.25 every time you use an ATM if you're not a customer of that bank.

Note that many online banks and brokerage firms reimburse these fees, as they don't have ATMs of their own. Online banks and brokerage firms also don't charge you when you use your ATM card outside your home country.

One final note regarding banking: It's possible to arrange to have your U.S. Social Security payment direct-deposited into your bank account each month, including, in many cases, your overseas bank account. Go here for details: www.ssa.gov/deposit /foreign.htm.

An Online Brokerage Account to Manage Your Investment Portfolios

All online brokerage accounts offer online access, but you should confirm that you can initiate international money transfers online. Additionally, given current SEC regulations, you'll want to maintain a U.S. address as the address of record for your brokerage account. Some financial institutions won't even allow you to make a stock trade from a foreign IP address even if you are in fact living in the United States, and changing your address with your broker to a foreign address likely will trigger a change in your account status and restrict new stock purchases. The simplest thing is to maintain a U.S. address.

If you don't have an online brokerage account but think you might ever want one, I suggest setting one up before you move overseas . . . again, using your U.S. address.

VoIP

As I've explained, VoIP stands for voice over Internet protocol, and it's the most affordable way to make international phone calls in most cases. In some cases, calls to anywhere in the world can even be free. Skype is the main VoIP service I use. It's free for calls between Skype accounts, it's super cheap for outgoing

calls (as little as 2.1¢ per minute for calls to landlines from anywhere in the world to the United States, Canada, and most of
western Europe, for example), and you can arrange a virtual
phone number for incoming calls (with whatever area code you
designate).

The downside is that Skype works through your computer.
Other VoIP services (Vonage, for example) allow you to connect
a regular phone to a router box, which is then connected to your
Internet service. You still need Internet service, but you don't
need a computer.

A Mail Forwarding Service

If you decide to use a private mailbox service, it can double as
a mail forwarding service for you. While we were living in Ireland, we used the UPS Store to arrange for our mail to be col-
lected and automatically forwarded to us once a month. This
works if you live in a place with physical addresses.

For most of Latin America, you'll need to choose a service out
of Miami that gives you a mailing address in Florida. They'll collect your mail and forward it to their office in the country where
you're residing. You can then either pick up your mail at their
office or, in most cases, have it delivered directly to your residence. You'll pay a monthly fee for this service (less than $25),
plus postage charges.

In our age of Internet shopping, these services also can receive
your online purchases and ship them to you almost anywhere in
the world, taking care of any required customs paperwork and
paying any import duties. Be sure to check the amount of associated import taxes before ordering. Depending where you're shipping to, certain categories of items may not be worth the extra
cost for the convenience of shopping online.

A Driver's License

Renew your driver's license just before leaving your home
country. You'll want to use it for renting cars and as a secondary
form of ID abroad. Plus, you may not be able to arrange for a

local driver's license in your new country of residence immediately. Sometimes a test or a waiting period is required. And in some countries you'll need to show proof of residency to be able to apply for a local driver's license; however, you may not have your residency visa until some months after your move.

For all these reasons, you should maintain your home country driver's license as long as possible. For a U.S. driver's license, this means you'll need an address in the state issuing the license. Note, though, that the address needn't necessarily be the same as your mailing address (see my comments on mail forwarding services above). If you don't have a virtual U.S. address (an address through a mail forwarding service), it can be possible to use the address of a family member or a friend in your home state for the address on your license. Some states don't mind this creative approach, but others do. Contact your state's Department of Motor Vehicles (DMV) in advance of your move to explain that you're planning to relocate abroad but would like to maintain your U.S. driver's license. Depending on the state, the DMV representative should be able to help you make that happen.

A Cell Phone

Here you have two needs: first, a cell phone to use while traveling around scouting potential retirement havens; second, a more permanent local cell phone in your new country of residence.

First, the short-term need. This can be addressed with your current cell phone if it allows for roaming in the countries where you intend to travel. Contact your carrier to find out. Some services don't work in some countries, and some services don't work in some countries until you contact the carrier to have a switch flipped.

This is not a long-term solution, however, as roaming charges can be expensive. In the long term, the cheaper option is local cell phone service. Unfortunately, most U.S. carriers "lock" their U.S. cell phones. This means that you won't be able to switch the SIM card in your U.S. cell phone with one from another carrier in another country. In other words, your U.S. cell phone is probably no good to you (short of its capacity for roaming). Sometimes you can manage to have your U.S. cell phone unlocked, either by your carrier or by going online and buying an unlock code, but this is a hassle and doesn't always work.

The easier option is to buy a new phone overseas. Pay-as-you-go phones are cheap and easy to come by in most of the world. You can shop for one in any electronics store. In Panama, for example, you can buy a low-end, no-tech but functional pay-as-you-go cell phone for $20 that comes with a voucher for $5 worth of calling credit.

Once you're more established in your new home country, you may want to switch from a pay-as-you-go phone to a cell phone plan. Qualifying for a monthly plan as a foreign resident can be complicated but worthwhile if you use your phone a lot.

In Europe, to qualify for a monthly plan, you'll need proof of address (for example, an electric bill) and a local bank account from which the phone service will be able to debit the amount of your bill each month.

A Laptop

This isn't absolutely necessary. You probably could get by using PCs in Internet cafés. But the more self-sufficiently mobile you are, the better. Alternatively, once you're set up in your new residence you could buy a local desktop computer, but it will likely come with an operating system in the language of the country you're in, as well as a non-English keyboard. You can request an English operating system and an English keyboard, but, depending on the country, these things may not be available at all or, at a minimum, will cost you more and take time to source.

Getting Paid While Working Overseas

If you'll be working from your laptop as a consultant or a writer, say, or providing some other service while living or traveling abroad, especially if the work will be done for non-U.S. companies, the easiest and most efficient way to get paid can be through PayPal. The company or individual paying you can send small amounts of money to you anywhere in the world quickly and cheaply via a PayPal account. If you'll be earning a few hundred dollars at a time (or less), the wire transfer fee associated with getting that amount to you wherever you happen to be can eat up most of the payment, whereas the cost of a transfer between two PayPal accounts can be zero.

Step 10: Consider Your Options for Unretiring Overseas

I made my first international move, from Baltimore, Maryland, to Waterford, Ireland, with the support of my longtime employer, who'd given me the marching orders to establish an EU base for that firm. I did not choose Waterford, but the idea of an adventure in the Old World was something I'd daydreamed about since I was a young girl. Waterford and Ireland were happy accidents. I made my second international move, from Waterford to Paris, again with the support of the firm I'd by that time become a partner in. However, this time I chose the destination. My family and I wanted to be in Paris, and my business partner accommodated the agenda.

My move from Paris to Panama was entirely my doing. The year before, I'd left the company that had taken me to Ireland and France. I'd retired early to find that retirement didn't suit me. I liked being in business and decided to start one of my own. Two minutes of discussion with Lief led us to agree that, if I wanted to pursue a business agenda, we'd need to leave France, perhaps the least entrepreneur-friendly country in the world. We knew from experience that Panama is one of the best places to start and run an Internet business of the kind I imagined, so we bought one-way tickets for Panama City.

For the next nine years, we hunkered down in Panama, raising our son and building the Live and Invest Overseas business. When both were mature enough to take their first independent steps, Lief and I planned our fourth international relocation. Our business base in Panama City remains, but Lief and I hang our hats these days again in Paris. Now that we've launched our son and established our business, we're transitioning to the long-anticipated next stage, for us the ultimate lifestyle. We travel back and forth regularly between Paris and Panama City, enjoying the delights of the City of Light while continuing to manage the growth of our business, which affords us many opportunities to rationalize travel elsewhere.

As we look ahead from this pivotal point in our lives, we imagine continued hard work, which we both enjoy, punctuated by regular travel. More than anything, Lief and I appreciate change, contrast, discovery, and the unexpected. Plus, we like history, architecture, long city walks, and extended café afternoons. This world of ours hides many spots for indulging in all those things. We look forward to getting to know as many of them as possible.

My point is that although, for more than thirty years, "retire overseas" has been my beat, it's never been my personal agenda. I've enjoyed a life of serial adventures overseas funded by enterprises that have allowed me to convert passions for travel and real estate into cash flow.

The dictionary defines "retire" as "to stop working willingly" and "retirement" as "being away from a busy life, a state of being withdrawn from the rest of the world or from a former busy life."

If traditional retirement is what you're after, no question, the opportunities overseas are diverse and appealing. I suggest many destinations in these pages where you could withdraw from the rest of the world and spend the rest of your days swinging in a hammock or bettering your golf game.

I'd like to suggest, though, that that's but one (I'd say limited) strategy. Why not think bigger and broader? Why wait until you have some magic number of dollars saved or invested to chase your dreams of cross-border adventure? Instead, use your imagination and your professional experiences and personal interests to conceive a strategy for earning the money you need to fund your adventures as you go. Not only is this approach more practical, as it allows you to control your income long-term and through retirement, but it's also immediate.

As I've explained, my retirement plan, which Lief and I are right now embarking on, has nothing to do with withdrawing from the world. I've been looking forward to this stage as a chance to be more engaged than ever, in the world, in life, and in the pursuit of happiness. My ideas for retirement are about moving around the world as whim and wanderlust dictate and settling in to get to know each place where I land, its people, and the local way of life. What goes on here? I'm always wondering about wherever in the world I happen to be. How do people spend their time here? How do they do what they do, and how might I participate?

I've taken to describing the lifestyle as "unretirement." Unretired, I'm working and productive but in control of my day and my time. I'm not tied to a conventional work schedule or to a conventional anything. I organize an unconventional schedule that allows me to indulge in the best of the place where I happen to be that day while still meeting all my deadlines and business-building objectives. I'm more productive than ever because I'm more content, less stressed, and less distracted by daydreams of the life I could be living.

Your unretirement plan likely will look different than mine. Not many are crazy enough to commit to what I committed to when I launched the Live and Invest Overseas business, but now that I'm in this thing, I want to see how far my team and I can take it. The point for you is that you can unretire at any age and with any level of income, assets, or savings, and you can unretire anywhere in the world that supports your unretirement agendas.

You could be unretired, period, living a *mas o menos* conventional retirement lifestyle but in a new country, meaning a lower cost of living and days filled with adventure and the exotic. You could be unretired and earning an income (think laptop business). You could be an unretired entrepreneur like me. You could be unretired for fun and profit, investing (in real estate, say) to generate cash flow to support yourself as you embrace this free and flexible lifestyle.

You could unretire with school-aged children or your aging parents. You could unretire to a penthouse or live off-grid and be self-sufficient. Bottom line, unretirement is about taking control of your life and how you spend your days, making it possible for you to spend them wherever you decide you'd really like to spend them and filling them with discovery and adventure rather than business meetings and a daily commute.

Any of the places I introduce in these pages would make for great unretirement locales, as would many other spots across the globe. You can unretire almost anywhere on the map that grabs your attention. And you can do it now.

PART II

LOOKING FOR
SOMETHING SPECIFIC

The world's best place to live? There's no such thing. This isn't a one-size-fits-all program. The appealing options for a new life overseas are many. You can be spoiled for choice, even overwhelmed trying to make a decision.

It helps if you can clarify a primary agenda. Here are shortcuts, the most common reasons for seeking out a new life overseas . . . and where best to look in each case to find a lifestyle that's sure to satisfy those objectives.

Cheap Living

Cuenca, Ecuador • Chiang Mai, Thailand • León, Nicaragua

About a month before our move from France to Panama, Lief presented me with a budget, showing that our cost of living in Panama City would be more or less on par with what it had been in Paris. I suggested that my husband, an accountant by training, double-check his figures. Alas, upon closer inspection (and holding aside the cost of housing, which is best considered separately), I realized that Lief was correct. His figures showed that our day-to-day cost of living would be the same in Panama as it had been in France.

On one hand, this is a comment on how affordable Paris can be. Paris is a place where even a modest lifestyle can feel rich and where some of the greatest pleasures—strolls along the Seine, picnics in the Luxembourg Gardens—come free. Paris is also a city where a car is an unnecessary liability. We spent four years in Paris when our children were young happily auto-free, and now that we're back, we have no intention of investing in a car. We walk nearly everywhere. The butcher, the baker, the grocer, and the wine shop are all less than fifteen minutes' walk from our apartment, as are the Tuileries Garden, the Louvre, the Latin Quarter, six movie theaters, and at least a dozen cafés and restaurants. When we want to venture beyond our quartier, we duck into the nearest Métro station, which is never far. For less than $2, we can get quickly and easily from anywhere to any location in the city where we might be headed.

Other things in Paris can be cheap, too, including telephone, cable, and Internet. Get this: We've bought a package from Orange that includes phone, cable, and Internet. Our phone service allows unlimited free calls anytime to anywhere in North America, the Caribbean, and Europe, and the total cost of the package—for all services—is 42 euros per months. Right now, that's less than $50.

You can get by as well in Panama City without a car, but it's a hassle (though less so now, thanks to Uber). Plus, sometimes one of the best things about living in Panama City is the chance to escape it for a weekend at the beach or in the mountains (both of which can be as little as two hours away). You can rent a car every time you want to explore beyond the capital, of course, but eventually, in Panama, you're probably going to want to invest in a vehicle of your own. Which means monthly insurance, gas, and maintenance expenses, and maybe the cost of a driver. I drove the first year after we bought our first car but then swore off it. Panamanian drivers terrified me.

Our basic phone, cable, and Internet package in Panama City cost about $90 per month, not including international phone calls, which, again, in Paris are mostly free with our service package. In Paris, we'll pay for heat maybe six months a year. In Panama City, we paid for air-conditioning year-round.

In Paris our family of four, when we were living here with our kids, spent 250 euros a week on groceries. In Panama City, Lief, Jackson, and I (by the time we moved to Panama, our daughter was off to university) spent about $250 a week. You could spend half that much to eat in Panama, maybe less than that even. We admit it. In Panama City, we shopped indulgently. We frequented the big U.S.-style grocery story Riba Smith rather than the more local and cheaper Super 99. We bought Entenmann's pound cake and Aunt Jemima syrup for our pancakes. We splurged on Tropicana orange juice, rather than buying the local brand.

On the other hand, in Panama City we found bargains—like Moët's exported champagne (exported from Argentina, not France, so technically not champagne but still very quaffable), sold throughout the city for only $12 a bottle. Lief likes sangria and buys a local brand for about $3 a bottle. Other great buys in this town include men's haircuts (Lief was able to have his hair cut for $10 or less, whereas he pays 30 euros or more in Paris), movie tickets ($4 to see a new-release movie in English on Wednesdays), taxis (less than $2 for a ride across town), and film processing ($5 per roll, compared with $40 or more a roll in Paris!). For as little as $20, you can buy a cell phone that comes with $5 worth of phone credit.

While in Panama, I enjoyed full-time, six-days-a-week help around the house. We paid top dollar: $400 a month. In Paris, I've found someone who comes once a week for three hours for 45 euros. We've kept the same health insurance as we've moved from Paris to Panama and back. It's a high-deductible international policy from Bupa that costs less than $150 per month for each of us.

Then there's housing. Again, this is the most significant part of any budget and best considered apart from your other living expenses. In Paris, you could spend as much as $2,000+ per square foot to buy an apartment in one of the city's prime neighborhoods and up to $25,000 per month or more to rent one. You could also buy or rent for a fraction of those prices. It depends on what kind of apartment you want, what size, and in which arrondissement you'd like it to be located.

When we contacted a Panama real estate agent a few months in advance of our move to Panama City years ago, to begin exploring housing options, we were surprised by his response. He told us about places for rent for $8,000 a month and for sale for $500,000, $800,000, even a million dollars and more.

Remember, this was a decade ago. I know of people renting apartments in this city today for less than $500 a month, and Lief told me the other day about a woman he knows who has just bought a two-bedroom apartment, off the water, in an out-of-the-way neighborhood, for less than $120,000. I'm going to admit my bias. I don't think I'd want to live in any apartment renting today in Panama City for less than $500 per month or selling for $120,000. But those options are available.

I also know people today renting apartments at Panama City's poshest addresses for $8,000 or $10,000 per month or more. We were able to find a nicely appointed three-bedroom apartment, located on Avenida Balboa, with the Cinta Costera park and recreation area on our doorstep, for $3,000 per month, a bargain and a find in today's Panama City market. To continue drawing our comparison of Panama versus Paris, you could rent a comfortable (though much smaller) place in a nice neighborhood in Paris for a similar amount.

In other words, at the current rate of exchange between the U.S. dollar and the euro, as Lief has now long observed, when all is said and done, our cost of living in Paris is only a little higher than our cost of living in Panama City. Does that mean it would cost you $5,000 a month to live in Panama City, as it has cost us? Only if you want to live just the way we lived. In other words, the answer is probably no. You could live in this city comfortably on a third as much or less.

To complicate the issue further, remember that Panama City isn't Panama. As I've explained, you've got to thin-slice your retirement havens. In fact, it's not possible to talk about the cost of living in Panama. You've got to look at the cost of living in Panama City, as we've just done, then consider the costs of living elsewhere in this beautiful little country, for they vary dramatically region to region.

Take Las Tablas, for example. This is a small town on the Pacific coast about three and a half hours' drive from Panama City. A friend lives here on $1,100 a month. I've had her verify her expenses, and I've checked her figures. No kidding, Rebecca is living well in this safe, friendly, charming colonial town, within two minutes' walk of the beach, for $1,100 a month, including rent and full-time household help. She spends her free time fish-ing and swimming. As she explains, she couldn't be happier.

You can find all of life's necessities in Las Tablas. For little indulgences, you've got to come to the big city, so a few times a month, Rebecca makes the drive to Panama City for shopping and a night out. Sometimes she takes the bus. A ticket from Las Tablas to Panama City costs only $10.

Everything is affordable in Las Tablas, but what makes the cost of living here (and elsewhere in the interior of Panama) so appeal-ing is the cost of housing. Unlike in Panama City, where a decent place to live will cost you, say, $1,500 a month or more, in Las Tablas you can rent a little house near the beach for $500. Yes, sure, you could spend more. And, no, you aren't going to find rentals at this price on the Internet or through a broker. You need to be connected on the ground, and you need to be able to com-municate directly with the property's owner in Spanish. But Re-becca did it, and you could, too. Meaning you could live a simple, sweet life at the beach in this safe and friendly little town for less than $1,000 a month. It would be a modest, careful life but more interesting, I'd suggest, than any life you might live on $1,000 per month stateside.

You have to remember the bigger-picture context and also the real point. Moving overseas can mean a dramatically reduced cost of living, but that's not the beginning and the end of the story. The benefits of taking your life global are many beyond a reduced budget.

Living on the cheap in Las Tablas, for example, means, big-ger picture, living in Panama. Panama offers many advantages. It's a convenient place to get to and from and but a few hours' flight from key points in the States. It's a travel hub for the Amer-icas in general. It's a tax haven. It uses the U.S. dollar for its cur-rency, so Americans have no exchange-rate concern. It boasts the most developed infrastructure in the region and world-class health care in Panama City. Its Friendly Nations visa program means this is perhaps the easiest place in the world today to show up and obtain legal residency and a work permit.

For all these reasons, Panama today is the best place in the world to start an Internet business, but is it a bargain destination?

You're beginning to understand why it's not easy to give a cut-and-dried answer to that question. First, any worthwhile response must be very localized. The cost of living in Las Tablas bears little resemblance to the cost of living in Panama City, and a monthly budget for living in either of those places would be different, again, from one for living in Boquete, a mountain town in Panama's interior highlands.

Furthermore, and just as important, cost of living is subjective. You have your notions about what is expensive, and I have mine. Our ideas are based on our experience and our frames of reference. I'd call Las Tablas a screaming bargain. You could be living now in a small town in Iowa or maybe Detroit. In which case, you might agree that Las Tablas is a cheap place to live, or you might not. On the other hand, if you currently call Newport Beach home, even top-of-the-line Panama City living could promise welcome relief for your budget.

A couple of years ago, a reader wrote to me from Uruguay to alert me that the cost of living was on the rise in that country. "The cost of a gardener has doubled in the past two and a half years," he complained. "It's now about $96 a month." To him, $96 a month for a gardener seemed expensive, because he'd become accustomed to enjoying that service for much less. It was hard for me, reading his letter in Paris, where I was paying about half that amount for but three hours of any workman's labor, to sympathize.

Cost of living is both relative and manageable within boundaries. Bottom line, you can control how much it costs you to live somewhere. A few places are absolutely expensive and won't work for you if budget is a chief concern—Monte Carlo, for example. But in most of the world your lifestyle can be adjusted to fit your allowable monthly spending. This is key, maybe the most important point to keep in mind as you think through what your cost of living will be in your new home, be it Paris, Panama City, or Chiang Mai. Your lifestyle can expand or contract according to your budget and to accommodate your financial constraints. We spent as much to live in Panama as it costs us to live in France, and I'd bet that if we set our minds to it, we could live on the same budget in Thailand. On the other hand, I have a friend living in Phuket, Thailand, right now on less than $800 a month.

As you try to spreadsheet your cost of living in your chosen overseas haven, remember our discussions in Part I. Be honest with yourself. What are you absolutely not prepared to give up, no matter what the cost? Again, we spent nearly as much to live in Panama City as we spend to live in Paris. That's because of how we choose to live. We could have rented a more local-style apartment for a third what we spent to live where we chose to live. We could have shopped exclusively at the local farmers' markets rather than the Riba Smith superstore. We could have used less air-conditioning. We could have gone without full-time household help. We could have forgone dinners out and our regular weekend beach escapes. We could have made some or all of those changes if we needed to.

But here are things I've learned about myself: I'm Maytag's biggest fan. I won't settle for a locally made washing machine anywhere in the world. Everywhere we've lived, we've paid to have full-size Maytag washers and dryers shipped from the States. This has come at a cost, but I don't want to spend my days messing with the ridiculously tiny and inefficient washing and drying machines common in most countries beyond North American borders.

I like to take weekend trips with the kids—to the beach, to the mountains, to go hiking, to explore archaeological ruins. In Panama, this meant investing in a four-wheel-drive SUV. I like good wine. Lief is happy with his $3-a-bottle sangria, but, I admit, I splurge on more expensive vintages. I like to read magazines. Online reading and Internet research is great, but on Sunday afternoons, I like to sit on the balcony and read *The Economist* or *Vanity Fair*. Neither was available for sale on any newsstand in Panama, so I paid to have them delivered via a Miami mail forwarding service.

The point of this take-your-life-overseas exercise isn't misery or regret. You don't want to go through all the hassle (yes, this adventure comes with hassles) of setting yourself up in a new life you don't like. The point is to launch a new life someplace exciting, exotic, interesting, friendly, maybe sunny, maybe super cheap that includes as many of the things you like as possible and avoids as many of the things you don't like as possible. No place is perfect, and nowhere will you be able to bring along every comfort and convenience you're accustomed to back home. Neither should you want to. You're setting off for an adventure. Discovering the differences is part of the fun.

But what changes would make you miserable? What sacrifices are you not willing to make? Identify them, find the cost of preserving those indulgences or conveniences in the retirement haven you're considering, then see if your budget will accommodate them.

What should you take away from all this? Bottom line, yes, indeed, it is possible for you to reduce your cost of living, maybe significantly, by retiring overseas. Reduce it by how much? That depends on all the things I'm outlining here.

To the point, allow me now to introduce you to three of the world's most affordable places to live right now. . . .

Cheap Living Pick #1: Cuenca, Ecuador

Cuenca, Ecuador, is the most affordable place you'd want to live in Latin America. Other places may be a bit cheaper, including some places elsewhere in Ecuador, but you'd be removed from the conveniences of a city, you wouldn't have access to certain services, amenities, and conveniences that make life comfortable, and your standard of living might be reduced. In Cuenca, you could live well, perhaps better than you're living now. Your life could be enriched, your breadth of experience expanded. All at an almost unbelievably low cost. Cuenca amounts to the world's best quality of life buy for the money.

How much, specifically, do you need to live here? About five years ago, a friend, Christian, retired to Cuenca from New York. Christian and his wife have been living comfortably, happily, and well in Cuenca for the past five years on a budget of about $1,145 per month, including the cost of renting an apartment but not including the cost of household help. If cost of living is your primary concern, you probably won't want a maid, but if you do, in Cuenca, plan on spending around $200 per month to employ one full time.

Christian's monthly budget includes $400 for rent (for a modern apartment in a building with a doorman and underground parking); $150 for HOA (or building maintenance) fees (often paid by the renter in Ecuador); $40 for transportation (Christian does not own a car but uses taxis and buses to get around the city); $5 for gas (used for hot water and for cooking); $40 for electricity and water; $20 for telephone; $35 for Internet; $25 for cable TV; $250 for groceries; and $180 for entertainment (concerts, theater, and other cultural activities are often free in this city).

Christian's cost of living is certainly affordable, but you could live in Cuenca for less. To cut costs further, you could rent an apartment farther from the center of town for as little as $260 per month. You'd be in an older building with no doorman or garage. You'd save $140 on rent and $150 on HOA fees, as in an older building, you probably wouldn't incur them.

Invest in a home of your own in Cuenca, an apartment or one of the charming old colonial houses the city is known for, and you could live on as little as $700 a month. Assuming all other expenses remain the same, you'd have no rent and no HOA fee, but you would have property taxes (probably less than $50 a month), and if you bought a house rather than a condo, you might want to invest in homeowner's insurance (about $50 a month). If your budget allows for it, you could add $100 per month for in-country travel. This should buy you four in-Ecuador vacations per year.

Remember, Ecuador, like Panama, uses the U.S. dollar. This eliminates the variable of exchange rate fluctuations . . . which can, in some countries at some times, affect your cost of living dramatically for better or for worse. Choosing a country that uses the U.S. dollar as its currency means an expat with U.S. dollar–based income isn't hurt when the dollar falls against the local currency. But it also means the U.S. expat doesn't benefit when the dollar surges against the local currency—as is the case in many countries right now. This exchange rate factor means that U.S. dollar holders today are able to better afford many places, including many places in Europe, that they might historically have dismissed out of hand as too expensive.

Cheap Living Pick #2: Chiang Mai, Thailand

This is another place you could embrace an exotic and outside-the-box lifestyle on the cheap: Chiang Mai, Thailand. Here a couple could live for as little as $1,300 per month if you rent or for as little as $850 per month if you own your own apartment or condo. Our friends Paul and Vicki have been spending time in Chiang Mai for more than two decades. "We know a single man," Paul explains, "an American, who lives on $200 a month, with half that going for rent. He gets around on a bicycle and eats at noodle stalls or free when a temple offers lunch. He makes a sport of spending as little as possible.

"We also know a Thai American woman," Paul continues, "who bought an apartment in a small town fifteen kilometers from Chiang Mai. She manages on $600 a month Social Security and, as she is Thai and over sixty, enjoys free government health care. Another couple rents a place in the countryside twelve kilometers from old town Chiang Mai. They pay $135 a month for a small home and garden."

But those are special cases, exceptions. The typical expat retiree in Chiang Mai should start with a bigger budget, about $1,300 to $1,400 a month, including rent. House and apartment rents vary greatly, as they do everywhere, and you'll spend more on rent, for example, living in Chiang Mai proper rather than outside the city.

Here's how an average budget for a retired couple living in Chiang Mai breaks down: $450 for a comfortable apartment; $105 for transportation (it costs 60¢ to ride the local bus; the average taxi ride is $2.50); $80 for electricity (depending on your use of air-conditioning), water, and gas; $18 for telephone (for a cell phone, depending on use); $30 for Internet; $30 for cable TV (including English-language movies); $330 for groceries (you can eat very cheaply in this country); $275 for entertainment (including meals out).

Foreigners cannot own land in Thailand without putting some kind of workaround in place (enlisting a Thai partner, for example), which is something I do not recommend. However, you could own an apartment or a condo. In this case, you'd have no rent. You wouldn't pay property taxes, as Thailand doesn't impose them on owner-occupied real estate. However, you would be liable for an HOA fee (of about $75 a month) and homeowner's insurance (which would cost about $35 a month).

Note that these are costs for Chiang Mai. As in Panama, where the cost of living varies dramatically between Panama City and Las Tablas, in Thailand, the cost of living in Bangkok is much greater than anywhere else in the country. In the capital, you should figure more than double what I'm quoting here for rent, transportation, eating out, and entertainment.

Cheap Living Pick #3: León, Nicaragua

If you've read about Nicaragua as a retirement haven, you've probably read about colonial Granada, sometimes referred to as the country's jewel and certainly its best-known city. I'm a big fan of Granada, with its largely renovated colonial center, centuries-old churches, markets, restaurants, and established expat community. It's probably my favorite city in this part of the world. I'll tell you more about it in Part III.

However, if budget is your primary concern, you could look to Granada's sister colonial city, León, instead.

Granada, as I said, is home to hundreds of expat retirees, from North America and Europe, who've been at work fixing up the city's old haciendas and opening taverns and eateries in the town center for the past couple of decades. They've added a new and appealing dimension to life in Granada, and as a result, the cost of living in this city—specifically the cost of housing—has risen significantly.

In León, Nicaraguans go about their business blissfully separate from the bustle (and the inflated economy) of expat retiree life in Granada. León is one of the oldest cities in the Americas (founded in 1524), and life here remains simple and sweet, relaxed and unhurried . . . and very local.

How much to live here? All things considered, a budget of about $1,200 per month could keep you nicely, including rent of about $400, which should be enough to afford you a comfortable, high-end home. HOA fees are not commonly paid by apartment renters, as they are in Ecuador. This would buy you an expat-standard life; as anywhere, you could live like a local for considerably less.

León has most of what you'd need right in town, and it's a city laid out for walking. You could live here without investing in a car. For longer distances, buses and taxis are easy to come by and cheap.

Here's how an average budget for retired life in León would break down: $400 a month for rent; $50 a month for transportation; $10 a month for gas (used for hot water and cooking); $135 for electricity; $30 a month for telephone; $43 a month for Internet and cable TV (which come bundled); $300 for groceries; and $150 for entertainment.

Again, all that totals about $1,200. How does that compare with the cost of living in Granada? Most costs are similar. Internet, cable, telephone, electricity, and gas will cost you more or less the same anywhere in the country. Your grocery and entertainment expenses could be lower in León than in Granada—first, because the lack of an expat population means prices in León are more local level, and second, because your entertainment options would be more limited in León. Just not as much in the way of nightlife, for example, to spend money on.

However, while a budget of $1,200 a month could do you in León, you should figure $2,100 a month at least for a comfortable standard of living in Granada. Nine hundred dollars more a month? Yes, and nearly all of it spent on rent. The supply of available expat-standard housing in Granada is limited. Expat investors have been renovating this city's classic colonial-style haciendas for years, but there are only so many of them. Growing demand means you should plan on $1,200 to $1,500 per month to rent one.

This reinforces the point I've been making about priorities. What is more important to you? A lower cost of living . . . or a more developed, more fully appointed, more expat-friendly lifestyle? If your budget is strictly limited, that's your answer.

Note that while, as we've mentioned, Ecuador and Panama use the U.S. dollar as their currency, Nicaragua has its own córdoba, which the Nicaraguan government sets to depreciate against the U.S. dollar at a slow and stable rate. So while a fluctuating dollar can at times erode the buying power of the U.S. expat abroad, that's not a concern in Nicaragua.

Luxury Living on a Budget

Paris, France • Buenos Aires, Argentina
• Kuala Lumpur, Malaysia

In some places around the world, you aren't going to live the life of the rich and famous no matter how much money you're willing to spend trying. In Nicaragua, Belize, and the Dominican Republic, for example, the luxe life can't be bought. It doesn't exist. Places like these, with their long coasts and year-round sunshine, offer blissful escape beneath the palms or a view of the crashing Pacific from your bedroom window. These countries, though, do not boast theaters or art galleries, high-end shopping malls or restaurants with haute cuisine on the menus and well-stocked wine cellars.

That is not to say you can't enjoy a luxury lifestyle in your new life overseas, even on a budget. Before we consider where that might be possible, though, let's define "luxury." Like cost of living, it's relative.

Luxury is not the same as jet set. Living the jet-set life, you'd expect limos and private planes, an entourage, and connections that'd get you jumped to the front of any queue. That's something else. I'd say that, for a place to qualify as luxury, it must allow you access to four- and five-star restaurants with wine lists to match; malls and boutiques offering internationally recognized brand-name indulgences; live theater; movie cinemas showing first-run and foreign flicks; an artist community; affordable help around the house and a private driver; to-your-door delivery services (from grocery stores and restaurants); specialty food shops; wine stores offering good vintages from around the world; English-language bookstores; and spa and salon services.

As well, for me, for a place to qualify as luxury it must have more than these commercial trappings. It needs also history and an ambience of charm and culture, plus parks, squares, and plazas, places to walk and wander while enjoying the scenery, the architecture, and the people.

If your life included all those things, you'd think of it as luxurious, wouldn't you? I would. Now, where can you not only find these things but also afford them?

Luxury Living on a Budget Pick #1: Paris, France

Hands down, no contest, the best place in the world to seek out a lifestyle of this description is Paris, France. Whatever your idea of the high life, you can find it in the City of Light, and as I've explained, the great thing about Paris is that some of the best it has to offer comes free. The sweetest pleasures of life are here for the taking. Picnics in the Luxembourg Gardens, long walks along the Seine, afternoons lost among the cobblestones of the Latin Quarter. These things cost not a sou.

Most museums, including the Louvre and the Musée d'Orsay, forgo admission fees one day a month. The Métro will transport you from restaurant to nightclub, from museum to café, for less than $2, and even the chicest Parisians don't mind using it for transport around their city.

Paris is a never-ending feast of gallery openings and special performances, exhibitions and celebrations, many available for little cost. You can join conversation groups, discussion groups, book clubs, and cooking classes. You can enjoy prix fixe meals for $25 or less, and you can spend hours in a café, seeing and being seen, for the price of but a single café au lait.

The more practical necessities of life don't come free in Paris, but they are more affordable than you might imagine. France boasts perhaps the world's best infrastructure (after Switzerland, maybe), and it's a bargain. Cable TV, Internet, and telephone, as well as the Métro, the bus, and the RER train system, are likely less costly than comparable services wherever you're living now.

I've spoken generally about the cost of living in Paris already, based on my family's experience. Thinking in a more general context, I'd revise the budget as follows: $85 a month for transportation (taxis and the Métro); $90 a month for gas and electricity; $50 a month for telephone, Internet, and cable TV; $700 a month for groceries (delivered free to your apartment if you like); $350 for entertainment and eating out (certainly you could spend more than this, but $350 would allow you to eat out a few times a month at moderately priced restaurants, to go to the theater once a month, and to see a movie). That's a total of $1,275 per month.

Now, housing. An apartment in central Paris, just off the river, won't come cheap, but outside this zone you could rent a small furnished apartment for as little as $1,500 a month. Build your budget out from there. How much luxury are you in the market for? Regular spa treatments, expensive bottles of wine with dinner each night, and regular shopping at Cartier and Prada, of course, would require a more expansive nest egg. But all those things are available, and even indulging in them only now and then would make life feel special.

Luxury Living on a Budget Pick #2: Buenos Aires, Argentina

My second pick for living the ultra-good life on a budget is the Paris of South America, Buenos Aires, Argentina. With few exceptions, anything available in Paris is available as well in Buenos Aires, at lesser cost and with a Latin edge, including five-star restaurants, nightclubs, comedy clubs, open-air cafés, world-class live theater and ballet, art galleries, museums, indoor shopping malls and outdoor antiques markets, European-style parks, plazas, and gardens, plus classic architecture of the kind found in but a handful of cities around the world. If you want to live a life filled with art and history, culture and interesting company, but you can't afford Paris, look to Buenos Aires.

In this city, not only could you enrich your life culturally and socially, but you could pamper yourself as well. In Paris, spa therapies and massage treatments are real indulgences. In Buenos Aires, you could make them a regular part of your routine.

A basic budget for retirement in one of this eclectic city's best neighborhoods would be as little as $2,000 a month, with about half that given over to rent. As with Paris, you could build out your luxury retirement budget from there.

Note that this $2,000-a-month budget includes rent of about $1,000 a month for an apartment in the Recoleta or the Palermo District, two of the chicest neighborhoods in Buenos Aires. The rents reflect this. Settle instead in Barrio Norte, for example, a more up-and-coming area, and your rent could be as much as a third less.

Other expenses break down like this: $70 for transportation (bus and taxi fares); $50 for gas (used for heating and cooking);

$65 for electricity; $25 for telephone; $40 for Internet; $30 for cable TV; $400 for groceries; and $320 for entertainment. If you invest in an apartment of your own, you'd have no rent, of course. Buenos Aires is a place where owning a car can be more a liability than a convenience. It's also expensive. Better to go without one.

Luxury Living on a Budget Pick #3: Kuala Lumpur, Malaysia

The very good life is available at even less cost in Kuala Lumpur.

This is a city with a thriving nightlife—bars, clubs, floor shows, music bars—as well as a national opera and symphony, regular concerts, theater, dancing, museums, galleries, five-star restaurants, and international brand-name shopping. In other words, Kuala Lumpur boasts all the trappings of luxury as I defined them above, with an Asian twist. Perhaps the best part is that you can enjoy it all on a budget of as little as $1,460 per month, including $700 a month for rent. In truth, your rent could be considerably less than this, even for what would qualify as a luxurious rental. I know of an 1,100-square-foot condominium in a good area of the city, for example, partly furnished, with a swimming pool and tennis court, available for rent for less than $400 per month.

Specifically, other monthly costs for living in Kuala Lumpur break down as follows: $95 for transportation (buses, trains, and taxis); $10 for gas (used for cooking); $65 for electricity; $22 for telephone; $32 for Internet; $36 for cable TV; $300 for groceries; and $200 for entertainment (eating out, movies, etc.).

Retire to the Beach

Ambergris Caye, Belize • Las Terrenas, Dominican Republic • Las Tablas, Panama

If your heart is set on a new life at the beach and that's your clear and driving agenda, here are the top three places to consider. These spots boast world-class sea, sand, sun, and surf, plus these locations make sense in the bigger picture as well. Each of my top beach picks is in a country that offers important advantages for expats and foreign retirees in general.

Beach Pick #1: Ambergris Caye, Belize

Ambergris Caye, Belize, is my number one choice for a quintessentially Caribbean lifestyle. Madonna's "La Isla Bonita" and several seasons of *Temptation Island* put little Ambergris on America's radar. Before it found itself in the spotlight, this unassuming island outpost was the well-guarded secret of serious divers. The reef and the Blue Hole are still important parts of Ambergris's appeal, but today those natural wonders are supported by a fully fledged expat community and all the accoutrements that go with it. Former fishing village San Pedro Town, the island's only actual population center, is today a sandy, chic beach town of white picket fences, wine and cheese shops, delis, golf cart rental agencies (a golf cart is the best choice for getting around the island), bakeries, and art galleries. Demand continues to expand, and this is a great place to start an expat-oriented business.

Genuinely welcoming and friendly San Pedranos have accommodated all the expat attention and population, but they haven't sold out. Ambergris retains authentic Belizean undertones. The downside to life on Ambergris? This is a little island. Not everyone is cut out for life on a little island. When Ambergris begins to feel claustrophobic, you can hop a flight to the mainland for a rain forest escape.

Beach Pick #2: Las Terrenas, Dominican Republic

The Dominican Republic is known for its beaches, which are world class and attract big volumes of tourists every year. These powdery coasts, though, make sense not only as a vacation spot but also as a place to consider for the longer term, for there's much more to this country than its beaches.

The Dominican Republic is small, about twice the size of the state of New Hampshire, yet it offers an estimated one thousand miles of pristine, white-sand beaches, most of them completely people-free. The tourists congregate in the resort areas. Travel just a few miles away in either direction, and you find yourself completely alone on some of the most picturesque stretches of sand you will ever lay eyes on.

My favorite coastal spot in the Dominican Republic is Las Terrenas. This isn't your typical Caribbean getaway but more international than you might expect, more cosmopolitan. Have a craving for blue cheese, authentic French baguettes, or fresh gnocchi? You can find all of these things here. The French and Italians began settling in Las Terrenas decades ago and have since developed an extensive and diverse culinary, business, and service infrastructure geared toward their fellow expats.

And now, thanks to recently enacted legislation, this island nation is a far more tax-advantaged choice. In addition, the Dominican Republic offers a competitive retirement residency option. This fast-track program means that your visa can be processed in as little as forty-five days. Once you've qualified (by showing a minimum pension income of $1,500 per month), you're exempt from tax on dividend and interest income (both foreign and from within the Dominican Republic); you're 50 percent exempt from annual property tax; and you're eligible to import personal and household belongings, including a car, into the country duty-free, among other benefits.

Beach Pick #3: Las Tablas, Panama

Within a twenty-minute drive of the little town of Las Tablas, Panama, you can reach five different beaches, all beautiful, all undiscovered. This is a big part of the reason why dozens of U.S. and Canadian expats have settled in this part of Panama's Azuero Peninsula, about four hours west of Panama City. The other draw is the cost of living. It's dramatically lower in this region than in this country's capital city.

It's when you put Las Tablas beach living into a broader perspective that retiring to this unassuming beach town can become an irresistible notion. Panama offers the world's best *pensionado* program for foreign retirees. It's an easy place to acquire foreign residency, a tax haven (even as an American you could live here tax-free), and a travel hub, and it boasts the most developed infrastructure in the region, not only in Panama City but throughout the country. Even on the relatively remote Azuero Peninsula, where you find Las Tablas, the roads are paved, the Internet connection and the electricity are reliable, and you even find things like streetlights and fire hydrants. Remote beach living in Panama can be more convenient and more advantageous than living in the center of the capital city in neighboring countries.

Escape to the Mountains

El Valle de Antón, Panama • Istria, Croatia
• Medellín, Colombia

On the other hand, beach living has its downsides. Seawater and sand take their toll—on the exterior of your house, your pool furniture, your car. Maybe it's not sun and surf, therefore, that you seek, but mountain escape. The weather's better (cooler and less humid) at higher altitudes, and the year-round view from your bedroom window could be of wildflowers and waterfalls. You wouldn't spend your days fishing, boating, snorkeling, or diving, but instead, perhaps, hiking, bird-watching, gardening, and horseback riding.

If that describes your idea of the ideal lifestyle, here's where to find it.

Mountains Pick #1: El Valle de Antón, Panama

El Valle de Antón sits in a volcanic crater about two hours outside Panama City. All around the city tower jagged 10,000-foot-high mountains covered in a humid cloud forest that tumbles down to the flat but equally green and fertile crater floor. El Valle itself sits approximately 2,000 feet above sea level, in the province of Coclé. The population of almost 7,000 is made up of natives (descended from the Guaymí tribes), retired and working Panamanians, and retired and in-business expats. It's an enclave with a surprisingly international feel.

El Valle's primary attraction is its altitude, which offers cool respite from the heat and humidity of Panama City. Its other appeal is its vistas. You've never seen such stretches of verdant green. While there is a small expat population in El Valle, this town is a well-kept Panamanian secret. For generations, Panamanians from the capital have looked to El Valle for regular weekend and holiday escape. As a result, this is a top mountain choice for going local. Living in El Valle, you'd have to learn to speak Spanish and to assimilate among the friendly and welcoming Panamanian community.

Mountains Pick #2: Istria, Croatia

This region of Croatia, a triangular-shaped peninsula running alongside the coast of Italy (it was in fact part of Italy briefly early in the twentieth century), is a beguiling hinterland region, a patchwork of meadows, vineyards, and olive groves. Its rolling hills and mountainsides are dotted with white-stone villages, some dating to the Middle Ages. This is Europe's undiscovered Riviera, the "New Tuscany."

I'd say, though, that it's better than that region of Italy it's so often compared with. Istria is less discovered, less touristy, and more green, and it boasts better infrastructure. Croatia's war of independence ended in late 1995. Since then, the Croatians have been working ambitiously and aggressively to rebuild their country. Croatia's highways, bridges, and mountain tunnels are state of the art, while the towns, villages, and olive groves they traverse in Istria are ancient.

And while Istria is without question a place to seek out pastoral living at its best, it's also an increasingly cosmopolitan region, with world-famous truffles festivals every fall (when hundreds of truffle hunters and their sniffing dogs trawl Istria's woodlands in search of the white and black truffles the area is famous for); the internationally recognized New Wine Festivity, at the end of fall (when Istria's best winemakers present their offerings); and an annual summer film festival that attracts the international jet set.

For all these reasons, it's my top choice for mountain living in Europe.

Mountains Pick #3: Medellín, Colombia

Twenty years ago if you told anyone inside or outside Colombia that drug- and crime-ridden Medellín would be cleaned up and considered high tech and sought after just two decades later, no one would have believed you, but that is exactly what has happened. Medellín is not only no longer unsafe or unsavory, but it also is establishing a name for itself as one of the world's most progressive cities.

Medellín has many things going for it, including its geography. This pretty, tidy city has a near-perfect climate, thanks to its elevation (about 5,000 feet). This city, therefore, is my top pick for someone looking for the mild temperatures and impressive vistas that come with mountain living and who also appreciates Euro chic but doesn't want to travel all the way to Europe.

Top Choices with School-Aged Children

Panama City, Panama • Montevideo, Uruguay

My daughter, Kaitlin, age nine at the time, cried herself to sleep every night during our first year living in Waterford. She was fiercely opposed to leaving her grandmother, her cousins, her friends, and her school in Baltimore behind, and she made sure we were painfully aware of that fact every single day. "You've ruined my life!" she'd sob night after night as she fled from the dinner table to her bedroom and slammed the door.

My husband and I, of course, thought we were doing precisely the opposite. We believed we were enriching Kaitlin's life and expanding her horizons. But I have to admit, some nights I'd lie awake wondering if maybe Kaitlin wasn't right. Maybe launching a new life in a foreign country at age nine would translate into years of psychotherapy down the road.

Our first year in Paris when our children were young, it was Kaitlin's little brother, Jackson, age four at the time and born in Ireland, who struggled through the transition. "Give him six weeks," his preschool teacher advised me every morning when I dropped him off. "At this age, he'll adapt very quickly. In six weeks, he'll speak French, and he'll be fine. You'll see."

Meantime, every morning, as I'd turn to leave, Jackson would wrap his arms around my ankles, crying and begging, "Please don't make me stay here. They don't have an English voice, and I can't find my French voice." I'd pull myself free and race out the door and down the street, fighting back tears myself and wondering, again, if moving around the world with kids was really such a good idea. Six agonizing weeks later, though, and voilà, seemingly overnight, Jackson spoke French. He'd adjusted; he'd made friends.

In truth, our lifestyle has been easier for Jack to handle than Kaitlin. While Jack was born into it, Kaitlin might say she was yanked. On the other hand, it was Kaitlin's idea to move from Waterford to Paris. Kids in Ireland take what is called a "gap year" at age fifteen, between what would be their freshman and sophomore years of high school in the States. For this year, many study or take internships abroad. As they approached their gap year, Kaitlin's friends began making plans to attend school in the United States, Britain, and elsewhere. Kaitlin decided she'd like to spend the year in Paris.

We'd been enjoying Irish country life, but by this time we were wanting for more cosmopolitan distractions. We took Kaitlin's suggestion, therefore, as an opportunity for another family move. In the essay Kaitlin prepared as part of her admissions application for St. John's College in Annapolis three years later, she wrote: "I fought against my family's move to Ireland and resisted life in that country completely. But, if not for Ireland, I probably wouldn't have gone to Paris. And now I can't imagine not having had the chance to live in Paris."

Today Kaitlin is grown and married and working as the editorial director for my Live and Invest Overseas business. She and her husband have been based in Panama City, with Lief and me, since Kaitlin graduated from college. And as I write, they are preparing for their own return to Paris. Within the next eighteen months, the young couple will rejoin Lief and me, this time in the City of Light, where we're expanding our Live and Invest Overseas operations.

Also as I write, Jackson has just finished high school. He sat for his French baccalaureate exams last month, passed (with high marks—I feel, as his mother, compelled to mention), and is taking the summer off before embarking on a gap year of internships in Lisbon, Portugal; Montevideo, Uruguay; Medellín, Colombia; and Cayo, Belize. Then he'll be off to the States, like his sister, for college. He has his sights set on New York University. After college, Jackson, again like his sister, intends to return to Paris. Born in Ireland, raised between France and Panama, Jackson considers Paris his hometown.

All along the way I've worried that my children might suffer as a result of the globe-trotting lifestyle their parents chose for them. Now, with some perspective gained from the passage of time, I'm more confident than ever that the lives we've lived these past twenty years with our two children did them much more good than harm.

The advantages of raising children abroad are many, from a second (or even third) language to a second passport. Children raised overseas are generally self-confident, open-minded, and resourceful. They learn to make friends easily and adjust quickly to change. I make all these points based on now two decades of experience raising two children across four countries.

That's not to say raising kids in another country is easy. If you're considering making an international move with children, they—specifically, the options for their education—become your priority. Moving with children also means that you must move there full time, or at least that you must schedule your part-time life in your chosen haven around their school calendar.

The fundamental education choice you must make is whether to send your child to a local school (where, unless you're moving to Belize or Ireland, for example, he'll need to learn to speak the local language fluently), to a bilingual international school (where he'll have the opportunity to learn the new language but will take classes in his native tongue as well), or to an American or British school (where he'll be largely insulated from the local culture and community).

Just as we've chosen to go local with our lifestyles overseas, we've also gone local with our children's education. Why drag the kid to a new country only to enroll him in a school that could as easily be located in any U.S. suburb? We considered this question head-on in Paris, where the American School of Paris was one of our options for Kaitlin's education. Kaitlin and I visited together, and we both had the same reaction. The American School of Paris could be the American School of Any American Town. Every student is from the States, as is every member of the faculty. English is the only language spoken. The curriculum, the calendar, the special events—everything about the school is as it would be stateside. Nothing wrong with this per se, but it seemed a shame to us for Kaitlin to miss out on the chance to learn French, to make friends from all over the world, and to become part of the Paris teenager scene.

Another plus of going local with your child's schooling overseas is the cost. In most of the world (France is an exception; in France a public school education is as good or better than one your child might get from any private school), the local public schools probably don't offer the standard of education you're looking for. You'll be delighted, therefore, to learn that private schools in many countries are a bargain compared with the cost of private schools in the States. Tuition at Jackson's private French school in Panama City was about $7,000 per year. At Kaitlin's private elementary school in Waterford, Ireland, the tuition was less than $2,000 per year.

In addition to schooling options, when you're moving with children, you also must consider health care and local kid-friendly opportunities. Are there parks, playgrounds, private tutors, and places where the child could go to, say, study the guitar, learn to dance, or take karate lessons?

Likewise, you should also think about residency options. With a child, you can't easily reside under the radar or come and go so as not to exceed the time-in-country restrictions of a tourist visa. I don't recommend residing overseas without proper papers under any circumstances, of course, but over the years, I've known expats in France, Panama, Thailand, and elsewhere who've never gotten around to legalizing their stays. Often this is not a big deal. With school-aged children, it can be more difficult. This restriction, especially, can take a number of countries off the list of options, as it would be difficult or even impossible to organize legal residency for you and your family.

Moving abroad with children, you might be concerned about

their ability to adapt and to adjust. This has been my biggest worry. Having now moved my then nine-year-old daughter from the States to Ireland, then my then fourteen-year-old daughter and four-year-old son from Ireland to France, and then most recently, my then eight-year-old son from France to Panama, I can tell you this: Your children will be fine. The truth is, their move will be harder on you than it will be on them. They will learn the new language quicker than you will, they will make new friends more easily, and they will assimilate more readily.

Our first six months in Paris, Kaitlin would sit at the dining room table after dinner doing her homework—all in French. Before our arrival there, she'd never studied the language. Then, overnight, she was studying in the language, doing high school math in French. The work would take her hours, after which she'd retire, exhausted and nearly in tears. Then she'd have to get up the next morning to return to school, where, again, all lectures, presentations, and course materials were in French. This shouldn't be so hard on her, the mother in me couldn't help but observe. I made an appointment to meet with her adviser at school, who said this: "Kaitlin is struggling, yes. But you must let her struggle. It is good for her."

This is the last thing a child wants to hear and the hardest thing for a parent to accept. But I tell you now, it is the right thing, the true thing. After six months of exhausting effort, Kaitlin was bilingual. She retains this asset, and already it has opened doors for her. During her first year of college back in the United States, it was her overseas experience and her second language that helped her to land a part-time job in a chic photography gallery.

Don't worry about how your children will adjust. Worry about how you'll survive the adjustment period.

If you're considering making an overseas move with children, here are my two top recommendations.

School-Aged Children Pick #1: Panama City, Panama

Panama City is home to more than a dozen international-standard schools that could make good choices for your child's elementary and secondary education. Tuitions at these schools have increased sharply over the past decade, as Panama City's expat population, including the numbers of executives and entrepreneurs with young children, has exploded. These international-standard schooling options can still be more affordable than private schools in the United States, but they are not the bargain they were when we moved to Panama City with young Jackson in 2008. Plus, some of them now charge onetime enrollment fees (as high as $12,000). Among the many current options for where you could send your kids to school in this city are the Academia Interamericana de Panamá (tuition averages $6,500 per year, depending on the grade); the Canadian International School Panama (tuition is $2,000 per year); Colegio De La Salle Panamá (tuition is $2,800 per year); the Metropolitan School of Panama (tuition for grades K–5, $13,107; tuition for grades 6–12, $14,856); Balboa Academy (considered by many the top choice in the city; tuition for grades K–5, $11,264; tuition for grades 6–12, $12,456); and the French School of Panama (also called Lycée Français Paul Gauguin, administered by the French Ministry of Education; tuition is $7,000 per year). We chose the French School for Jackson because all of the teachers and much of the other staff came from France. For Lief and me this was an important consideration and point of comparison with the other international schooling options, whose faculties and staffs are mostly Panamanian.

Panama City boasts the best health care in the region and the state-of-the-art Hospital Punta Pacífica, affiliated with Johns Hopkins Medicine International in the States. The standard of care for your child would be what you're accustomed to back home.

Panama City is also home to the extensive Cinta Costera park and recreation area that fronts the entire downtown of the city, as well as Parque Omar, an oasis of trees and shade, with areas for soccer, baseball, bike riding, tennis, skating, karate, even a public swimming pool, and several other big parks throughout the city. At home in Panama City from the age of eight, Jackson found many spots for skateboarding, riding bikes, and shooting hoops with his friends.

It's also possible in Panama City to find organized team sports

(Jackson played on basketball and soccer teams), Scout troops, and most any kind of individual instruction your child might be interested in. During our nine years in Panama, Jackson took private lessons in guitar, piano, martial arts, fencing, tennis, and golf.

In addition, Panama is in the Central Time Zone, meaning it'd be convenient for your child to stay in touch with family back in the United States by phone, and but a few hours by air from key points in the States, meaning he or she could easily return home for holidays and regular visits.

School-Aged Children Pick #2: Montevideo, Uruguay

Uruguay, too, is home to top international education options, in both Montevideo and Punta del Este, on the coast. Choices in the capital include the British Schools; the Uruguayan American School; the Lycée Français Jules Supervielle (a French/ Spanish school); and the Escuela Integral Hebreo Uruguaya (a Hebrew school). In Punta del Este, your child could attend St. Clare's College for bilingual primary and secondary education; costs range from $7,865 and $11,250, depending on the grade.

Friends who've relocated to this country with their families report that life here is like life in the United States in the 1950s. There's a peace and an innocence about Uruguay that make it a great place to raise children. Certainly it's one of the safest places on the planet, far and happily removed from global tensions and strife.

Entrepreneurs Welcome

Panama City, Panama

In this day and age, you could start a business anywhere. Therefore, before you can determine where best you might indulge your entrepreneurial inclinations, be clear in your agenda. Are you moving to a new country to start a business? Or are you interested in retiring overseas and thinking that, once there, you'd like to find a productive (and maybe profitable) way to fill your days? Then, as important a consideration, will your business be local or international? Will you have a storefront (perhaps retail) or an office where customers or clients will visit, or are you thinking more along the lines of an Internet or consulting enterprise? And finally (and very important), will you need to hire staff?

Local options can be restricted in some jurisdictions. In Panama, for example, retail is protected, meaning foreigners can't buy or start a retail business. And Europe in general is a challenging place to try to be a small retail business owner. For the most part, though, you could open a dive shop (renting out dive and snorkel gear to tourists), a coffeehouse, a gift shop, a bar, or a bed-and-breakfast most places in the world. If this is your idea, to pursue a hobby/business dream you've harbored for years, you should make your destination decision based on all the other factors we've been discussing. Live where you want to live. Then once you are there, see what kind of entrepreneurial mischief you can get up to. You could open an art gallery or start a small school (as a friend of mine did in San José, Costa Rica); you could buy a small existing business or become a local service provider. (Set yourself up as a construction consultant, for example; there is a big demand for this in emerging markets where local construction standards, for everything from bathrooms to swimming pools, are not what developed-world buyers demand.)

Anyone reared, schooled, and trained in the first world has a serious leg up on the local competition in a developing nation. Growing up in the United States, for example, you've encountered innumerable business ideas. You've had the opportunity to watch some businesses grow and others fail. You understand why some enterprises succeed while others do not. You bring that experience and judgment with you overseas. On the other hand, note that to compete locally, you'll need strong local-language skills.

The underlying point, though, is not to allow a secondary agenda to determine what should be a bigger-picture decision. Live where you want to live and allow the business agenda to follow organically.

If, however, you're moving for the purpose of starting a business, then put the business requirements first. The ease and the costs of incorporating; corporate and income tax rates; the infrastructure; and the local English-speaking labor pool—these things become top priorities.

It's not difficult or costly to incorporate in most countries, and if you're running a nonlocal business, you shouldn't need a business license. Most countries do not tax foreign-source income, so tax planning is an option just about anywhere, to greater and lesser extents.

Infrastructure—that is, reliable Internet and electricity—is key for any business, for a business that can't communicate with clients and customers isn't in business very long. Outside of Europe, Panama and Malaysia sit at the top of the Best Infrastructure list, followed by Uruguay and Argentina. The Dominican Republic, Nicaragua, and Ecuador fall short here. I've operated businesses in Nicaragua and Ecuador and don't recommend it. You spend an inordinate amount of your time repairing your Internet connection, waiting for the electricity to come back on, and standing in line waiting for your turn to debate and deliberate (again and endlessly) with the local bureaucrats.

The real sticky wicket, though, is local labor law. If your international operation will not require local staff, then your choices for where to base yourself remain wide open. If you won't have to hire employees in-country, you can operate anywhere. I have a friend who is self-employed in an international business that requires no employees. He likes the Cayman Islands. This is not a budget destination, but cost of living is not an issue for my friend, so he's moving, with his business, to the Caymans. He's delighted. He's managed to find a way to pursue his income objectives in the place where he wants to spend his time.

If yours, though, is an international business that requires local staffing, then the decision-making process becomes all about things like employment law, labor costs, and employer taxes and social charges you would be liable for.

The most important thing to understand about employment law is that nowhere in the world does it favor the employer as much as it does in the United States. I ran a division of an international publishing company for about twenty-three years, the first thirteen of them stateside. Then I moved, with that business, to Ireland, where I came face-to-face for the first time with non-U.S. labor law. My most important lesson: In a jurisdiction like Ireland (the rest of Europe also qualifies), it's not possible to fire someone.

The in-house attorney for the company I worked for in the States reminded managers regularly that the business operated on a hire-at-will, fire-at-will basis. "You can fire someone because you don't like the color of the tie he wears to work one day," he'd joke. Depending on the state where you're doing business, it can in fact be almost that easy to disengage a U.S. employee.

In Ireland, the rest of Europe, and indeed, to greater and lesser extents, the rest of the world, I've learned, mostly the hard way, not only can you not fire at will, often you can't fire at all. In France, super-small owner- and family-run enterprises are common, because people are afraid to take on employees. There, when you hire someone, you hire him for life. That employee becomes your very long-term liability.

Furthermore, that employee (like all employees in France) assumes that the employer is the bad guy. In all Europe, the burden is on the employer to take care of his employees, but in France the relationship is more tense. It's not so much parent and child as it is Mean Mr. Capitalist and Victim. If you want to start a business that will require local hires, don't move to France. In fact, I'd steer clear of Europe altogether. Otherwise, you're creating additional and costly challenges and headaches, stacking the deck against your chances of success.

In Panama and throughout Latin America, too, labor laws favor the employee, but not nearly as aggressively as in Europe. In Panama, for example, it can be possible to fire someone when you want to. You, as the employer, are responsible for making a severance payout according to legislated formulas. As in Europe, the amount of the payout is predicated on the employee's salary, meaning that, in the Americas, severance payments aren't typically enough to break a business's back, as they can be in Euro-land.

Anywhere outside the States, you, as the employer, are liable for social benefits charges and fees, comparable to, though often more onerous than, Social Security in the United States. Again, though, these fees are predicated on salary, meaning that in Latin America, while as percentages they can seem burdensome, as whole numbers they're manageable.

This gets to one of the key benefits of doing business in Latin America: the cost of labor. It's low. I'm right now having flood damage repaired in a house I own in Granada, Nicaragua. The roof was blown off in a storm, and I was negligent in having it repaired. Meantime, the rains came, and over months, the wood moldings around the windows and the doors rotted away. This is a two-story, 2,300-square-foot house with many large windows. I've just had a quote for the cost of the labor required to tear out and replace all the rotted window frames and doorframes. The quote is for $450.

Again, labor costs in Latin America and South America are one big advantage of doing business here. Note, though, that depending on the type of business you want to run, your labor costs may be higher than average. I'm sure the carpenter being called in to replace the rotted wood in my house in Nicaragua doesn't speak English. English-speaking labor, if you require it, comes at a premium in this part of the world.

Taking all these issues into account, where should you think about basing your international business if it requires staffing? Panama. It checks every box you need checked. The IT infrastructure is first-rate and reliable. The time zone is convenient if your clients, customers, or vendors are based in the United States or Europe. The educated and English-speaking labor pool is big, and it comes at an affordable cost; the current minimum wage in Panama City is $3.25 per hour (less outside the capital city). An English-speaking midlevel manager makes $1,500 a month; you can hire an English-speaking personal assistant for $1,000 a month. Call centers start their English-speaking staff at $800 a month.

I've started and operated businesses in eight countries. If today I was to launch an international business that did not require any local employees, I'd do it in Paris, because this is where I want to be based. However, the international publishing company I'm running does need local staff, which is one of the primary reasons we moved from Paris to Panama in the first place. In Panama City today you can find the staff you need for any kind or size of business you want to run. This city is attracting educated, English-speaking talent from around the world, but especially from North America and Europe. Panama City is awash these days in twenty- and thirtysomething digital nomads and all manner of opportunity seekers. This is one of the many reasons global businesses from Dell and Nike to Estée Lauder and Procter & Gamble are choosing to base themselves in Panama's capital city; they know they can find the employees they need. If they're comfortable Panama City is the place for them to locate, you can be, too.

For all the reasons I've cited already, Europe in general is not a good choice from a doing-business point of view. What about Asia? Here, the top option would be Singapore. This tiny city-state is an ultramodern country of skyscrapers, well-maintained parks and greenbelts, clean air, and prosperity. Ancient restored Chinese-style shop houses and nineteenth-century colonial buildings lie in the shadows of towering high-rise condominiums, financial companies, banks, and global corporations.

Singapore was a British colony until 1963, when it became an independent republic. Today, many stately British buildings remain in use, tucked away among the skyscrapers, serving as government buildings, banks, theaters, and museums. Along with these buildings, Britain left another legacy—her language. Although the dialect is uniquely Singaporean, English remains the de facto language. The country is safe and comfortable. Crime is almost nonexistent. The public transportation system is one of the best in the world. Public buses are even equipped with GPS systems that let riders view where they are along the route at any given moment.

In other words, Singapore has much to recommend it for the would-be entrepreneur. The telecom infrastructure, especially, is solid, and the banking industry has earned the country the reputation of being the Switzerland of Asia. But there are serious disadvantages, as well.

If you're planning to operate a business that targets the U.S. market, the biggest disadvantage is the time-zone difference. Maybe you could handle working until two A.M. for a few months, but that gets old quickly. This is one important reason I recommend Latin America in general over other regions worldwide. It's generally in the Central Time Zone.

The other big downside to Singapore is the cost—of living, of doing business, of labor, of everything. Singapore is not a low-cost anything, and it is usually at or near the top of any World's Most Expensive Cities list. In other words, Singapore could be a great place to live and start a business if you've got the budget for it.

Moving to any new country to launch a new business is no easy thing. Over the years, doing this again and again, in eight jurisdictions now, I've been uncertain, nervous, intimidated, afraid, lonely, confused . . . yet I've continued to pursue this life as part of the laptop-toting expat entrepreneur revolution because it comes with serious advantages. As an entrepreneur abroad, you have complete freedom and flexibility, independence and autonomy. You're able to take what you want to do, what you love to do, and convert it into an income that allows you to live where you want to live. You live where you want, how you want, all the while having the adventure of a lifetime.

Best Health Care

Paris, France • Panama City, Panama • Kuala Lumpur, Malaysia

Belize is the only country on my World's Best Places to Live list that doesn't boast what generally could be described as international-standard health care. In every other country, at least in the capital city, you'll find at least one state-of-the-art hospital with at least some English-speaking doctors, nurses, and other medical staff. Even Managua, Nicaragua, for example, boasts the Hospital Metropolitano Vivian Pellas, brand-new and fully equipped to twenty-first-century standards.

If you don't want to limit your options to the capital or another major city, as you may have to do in Latin America, look to France, which boasts the best health care in the world. If you don't want or can't afford Europe, put Panama in the Americas or Malaysia in Asia at the top of your list. Both these countries offer first-world care at third-world prices.

Best Health Care Pick #1: Paris, France

For years, the World Health Organization published an index rating ranking the quality of the health care in all the countries of the world, and year after year, France came out the winner.

Medical care in France is top-notch. While France offers free health care for residents who pay into the social security system, this requires not only formal residency status in France but also entering the French tax system (which is something best avoided).

The best option, unless you're a passport-carrying member of the European Union, is to choose France as a part-time retirement home. Spend up to six months a year in Paris or along this country's sunny Mediterranean coast and carry an international insurance policy (through Cigna, for example) that covers you during your stay. You'll enjoy the world's best health care at least part of the year.

Best Health Care Pick #2: Panama City, Panama

For top-notch health care at a more affordable cost, look to Panama. A complete blood workup at Panama City's Hospital Punta Pacífica, affiliated with Johns Hopkins Medicine International, is $40. A full physical with an English-speaking doctor, likely trained in the United States, is $50. While a home-care nurse can charge $40 an hour in the States, in Panama City you could engage one for about $40 a day.

I recently spent the day in the emergency room of Panama City's other top choice for health care, the Paitilla Medical Center, for the treatment of a spider bite on my foot. I'd had an allergic reaction to the bite, plus the area had become infected. The entire day's adventure, including blood work and other lab tests, injections for the infection and the allergic reaction, and the kind care of an English-speaking doctor who knew what he was doing, came to a grand total of $70.

Certainly the country's best medical facilities are located in Panama City, and if health care is a concern, you should stick close to the capital. However, the standard of care elsewhere also can be good or at least acceptable. I tumbled off a motorbike while riding in the mountains around Boquete years ago and landed on my head. I was unconscious for an hour, and when I came to, I couldn't remember who or where I was. It turned out not to be as scary an experience as that might sound, but I did have a concussion and lots of gashes and scrapes. I was taken to the medical center in David, the nearest big city, capital of this country's Chiriquí Province. While David is a big city within the context of Panama, this is a hinterland region, very rural. Yet the U.S.-trained doctor on duty spoke perfect English and had access to the equipment he needed to care for my injuries. I spent the night in the clinic, then was released to a friend's care. The bill for the entire experience was less than $300.

You can arrange local Panama health insurance (with a zero annual deductible) for $170 a month or less, depending on your age. Note, though, that most local Panamanian health insurance plans accept new applicants only through age sixty-four.

Best Health Care Pick #3: Kuala Lumpur, Malaysia

Health care in Malaysia is modern, efficient, and super cheap. You won't be able to get local Malaysian health insurance over the age of sixty. Your options are to carry an international policy or to go naked—that is, to pay your medical costs out of pocket. This can be a reasonable choice in this country, where a doctor's visit that might cost $150 in the States costs less than $15. A complete dental examination is about $25 (compared with, say, $150 in the States), and a crown costs less than $300 (compared with $500 to $1,000 stateside). Most prescription medications can be easily obtained at pharmacies without a prescription and at super bargain prices.

Great Weather

*Eternal Spring: Cuenca, Ecuador • Tropical Weather
That's Not Too Hot, Not Too Humid: El Valle de Antón,
Panama • Four Mild Seasons: La Barra, Uruguay; Istria, Croatia*

What's your idea of the perfect climate? Temperatures in the mid-70s year-round? Or are you more comfortable in the tropics, as long as the humidity isn't too great? Perhaps you enjoy a change of seasons, as long as winter doesn't mean snow, and summer isn't so unbearable that you never want to venture far from air-conditioning?

Having grown up in Baltimore, Maryland, I'm okay with hot, even a little steamy. Lief, who grew up in the Arizona desert, can't tolerate humidity. We do okay in Panama City, because I appreciate the sizzling sun, and when things become too sticky for Lief, we can escape a couple of hours inland to the mountains or to the breeze-swept beaches along the country's Pacific coast. Boquete, in the highlands, can be downright chilly. Houses sometimes come with fireplaces.

Bear in mind that the temperature, the level of humidity, the amount of rainfall, the length of the day, and the duration of each season can vary dramatically from one region of a country to another. In other words, as with everything we're considering, you can't talk about the weather in Portugal or Thailand. You've got to look at the climate in Lisbon or the Algarve, in Bangkok or Chiang Mai, just as, if you were planning your retirement stateside, you might weigh the weather in Phoenix against that in Seattle.

Here's my guide to the world's best weather, whatever you interpret that to be.

Eternal Spring: Cuenca, Ecuador

Located in the northwest corner of South America, Ecuador lies directly on the equator. Cuenca, Ecuador's third-largest city, sits high in an Andean valley, about 8,200 feet above sea level. Just 2.5 degrees south of the equator, it offers pleasant temperatures year-round and little seasonal variation, both thanks to its altitude. In Cuenca you can live without heat or air-conditioning; they're never necessary.

Don't choose Cuenca, though, without visiting first. Many people are unaffected by high altitude, but others notice it. If you find yourself short of breath, you should recover from the worst of it in a few days and be at your full physical capacity in a few weeks. But if you have difficulty breathing at sea level, a chronic heart condition, or asthma, then life at this altitude is not for you. And even if you don't have a chronic condition that might be adversely affected by high elevations, you still might find that life in the clouds doesn't suit you. It doesn't work for me. I spend the first week of every visit to high-altitude Ecuador sick in bed, and even during extended stays, never adjust completely.

Tropical Weather That's Not Too Hot, Not Too Humid: El Valle de Antón, Panama

El Valle de Antón is conveniently positioned not too far from Panama City yet at an altitude that makes the weather generally cooler and less humid. The mountain valley lies at approximately 2,000 feet and boasts springlike temperatures year-round. The year-round average high is 68 degrees Fahrenheit, and the average nighttime minimum is 61 degrees. Summer and winter temperatures vary little. The major difference season to season is the amount of wind and rainfall.

The dry season runs mid-December to mid-April, the wet season May to early December. During the wet (also called the winter) season, when it rains, the water can fall from the sky in what seems like a vertical river. But the downpours stop as abruptly as they start, the water drains away, the sun comes out, everyone jumps on their bicycle, and life goes on as before. The well-constructed drainage channels (all covered with emerald green mosses, lichens, and ferns) that run alongside every road cope remarkably well with the sudden deluges. It's rarely uncomfortably hot. Sometimes at night you'll even want a comforter on your bed.

Four Mild Seasons Pick #1: La Barra, Uruguay

Uruguay has four distinct seasons, and its 41-inch rainfall is spread evenly throughout the year. There's no wet or dry season, though rain is uncommon in the midsummer months of January and February (remember, the seasons down here at the bottom of the world are the reverse of those in North America). The average daytime high temperature is about 82 degrees Fahrenheit in midsummer, with the average low around 65. In midwinter, highs run around 60 degrees, with lows near 42. Frost is rare, and it never snows. Few people use air-conditioning, thanks to the ocean breezes, and evenings are cool. You will, though, use the heat in the wintertime.

Four Mild Seasons Pick #2: Istria, Croatia

Istria, too, sees four seasons, with dry and warm summers, plus an average of 2,400 hours of sunshine every year. Winters are mild and pleasant. You can expect rain at this time of year, but snowfalls are rare. You won't be swimming in the Adriatic in winter or early spring, but the sea is rarely too cold to keep you from sailing or fishing. The leaves on the trees turn red and gold in autumn, just as they do on the East Coast of the United States, and springtime is a delight. These distinct seasonal variations, very similar to seasonal changes in Maryland, where I grew up, are one of the things I enjoy most about this region.

No Language Barrier

Belize • Ireland

You could retire to most of the countries on my Best Places to Launch Your New Life Overseas list and, at least in particular cities and regions, get by without learning the local language. In Paris, Panama City, the Algarve, and Kuala Lumpur, for example, many of the locals speak English; certainly enough of them speak it well enough that you could survive without making any real effort to communicate in the local lingo. And, in a place like Ajijic, Mexico, or Boquete, Panama, you could insulate yourself from the local population, make a new life among fellow expats, and avoid the language issue altogether. I know many who've lived for years in these towns without acquiring more than a handful of local words.

In fact, I don't speak Spanish; Lief does. On the other hand, while Lief speaks only a couple of dozen French words, I do okay in French; Lief manages our in-country affairs in Panama and the rest of the Spanish-speaking world, and I take the lead in France.

So, yes, you could get by without learning the language in the places I recommend for your overseas adventures. You could count on a spouse, a friend, an assistant, or a translator. But your experience of the place will not be the same as it would be if you made the effort to learn to communicate with your new neighbors in their native language. Even a little effort is appreciated. Lief's couple of dozen French words and my smattering of Spanish allow us to keep face. We can say hello, good-bye, thank you, and please. We can give a taxi driver directions and order dinner in a restaurant where the waiter speaks no English. We can ask for help or for a beer at the bar. If you're thinking of retiring to a country where the language is something other than English, you should be prepared to make the effort to speak the local language at least at this level.

The more effort you make and the more of the second language you pick up, the more you'll be able to penetrate beneath the surface of the place and become part of the local community. If you have no interest in doing this and flat out don't want to hassle with the challenge at this point in your life, I recommend you consider places where language isn't an issue.

You may sometimes still feel like you need a translator, but in one of the countries on my Best Places list, the language is English. Yes, in Belize they speak our native tongue with a twist, but no language classes (or translation of documents related to the purchase of a piece of real estate, for example, or the installation of your Internet service) will be required.

Part-Time Retirement Overseas

Mendoza, Argentina • Istria, Croatia • Mazatlán, Mexico
• Chiang Mai, Thailand • La Barra, Uruguay

If you're considering options overseas for reinventing your life in retirement, a full-time, all-or-nothing move may be more than you're up for, especially at first. And maybe you'll never be prepared to cut the ties back home with your children, your grandchildren, the home you've lived in for decades, or any ongoing business concerns completely.

These are good reasons to retire overseas part-time. Two others are the weather (why not move south when the snow begins to fall up north?) and budget. If your retirement nest egg is modest, your prospects for retirement living in the United States may seem grim. On the other hand, if you spend half the year someplace where the cost of living is significantly reduced and rent out your U.S. home while you're away, your retirement funds could expand accordingly during the months you're stateside. Retirement could go from a source of concern to a cause for excitement.

Other places that make sense as part-time retirement choices are those where establishing full-time residency is a hassle or well-nigh impossible. You'll have your work cut out for you trying to organize full-time legal residency as a retiree in Croatia, for example. Many foreigners remain indefinitely in Thailand without formalizing their stays, making regular "visa runs," as they're called, every few months to refresh their tourist papers. I don't recommend this. It's easier and safer simply to limit your visit so that you don't overstay your tourist visa, making Thailand another good part-time choice.

Mazatlán, Mexico, could be the easiest part-time retire overseas option of all. You could drive back and forth between your part-time lives north and south of the border.

Easy Access to Home

Mexico • Panama • Nicaragua • Belize

Want to know that you could return home anytime? Then don't relocate "overseas," exactly. Don't put an ocean between your new home and your old one. Instead, consider top foreign locales in the same hemisphere with regular and convenient return flights to the States.

International accessibility can be deceptive. A place can seem close but in fact be difficult to get to. You can't look at a map and consider the distance between where you are and where you're considering going as the crow flies. When it comes to international travel, the distance between two points matters far less than the number of air carriers that service that route. If, for example, only one carrier serves the route you'll need to fly, you're going to have to pay monopoly pricing for every ticket you buy.

Also consider how regularly the route is served. Are there flights every day? More than once a day? Are they seasonal? Consider your stateside anchor point. Would you be able to fly direct between there and your new home? If not, what are the connection possibilities? Would they necessitate an overnight? To travel from the West Coast of the United States to the Dominican Republic, you'd have to take a red-eye and then connect in Newark for the last leg of the trip.

Think about departure and arrival times. International flights to Quito, for example, arrive late at night. This is your only option, making Ecuador, for me, a relatively inaccessible location. You arrive late at night in the capital. This, though, is likely not your final destination, meaning you'll have to include an overnight in the capital as part of every international excursion, then wake up the next morning and continue on to Cuenca or wherever you're ultimately headed.

An accessible international destination is one you can reach via more than one air carrier, each offering flights at least several times a week year-round, via routes and at times of day that make for convenient travel, not "I really don't *ever* want to have to go through that again" travel. Even more accessible is the international destination you can reach by car, which is why Mazatlán, Mexico, is my top pick if easy access is your priority.

Easy Access Pick #1: Mazatlán, Mexico

As I've mentioned, Mazatlán and other points along Mexico's Pacific coast qualify as among the most accessible "overseas" destinations of all. Never mind many flight options on multiple carriers (which exist); you can come and go from the United States to this part of Mexico whenever you want behind the wheel of your own car. Plus, hourly first-class bus service is available from the States to points throughout Mexico.

And, if you're up for it, you could even drive to Mazatlán from the United States—certainly a realistic option if you live in Texas or Arizona, for example.

Easy Access Pick #2: El Valle de Antón, Panama

Panama, the Hub of the Americas, is the most accessible country in the entire region. You can fly direct to Panama City's Tocumen International Airport from Newark and Houston, and on United; from Atlanta on Delta; and from Miami on American Airlines. Copa, the Panamanian national carrier, flies to an ever-expanding list of U.S. cities. In addition, from Panama City you can fly direct to almost any capital city in Latin America, and it's via Panama City that most intra–Latin America flights connect.

From Tocumen, El Valle is but a two-hour drive away on the very modern Pan-American Highway. Rent a car at the airport or take the bus; first-class bus service to El Valle operates regularly from the center of Panama City.

Easy Access Pick #3: Granada, Nicaragua

Granada, Nicaragua, is just fifty miles, via the Pan-American Highway, from the international airport in Managua, which is accessible from Miami on American Airlines; from Atlanta on Delta; and from Houston on United.

Tax-Friendly Jurisdiction

Belize • Panama • Uruguay • Malaysia

Most countries are relatively tax-friendly when it comes to retirees. That is to say, a foreign resident's pension or Social Security income is often not taxed. Remember, though, that you could owe tax in the United States on your retirement pension income; that tax obligation must always be considered as separate from and in addition to the local tax burden in your new jurisdiction. In other words, if you retire from the United States to Panama, while you'll owe no tax on your pension income in Panama, you could owe tax on it in the United States. The fundamental point, though, is that, if this is the only income you'll have as a retiree overseas, then tax planning isn't an issue for you. For you, one jurisdiction is as tax-efficient as another.

Things get more complicated when you have passive (investment) or earned (wages or business, including self-employment) income to report. The first thing to understand when considering your tax burden as an American planning a move overseas is that tax rules vary greatly jurisdiction to jurisdiction. Most countries (including the United States) tax residents on their worldwide income. These can be places where you want to avoid becoming resident at all costs. Unfortunately, as an American abroad, no matter where you go, you'll always carry your U.S. tax obligation. As long as you carry a blue passport with an eagle on the cover, you must file a U.S. tax return every year. This is not to say you will necessarily owe tax. Careful planning often can reduce or even eliminate your U.S. tax on earned income. Still, the filing requirement remains.

Some countries tax foreign residents on what's called a remittance basis, meaning they expect their share of any money you bring (remit) into the country. This can work to your advantage if you earn your money outside the country and are able to live on little. In this case, you could earn millions of dollars a year, from either passive or earned income, but as long as you kept most of your millions outside the jurisdiction where you're residing, you wouldn't owe any tax on it locally.

Again, as an American, you'd still have a tax obligation to Uncle Sam, but that's a separate matter. To the tax collector of the country where you're living, you'd owe tax on only the money you brought into that country each year to cover your living expenses.

Some countries tax foreign residents only on income earned locally. In this case, you could not only earn millions outside the country, you could even bring your millions into the country to spend as you like (theoretically speaking). As long as you didn't earn the money locally, the local tax collector would have no claim. This is as good as it gets from a tax-planning point of view.

Four key jurisdictions where this is the case are Belize, Panama, Uruguay, and Malaysia. As a foreign resident in any of these jurisdictions, you won't pay taxes on your pension income. In addition, in these four countries, neither will you pay income tax on any income from outside the country, be it passive or earned. If you have an investment account in the United States that earns you annual interest, for example, you'll pay no tax on that income to these countries' tax collectors.

Furthermore, the approach to taxation in these countries means that if you work as a consultant in one of them, with clients outside the country, you could pay zero local tax. A German fellow I met several years ago had set himself up in Kuala Lumpur, Malaysia. He was an engineering consultant whose clients were various companies in the Middle East. All his income was earned outside Malaysia, meaning he was liable for no income tax in the country. As he was German, living outside Germany, neither did he owe income tax in that country. He was living and working completely free of income tax.

Tax-Friendly Pick #1: Belize

Research Belize tax rates, and you'll find that they're high (at least after you hit a certain level of income) . . . for Belizean citizens living in the country. Don't be confused. Tax rates in a country for citizens of that country apply to citizens of that country only. Unless you acquire a Belize passport, these rules don't apply to you.

As a non-Belizean living in Belize, you're taxed on only income earned in Belize. Therefore, as a foreign resident in this country, you have a local tax liability only if you run a business or take a job. Two other critical taxes to consider when choosing a retirement jurisdiction are capital gains and inheritance taxes. Belize imposes neither. Furthermore, as I've explained, as a resident retiree in Belize, you're welcome to import personal belongings, household goods, a car, and even an airplane tax-free.

Tax-Friendly Pick #2: Panama

Panama doesn't differentiate between citizens and noncitizens for income tax purposes. As a resident, Panamanian or not, you pay taxes only on income derived directly from within Panama.

This means that, as a resident retiree in this country, you owe zero tax on any income (pension, earned, or passive) from outside Panama.

Panama has a top marginal tax bracket of 25 percent for income earned in Panama. Businesses pay a flat tax of 25 percent on net profits. Capital gains are taxed at 10 percent (again, this applies only to gains realized in Panama).

Tax-Friendly Pick #3: Uruguay

Uruguay also taxes residents only on income generated in the country. Individual income generated in Uruguay is taxed at up to a top marginal rate of 36 percent.

One downside to Uruguay is that the country imposes a wealth tax on all assets within Uruguay. This is something to be aware of if you decide to invest in property in this country. The wealth tax rate is low, starting at 0.7 percent and topping out at 1.5 percent. Exemptions apply, so the total actual tax should be minimal unless you buy an expensive piece of real estate.

Tax-Friendly Pick #4: Malaysia

As a resident, you are taxed only on income derived from within Malaysia, meaning that even income you remit to Malaysia is not taxed as long as it was earned outside the country. Income earned in Malaysia is taxed at marginal rates from 0 percent to 28 percent. The country imposes no wealth tax and no property tax. Capital gains are taxed on a sliding scale that is reduced to 5 percent for nonresidents and zero for permanent residents after you've held a piece of real estate for five years or longer.

Established Expat Community

Ajijic, Mexico • Boquete, Panama • Ambergris Caye, Belize

A friend who relocated his family from the United States to the South of France about the same time we moved from the States to Ireland once remarked, "You know, I think we're doing this the hard way. Here in France, we're scrambling to learn French so we can figure out what's going on, because we're always confused. We're trying to make friends and to find a place for ourselves in a French country community where families have known each other for generations. We don't understand French cultural nuances yet, so we're committing one faux pas after another. And we don't have any other Americans around to commiserate with, no one to show us the ropes. We've really jumped into the deep end of this living overseas thing.

"And you have, too, in Ireland. You aren't struggling with a new language [in fact, Lief and I would have argued that we were!], but you're on your own in a foreign community. You're living and working and sending your children to school among the Irish. You've plopped yourself down and are trying to fit in among the local community.

"It'd be a very different experience, I think," my friend continued, "to move as an expat into an expat community, a place like Lake Chapala, Mexico, for example, where you'd be surrounded by other people just like you, other people who've already done what you're doing and who could offer a word of advice when you needed one."

Which is better? Assimilating into the local culture or becoming part of the American Dream abroad? It's not a question of better or right but, as with so many things to do with relocating yourself to another country, a question of what you want. This is an entirely personal decision and one of the most important and fundamental choices you must make when planning for your new life overseas—to go local or not. If you decide you'd like to take the idea of living overseas for a test spin by settling, at least at first, in what would be very familiar surroundings, here are three top options.

Expat Community Pick #1: Ajijic, Mexico

Ajijic and the area around Lake Chapala, Mexico, host the most organized, developed expat community in the world. The Lake Chapala Society reports about 4,000 American and Canadian residents in Chapala proper. The Mexican government, meantime, estimates that nearly 20,000 expats reside full time in the state of Jalisco, the region where Lake Chapala sits. In other words, the path has been cut. Moving here, you could slide into a way of living not dramatically different from the life you left behind in the States. You wouldn't have to worry about learning the local language if you didn't want to. You wouldn't have to work to make a place for yourself among the local community, because this isn't a "local" community. This is an entire community of nonlocals. You could wander into the restaurant down the street anytime and find English-speaking companionship, someone to complain to about the bureaucracy at the Department of Immigration or the challenges of studying to take a driving test in Spanish. Retiring to Ajijic, you could make a very comfortable life for yourself in a place that's exotic, beautiful, safe, and very affordable.

Our friends Akaisha and Billy have taken this path. They've been in Chapala for years, where they live comfortably on less than $50 per day, including housing, food, transportation, entertainment, and in-country travel. They eat well, play tennis, socialize, and travel comfortably. As they put it themselves, they want for nothing.

Don't misunderstand. Ajijic isn't a retirement village. This isn't Sun City South, at least not formally. This is a legitimate Mexican town that, over the past four decades, has attracted such a volume of foreign retirees that it's become less Mexican and more friendly to foreign residents.

Expat Community Pick #2: Boquete, Panama

Boquete, Panama, is this country's gringolandia. More than ten thousand foreigners call this colorful mountain town home at least part of the year.

What's the attraction? Beautiful setting, good climate, straightforward *pensionado* rules (for all of Panama), yes, but mostly the draw in Boquete, as in Ajijic, is the established gringo community. This is a place to come to enjoy many of the benefits of being retired overseas without leaving behind too many of the comforts and conveniences of American suburban living. In one private gated residential community development I know in this region, for example, amenities include a golf course, stables, even a small central town created specifically for foreign residents; and construction, for both the shared amenities and the individual homes, is to U.S. standards, with U.S.-style finishes, fixtures, and fittings. In the town of Boquete itself, shops and services catering to the ever-growing foreign retiree population continue to open. In the U.S.-style restaurants serving American-style menus (featuring scrambled eggs for breakfast and cheeseburgers for lunch), you'll hear all-English conversation at the tables around you and all-American music on the speakers. People you pass on the street will greet you with a wave and a hi or a hello, assuming that that's how you'd like to be addressed and that you'll reply in kind.

Expat Community Pick #3: Ambergris Caye, Belize

The biggest and best known of the cays offshore from mainland Belize has evolved over the past two decades into the home of the biggest American expat community in the Caribbean. Life on Ambergris is all about the sun, the sand, and the sea, and the U.S. and other expats and retirees who've chosen to base themselves here couldn't be more welcoming of like-minded beach-loving expats who make their way to this island to join them. You could show up on Ambergris any given morning and have a dozen expat friends in time for happy hour that afternoon.

Fully Wired Location

Kuala Lumpur, Malaysia • Paris, France • Panama City, Panama

In many places around the world, including some places you might not expect (rural Ireland, for example), the infrastructure is not what you'd call first world or reliable. Some whole countries, such as Nicaragua and Ecuador, qualify as maddening on this score. The electricity can go out, and nobody is quite sure why or can say when it might be restored. And the same goes for the Internet connection. Sometimes your emails will go through, sometimes they won't, and again, nobody can explain the reason.

In European and other developed countries, you can expect the same reliable service for Internet, electricity, and phone that is available throughout the United States, even outside major cities. And the cost of this super-reliable service in Europe can surprise you, as it did us living in Paris.

In the less-developed countries on my Best Places list, high-speed Internet might be a misnomer. Sometimes you're lucky if you can get Internet access at all. In remote areas, your best option can be to install satellite Internet. The equipment cost for this can be hundreds of dollars or more, depending on the country, and the monthly fees start at $150 for what old-timers would call dial-up speeds.

In more developed cities and towns, if you can get cable, you can get true high-speed Internet. But what happens when the electricity goes out? Then you've got no service at all. Maybe you have electricity and the Internet company doesn't. Maybe vice versa. Either way, no electricity equals no connectivity.

Nicaragua experiences scheduled and nonscheduled brown-outs. My husband, Lief, lived and worked in a remote part of Argentina years ago; his office lost its telephone connection every time it rained (probably because a cable got wet). A storm blew out the transformer at the end of our lane in Ireland, and it took the electric company days to make the repairs; as the transformer serviced only a few houses in this remote region of the country, it wasn't a priority for them.

If the thought of dealing with these kinds of infrastructure frustrations makes your blood pressure rise, stick with the first world (France, for example, or Portugal) or a first-world city in a developing country—Panama City and Kuala Lumpur qualify. The latter are both bustling cities where businesses, banks, and government offices require and enjoy full-time connectivity, meaning you can, too.

Fully Wired Pick #1: Kuala Lumpur, Malaysia

Kuala Lumpur's city center is fully wired with fiber optics. The country runs on a 3G cell phone system. Internet cafés are everywhere, as are Wi-Fi hot spots (in cafés and coffee shops, for example, including Starbucks).

Fully Wired Pick #2: Paris, France

High-speed wireless Internet comes bundled with telephone and cable for a very low price in Paris. Traditional cell phone contracts require proof of address and a local bank account (so the cell phone provider can direct-debit your account every month for your cell charges), but you can get a pay-as-you-go phone more easily. Wi-Fi hot spots are everywhere throughout the city and often free. Electricity is very reliable and almost never goes out . . . though, coincidentally, it did for most of our neighborhood last night. Within minutes a crew of Électricité de France (EDF) guys were on the scene working diligently until the problem was resolved. Lief and I took it all in stride. We spend a lot of time in the developing world. Our neighbors, though, were appalled. As I said, this never happens in Paris. Local restaurants, unable to open to serve the Saturday-night crowd, were the real victims.

Fully Wired Pick #3: Panama City, Panama

High-speed Internet is readily available and reasonably priced, thanks to competition among four service providers. Cell phone costs have fallen and service has improved since the government gave concessions to two new cell companies, increasing the total number of cell providers in the country to four, all of which are competing aggressively for customers. Wi-Fi hot spots are available in some cafés and most hotel lobbies, and Internet cafés are everywhere now. Electric outages happen rarely, though more often during the rainy season, when lightning and heavy rains play havoc with the lines. Most new buildings, however, are equipped with generators that provide full power during outages, so you might not even realize it when they do take place.

Special Benefits for Foreign Retirees

Panama • Belize • Malaysia

American retirees are an increasingly sought-after commodity worldwide. Countries compete for U.S. retirees and their retirement income, rolling out the welcome mat by offering sometimes significant tax breaks, in-country discounts, and other perks once you've qualified for resident retiree status. Panama is the clear winner in this category. Its *pensionado* program of special benefits for retirees is the gold standard.

Costa Rica was the first country to make a concerted effort to attract foreign retirees with a program of special benefits. Its *pensionado* program was responsible for bringing tens of thousands of foreign retirees, including many Americans, to the country in the 1980s and 1990s. While the *pensionado* visa is still available in Costa Rica, many of the tax breaks and other special perks it once offered have been discontinued. Meantime, Costa Rica has become more expensive, both as a place to live and as a place to own a home. These are the reasons I don't include Costa Rica on any Best Places to Launch Your New Life Overseas list. It's perhaps the world's best-known overseas retirement haven but no longer one of the best.

Special Benefits Pick #1: Panama

Panama has picked up where Costa Rica left off. Its pensioner program offers some of the deepest retiree discounts available anywhere. Seniors (that is, women ages fifty-five and older and men ages sixty and older) get up to half off on nearly everything, including movies, motels, doctors' visits, plane tickets, professional services, and electric bills. Furthermore, friends who've acquired *pensionado* visa status in Panama assure me that the discounts are easily realized and that it's no big hassle to have your pensioner status recognized. One friend I had lunch with recently remarked, "The only thing I haven't been able to get a discount on so far are my gin and tonics at the bar down the street from my apartment. And I'm working on that."

If you are over age eighteen and receive a regular pension from Social Security, any government entity, the armed forces, or a private company, you qualify. In other words, you could qualify as a resident retiree in this country, and reap all the benefits of that status, as young as age eighteen. This isn't common or the norm, of course, but the point is that Panama is very open-minded and flexible on this point.

To qualify for *pensionado* residency status, your pension amount must be at least $1,000 per month, plus $250 per month for each dependent applying for residency status along with you, including your spouse and children younger than eighteen. Panama pensioner benefits are for life.

Specifically, these *pensionado* benefits include:

➤ 50 percent off entertainment anywhere in the country (movies, theaters, concerts, etc.)

➤ 30 percent off bus, boat, and train fares

➤ 25 percent off airline tickets

➤ 50 percent off hotel stays Monday through Thursday

➤ 30 percent off hotel stays Friday through Sunday

➤ 25 percent off at sit-down restaurants

➤ 15 percent off at fast-food restaurants

➤ 15 percent off hospital bills (if no insurance applies)

➤ 10 percent off prescription medications

➤ 20 percent off medical consultations

➤ 15 percent off dental and eye exams

➤ 20 percent off professional and technical services

➤ 25 percent off your electric bill (up to 600 kilowatts)

In addition, *pensionado* status entitles you to a onetime tax exemption on the importation of household goods (up to $10,000) and a tax exemption every two years on the importation or the in-country purchase of a new car. Plus, you'll never have to wait in line at the bank. Every bank has a special express line for retirees.

Special Benefits Pick #2: Belize

Another country that rolls out the welcome mat for foreign retirees is Belize. Twenty years ago, the government of this country enacted legislation to allow Qualified Retired Persons (QRPs) to obtain permanent residency in this country. In many ways, this program is the most efficient route to foreign residency anywhere in the Americas, and, while the QRP visa allows you full-time residency, you can enjoy the benefits of being a QRP even if you spend as little as thirty days a year in Belize.

Belize's QRP program not only offers the equivalent of a U.S. green card to foreign residents ages forty-five and older, but also grants a host of other incentives designed to encourage foreigners to come and bring their money. These incentives include a permanent exemption from all Belize taxes, including income tax, capital gains tax, estate tax, and import tax on household goods, automobiles, boats, even airplanes. The only requirements are that you or your spouse be forty-five years of age or older, that you consider yourself to be retired, and that you show that you have at least $2,000 a month in income to support yourself in Belize (from a pension or some other regular income).

One thing to keep in mind is that recent changes to the QRP prohibit those in the country under the program from operating a business.

Special Benefits Pick #3: Malaysia

Perhaps the biggest challenge to retiring in Asia, at least if you're interested in doing so full time, is obtaining a residency visa. In this part of the world, the best option usually is to retire part-time. Spend part of the year in Thailand, for example, and part of the year back in the States or perhaps in another chosen overseas Shangri-la (Argentina, for example, or Panama). The exception when it comes to ease of obtaining foreign residency (and enjoying any special benefits as a result of that status) in Asia is Malaysia, which makes it surprisingly easy for foreigners to live here long-term, and through its Malaysia My Second Home (MM2H) program (available without age restriction), offers tax and other incentives. The MM2H multiple-entry visa, good for up to ten years, allows your spouse, children, and parents to reside in Malaysia along with you and, under certain conditions, even allows you to hold part-time employment or to have a business in the country.

Perhaps the biggest benefit of MM2H status is the tax status it gives you. As an MM2H resident in Malaysia, all your foreign-source income, including pension, interest, and dividend income, as well as foreign-earned income, is exempt from Malaysian taxes. Note, though, that income from employment or business within Malaysia is taxable.

As an MM2H resident, you can import one automobile duty-free (as long as it was purchased before you made your application for MM2H status) or buy a locally made automobile free of import duty, excise duty, and sales tax (as long as you make the purchase within one year of your MM2H status and retain the vehicle in Malaysia for at least two years before selling it).

If you are over the age of fifty, as an MM2H resident, you can work in Malaysia up to twenty hours per week. You must submit an application to the government for this, along with an employment contract, résumé, and other documentation. The government will review the application to determine whether you would be filling a position in a critical sector—that is, a position that would be difficult or impossible to fill with a Malaysian. This can include jobs in the transport, travel, food, entertainment, health, and education fields.

If you are younger than fifty, you must be able to show that you have liquid assets of at least 500,000 Malaysian ringgit (about $117,000) and an offshore income of at least 10,000 ringgit (about $2,350) per month. In addition, you will need to open a fixed-deposit account with at least 300,000 ringgit ($70,000) at a Malaysian bank. This deposit will earn interest, exempt from Malaysian taxes. After you've resided in Malaysia for one year, you can withdraw half of your deposit to use toward the purchase of a home, education expenses for your children, or medical expenses. The remainder of the initial fixed deposit must remain in a Malaysian bank for the duration of your participation in the program.

If you are age fifty or older, you will need to show financial proof of only 350,000 ringgit in assets (about $81,500) or an offshore income of at least 10,000 ringgit a month. If you are retired, you must show proof of a monthly pension. In this case, you have the choice of opening a fixed-deposit account of at least 150,000 ringgit (about $35,000) or of showing the government proof of pension income of 10,000 ringgit a month.

After one year, 50,000 ringgit (about $11,600) of the fixed deposit can be withdrawn for approved expenses (as explained above), but the remainder of at least 100,000 ringgit (about

$23,200) must be maintained in a fixed-deposit account, again for the duration of your participation in the program.

Regardless of your age, you must submit a medical report from a Malaysian hospital or registered clinic, and you must have health insurance (you can purchase it locally or show proof of an international policy). If you can't get health insurance because of your age or medical condition, this requirement can be waived.

You won't be able to get local Malaysian health insurance if you're older than sixty (you'd have to opt for an international policy). However, health care is one of Malaysia's biggest bargains; a doctor's visit often costs less than $15.

It is possible to apply for MM2H status on your own, without the help of a licensed agent; however, as with Panama and Belize, given the amount of red tape involved, I recommend that you enlist the help of a Malaysian attorney or qualified immigration agent.

PART III

THE WORLD'S EIGHTEEN BEST PLACES TO REINVENT YOUR LIFE AND CHASE ADVENTURE OVERSEAS

Every country on my Best Places to Launch Your New Life Overseas list holds out an appealing lifestyle and a comfortable standard of living at an affordable cost. You're beginning to understand, however, that some countries make more or less sense than others, depending on your particular priorities and objectives, and no place is perfect. Therefore, in this part, I not only consider each of the countries on my list up close, but I also try to make it easy to compare and contrast each with the others. These comparisons are important, because few things are absolutely true. No country has absolutely perfect weather, for example. But some countries have better weather than others.

Specifically, I rate each country according to the fourteen key factors I described in Part I ("Step 1: Know Yourself") to address when considering any destination. Each country receives one to five stars in each category, five stars being the best, one star being not so good. For example, five stars in the Cost of Living or Cost of Housing category indicates that the country or its real estate is super affordable. One star in the Special Benefits for Foreign Retirees category indicates that the country offers few extras (tax breaks, travel discounts, etc.) for expats. Four or five stars in the Language category for a country where the language is not English means that you could live here and get along day to day without learning the local lingo if you wanted to. And so on.

I've also included cost of living overviews for each location. For more detailed budgets, see the Appendix on page 305.

Belize

Focus On: Ambergris Caye

➤ Cost of living: ***

➤ Cost of housing: ***

➤ Climate: ***

➤ Health care: **½

➤ Infrastructure: **

➤ Accessibility to the United States: ****

➤ Language: *****

➤ Culture, recreation, and entertainment: **½

➤ Residency: ***½

➤ Environment: *****

➤ Taxes: *****

➤ Special benefits for foreign retirees: ****

➤ Education and schools: *

Estimated Monthly Costs Living on Ambergris Caye: 4,340 Belize dollars

Focus On: Cayo (San Ignacio)

➤ Cost of living: ****

➤ Cost of housing: ****

➤ Climate: ****

➤ Health care: **½

➤ Infrastructure: **

➤ Accessibility to the United States: ****

➤ Language: *****

➤ Culture, recreation, and entertainment: **½

➤ Residency: ***½

➤ Environment: *****

➤ Taxes: *****

➤ Special benefits for foreign retirees: ****

➤ Education and schools: *

Estimated Monthly Costs Living in Cayo (San Ignacio): 2,990 Belize dollars

Cost of Housing

The cost of housing on Ambergris Caye is affordable but not super cheap. Remember, this island isn't so much Central American as it is Caribbean; it's also Belize's most touristy destination. Compared with other Caribbean island destinations, the cost of rentals on Ambergris isn't expensive. Compared with mainland Belize and some of the Central American outposts I'm describing in these pages, you wouldn't call it a bargain, either. In San Pedro Town, Ambergris Caye's only real town, you could rent a two-bedroom furnished apartment for $800 to $1,200 per month or a two-bedroom furnished house for about $1,000 to $1,500 per month. Note that the market for long-term rentals in San Pedro is thin. Most owners prefer to rent short-term on the tourist market rather than long-term to expats or retirees, since the yields renting short-term can be much greater.

Real estate values on Ambergris Caye appreciated dramatically from the mid-1990s through 2007, as this island, the setting for TV's *Temptation Island* series, gained increased recognition among the world's sunseekers. Then in 2008 they collapsed, but they have since recovered and continue to increase. You could spend more than $1 million to own a large and comfortable house on the water on Ambergris, but it's also possible to buy a one-bedroom condo for as little as $150,000 off the water or a two-bedroom condo on the water for about $250,000.

Climate

This is the tropical Caribbean. That is to say, temperatures in Belize are warm, generally 70 to 85 degrees Fahrenheit, and consistent year-round. Rainfall varies season to season; average is 8.5 inches in the wet season (May through November) and 3.8 inches in the dry season (December through April). Belize, especially Ambergris and the other outlying cays, sees hurricanes and tropical storms regularly; the season is June to November.

Health Care

Belize's health care system isn't up to American or European standards, but in almost every town you'll find doctors or clinics that can handle minor ailments and most emergencies. Treatment is inexpensive, but like the cost of living in general, it can be more expensive in Belize than elsewhere in Central America. The Belizean government has put a high priority on improving the country's medical facilities, goals have been set, and significant advances are under way.

Although you could certainly have a broken bone set or a cold attended to at a local clinic on Ambergris Caye or at a hospital in Belize City, for anything more serious you'd still likely want to travel to Mexico, Guatemala, or the United States for care. Just across the border to the north, in the Mexican state of Quintana Roo, for example, state-of-the-art facilities are available at very affordable prices, sometimes at a lesser cost than the cost of the lower-standard facilities and services in Belize. The other option is Guatemala City or Antigua in neighboring Guatemala. For this reason, as a retiree in Belize, you'll want to include evacuation coverage (that is, the option to be transported to an appropriate medical facility in another country for necessary care;

medical repatriation coverage allows for you to be transported to your home country, specifically, for necessary care) as part of your health insurance. These policies can vary greatly and come with restrictions. Do your homework before choosing one.

Pharmacies in Belize are well stocked, and prices for medicines are comparable to those in the United States.

Infrastructure

Belize's international airport sits about twenty minutes outside Belize City. Domestic airports are located in Belize City, Belmopan, Caye Caulker, Corozal Town, Dangriga, Orange Walk Town, Placencia, Punta Gorda Town, San Ignacio, and San Pedro Town on Ambergris Caye and can be the easiest way to hop around this little country. It's inexpensive and convenient to fly from one to the other, especially because Belize's road system is limited. There are three highways—one goes north, one goes south, and one goes west.

Bus travel is also an option. Buses are cheap and run to and from nearly anywhere on the mainland you'd want to travel (and can access by road). These buses, though, intended mainly as transportation for the locals, are crowded and hot, and the schedules are not easily available, readily understood, or generally reliable. In practice, the easiest way to catch one is to flag it down. Even if you buy a ticket in advance, you may have to fight for a seat or not be able to sit down at all. Keep an eye on your luggage as it's unloaded, as bags can go missing.

In Belize City and other cities of any size, taxis are easy to come by, but they are not metered. The price depends on the cabbie.

Accessibility to the United States

Direct flights are available daily to Belize's international airport from Atlanta, Dallas, Fort Lauderdale, Houston, and Miami. Weekly flights on Saturday from Los Angeles, Charlotte, and Denver make access from the West Coast of the United States even easier. Access to Belize is improving all the time; when these pages were published in their first edition, your options for getting between the United States and Belize were many fewer than they are today. The flight time from Belize City to Houston is two hours and thirty minutes; it's only two hours to Miami.

Language

It's English. Sometimes, especially in the south of the country around Dangriga, you'll have trouble following the conversation, but believe me, they're speaking English (with heavy Creole and Caribbean influences). Spanish is spoken widely, as well (many if not most Belizeans are bilingual), and in some small towns in the middle of the country, Spanish is the only language spoken. You're not likely to want to move to those towns.

Culture, Recreation, and Entertainment

What do you do for a night out in Belize? You head to the local bar for live music or you try your luck at one of the country's casinos (gambling is legal and a popular pastime throughout the country).

Belize's sunny days are best spent beachside on Ambergris Caye. Off this island's coast is the world's second-largest barrier reef, meaning the diving and snorkeling off these shores is among the best on the planet. The outlying islands, including Ambergris Caye, offer world-class boating and fishing. Inland, in the Cayo District, are Mayan ruins to explore, many still unexcavated, as well as hot springs; rivers for rafting and kayaking; national parks for hiking, climbing, and horseback riding; waterfalls; and the Mountain Pine Ridge, a large forest reserve and a good place for canopy tours and cave tubing.

Residency

Belize offers two paths to residency—its Qualified Retired Person (QRP) program and simple permanent residency. The QRP was set up in the late 1990s for the reasons many other countries since have offered similar programs—to entice retirees to move to the country and bring their retirement income with them. The QRP provides the equivalent of a U.S. green card to anyone who can show a minimum of $2,000 of income per month. Unlike most countries offering retirement residency programs, Belize allows you to use any reliable, provable income to meet the minimum. As a QRP, you need spend only thirty days a year in the country to maintain your residency status. Note that, as a QRP resident, you are prohibited from working in Belize in any fashion, including in your own business.

Permanent residency is available to anyone of any age. Qualifying is sublimely straightforward—no up-front investment requirement and no minimum monthly income requirement. You simply show up and enter Belize as a tourist. Then you renew your tourist visa every thirty days for twelve months. After a year you can apply for permanent residency, which is all but guaranteed. The downside to this approach is that you can't leave the country during the twelve-month tourist period except in case of an emergency.

Environment

With a low population density and no heavy industry, Belize has virtually no pollution. The rivers and air are clear and clean. Outside Belize City, it's very uncommon to see garbage in the streets, and the country and its population are green-conscious and ecofriendly. This country is a great choice for a healthy, natural lifestyle, even going completely off the grid. Local food production isn't 100 percent organic, but you can find organic options for most food items.

Taxes

> ➤ Personal income tax: 25 percent flat rate after the basic deduction for earned income; pensions are not taxed; interest paid to nonresidents and all dividend income are taxed at a rate of 15 percent

> ➤ Personal property or wealth tax: none

> ➤ Sales tax (GST): 12.5 percent on most goods

➤ Property tax: 1 to 1.5 percent of the assessed value of the property

➤ Property transfer tax: 8 percent of the value over US$10,000

➤ Capital gains tax: none

Special Benefits for Foreign Retirees

As a QRP resident of Belize, you enjoy a permanent exemption from all Belize taxes (including income, capital gains, and estate). In addition, you can import your household goods and personal belongings, including cars, boats, and airplanes, into the country duty-free.

Education and Schools

Belize is not a top choice if you're considering a move with school-aged children. Expats I've known living in the country with children typically have opted to educate them at boarding schools in the States or Europe, certainly beyond elementary school age.

At Home on Ambergris Caye

For many, the retirement dream is all about the Caribbean, and nothing else will do. If your overseas retirement fantasies are similarly aquamarine and sandy, put Ambergris Caye at the top of your list. The diving and snorkeling, the color and clarity of the water, and the abundance and variety of sea life in this country are unparalleled. This is quintessential Caribbean, still relatively undiscovered (despite the *Temptation Island* effect).

On Ambergris Caye, you'd live a simple and relaxed life by the water. There are but a handful of streets and very few cars on the island; people get around primarily by golf cart or their own two feet. At the same time, the established and growing expat community, one of the biggest in the Caribbean, continues to import services, products, and amenities to make life here more comfortable.

At Home in Cayo

An American friend living in Belize once told me, "A country never escapes its origins. The United States was founded by Puritans. Belize was founded by pirates." Most people you meet in this country have two common characteristics. They are hospitable, and they are fiercely independent. The average Belizean, including those who've adopted this country as their homeland, would choose to live in a humble home and off the land and sea rather than be beholden to someone. This country operates according to an old-school mentality that many of the world's more developed nations seem to have forgotten.

Belize is a nation of thinkers and doers, a country where you make your own way and where, while you're doing it, no one, including the Belize government, is making any attempt to thwart your efforts. This is a poor country. The government doesn't have enough money to get up to any real trouble.

All of this is nowhere more apparent than in Cayo. Cayo is a land of and for pioneers, a place where residents, both local and expat, make their own way and mind their own business, while at the same time being willing always to lend a hand to a neighbor. San Ignacio, Cayo's biggest town, is a kind of Mayberry in the rain forest where everyone knows everyone and life is simple, slow, and sweet. When you arrive in Cayo, it doesn't take long for any other reality you've brought with you to fade. In this frontier land, your mind and your body are occupied with challenge and discovery from sunup until you fall exhausted into your bed each evening.

The biggest downside to life in Cayo is the undeveloped infrastructure. This would not be a top choice for someone looking to run an Internet business or to earn his money as a day trader.

Colombia

Focus On: Medellín

➤ Cost of living: ***
➤ Cost of housing: ****

➤ Climate: ****

➤ Health care: ****

➤ Infrastructure: ****

➤ Accessibility to the United States: ***

➤ Language: **

➤ Culture, recreation, and entertainment: ****

➤ Residency: ****

➤ Environment: ***

➤ Taxes: **

➤ Special benefits for foreign retirees: *

➤ Education and schools: ****

Estimated Monthly Costs Living in Medellín: 5,497,000 Colombian pesos

Cost of Housing

At the time of this writing, the Colombian peso remains relatively weak against the U.S. and the Canadian dollars, making the cost of housing in Medellín low despite years of strong appreciation in this market. In U.S. dollar terms you can buy an apartment in Medellín today for not much more than it would have cost you in 2010.

Medellín offers several neighborhoods suitable for expat living, but most who migrate to this city choose to base themselves in either El Poblado, the city's best address, or Envigado, a more affordable suburb just south of Medellín proper.

Climate

Medellín offers a temperate climate year-round, with daily highs generally in the low to mid-80s and nightly lows in the low 60s. If you're looking for perennial spring (or summer, depending on your perspective), Medellín is the place for you. The only change in the weather throughout most of the year is the number of rainy days.

Health Care

Health care in Colombia is first-rate, and Medellín boasts some of the top-rated hospitals in all Latin America. You can also find English-speaking doctors with relative ease, as many physicians practicing in this city either grew up in or were trained in the United States.

The cost of health care in Colombia is relatively low compared with costs in North America, and the country, specifically Medellín, is a growing medical tourism destination.

Infrastructure

The quality of the infrastructure in Medellín in general is very good to excellent. The one challenge, thanks to a growing middle class, meaning more people than ever and more people every month can afford cars, is traffic jams. The city's road system was not designed to handle the current volume of traffic. Fortunately, taxis are plentiful and cheap, so you don't necessarily need to own a car. Uber is available in Medellín but not getting much traction because taxis are so user-friendly. Medellín also has a metro line running through the heart of the city, useful mostly for commuting.

Accessibility to the United States

Medellín is currently served by direct flights from the United States via Atlanta, Fort Lauderdale, Miami, and New York. You can also connect easily via Bogotá or Panama City.

Language

Spanish is the official language of Colombia, and the Colombian accent is considered by many to be the most pure and clear of any in Latin America. While you can and will find locals who speak English, you'll need to learn to speak at least some Spanish to make a go of life in Medellín. For many, this is the one serious downside to life in this pretty, friendly, welcoming, affordable, and safe city.

Culture, Recreation, and Entertainment

Medellín is both an industrial, economic, and financial center for Colombia and a literary and artistic one. Newspapers, radio networks, publishing houses, an annual poetry festival, an international jazz festival, an international tango festival, an annual book fair, and back in 1971, Colombia's answer to Woodstock, the Festival de Ancón—all have chosen Medellín as their base. The sculptor Fernando Botero is a son of Medellín, and the city's Botero Museum is fronted by an outdoor sculpture garden showcasing many of the artist's rotund creations.

Meantime, the city's temperate year-round climate and mountain setting mean you can enjoy the great outdoors twelve months a year . . . and the good folks of Medellín do just that. Residents of this city like to bike, skate, Rollerblade, and amble through their city and in the hills all around.

Residency

Colombia offers an attractive retiree (*pensionado*) residency program as well as good options for establishing residency through investment. The process in all cases is easy enough that you can complete it without using an attorney if you are adventurous and speak and read fluent Spanish.

The minimum retirement income to qualify under the *pensionado* program is three times Colombia's monthly minimum wage. As of this writing, that amounts to less than US$750 a month, one of the lowest minimum monthly requirements of any country offering such a program. The minimum wage is adjusted upward at the beginning of each year, and the exchange rate changes daily, so confirm the current requirement to make sure you qualify at the time of your application.

Residency-through-investment options start at 100 times the monthly minimum wage (around US$25,000) when investing in a private company in the country. You can also qualify for residency by investing in real estate.

Environment

Medellín is a city in a valley surrounded by high mountains. As a result, it suffers from a problem with air pollution. City municipalities continually implement plans to help mitigate the situation, including *pico y placa* programs that restrict driving during rush hours on specific days of the week based on your license plate number. Another program requires developers to create green space to maintain required ratios of parkland versus construction. This is having a positive effect both on air quality and the overall appeal of the city.

Taxes

➤ Personal income tax: top tax band—33 percent

➤ Personal property or wealth tax: none

➤ Sales tax: 19 percent

➤ Property tax: 0.3 to 3.3 percent

➤ Property transfer tax: 1.5 percent

➤ Capital gains tax: 10 percent (0 percent on gains from stocks on the local exchange)

Special Benefits for Foreign Retirees

Colombia offers no specific benefits for retirees.

Education and Schools

Medellín offers many bilingual school options and would be a great place to raise a family.

At Home in Medellín

Medellín is a city of parks and flowers, pretty, tidy, and pleasant. It is also one of the world's most progressive and innovative cities, with state-of-the-art infrastructure and environmentally conscious developers and city planners. Most every building is constructed of red brick and topped with red-clay roof tiles. The overall effect is delightful.

Thanks to its mountain setting, Medellín is one of a handful of cities around the world that qualifies as a land of eternal springtime. This means no heating or air-conditioning is required, and therefore, utility costs are low.

The European undertones in Medellín are strong, from the way the women dress to the way people greet you in passing on the street. This is South America, not Central America, and the differences between the two regions can be striking.

Thanks to the current exchange rate between the Colombian peso and the U.S. dollar, all of this is available to the expat or retiree at a dramatically discounted cost. At the current rate of exchange, Medellín is a more affordable place to live and to purchase property than Cuenca, Ecuador, for example, long recognized as one of the world's most affordable places to live or retire. It's possible today to enjoy a penthouse lifestyle in Medellín on a shoestring budget. If you like the idea of living large but your budget is small, put Medellín at the top of your list.

Dominican Republic

Focus On: Las Terrenas

➤ Cost of living: ****

➤ Cost of housing: ***

➤ Climate: ***

➤ Health care: **

➤ Infrastructure: ***

➤ Accessibility to the United States: ***

➤ Language: ***

➤ Culture, recreation, and entertainment: **

➤ Residency: *****

➤ Environment: ***

➤ Taxes: ****

➤ Special benefits for foreign retirees: **

➤ Education and schools: *

Estimated Monthly Costs Living in Las Terrenas: 74,660 Dominican pesos

Cost of Housing

You could purchase a two-bedroom house in the mountains outside town for as little as $70,000 or a two-bedroom condo in town with some ocean view for $140,000. Something on or across the street from the beach would start at $180,000. Long-term rentals are scarce due to the strength of the short-term rental market, but you could rent a furnished studio for as little as $500 a month or a furnished two-bedroom house for as little as $1,100 a month.

Climate

Both temperatures, which range from 70 to 85 degrees Fahrenheit, and rainfall are consistent year-round. The official Caribbean hurricane season is June to November; historically, tropical storms hit the Dominican Republic in August and September. The mountain range in the middle of the country breaks up or repels storms, so the island sees few actual hurricanes.

Health Care

The public health system in the Dominican Republic is deficient. Better not to avail yourself of its services unless you have no choice. Use the private health centers, which can be excellent, well equipped, and staffed by English-speaking doctors with good international credentials. Las Terrenas has a recently built hospital with modern facilities.

A visit with a private clinic doctor costs $6 to $45 (for a specialist). A private hospital stay is about $200 per day. You can buy local insurance for as little as $20 per month. You can also arrange local coverage that includes care at two Miami hospitals, where you'd be airlifted in case of a serious emergency, as well as in the Dominican Republic; the cost of this special coverage is $75 per month.

Infrastructure

The Dominican Republic's main international airports are in Punta Cana, Puerto Plata, and the capital, Santo Domingo. The Samaná El Catey International Airport is just thirty minutes from Las Terrenas but offers only limited service from Canada.

The public metro in Santo Domingo provides reliable transportation around the city. Public buses are a good and cheap way to travel from city to city, as long as you don't expect them to stick tightly to their schedules. Buses can take an indefinite, undisclosed amount of time to get from one point to another. Taxis are the most common means of transportation, even among the locals, which means the fares are cheap and convenient. The taxis in Las Terrenas are mostly motor scooters. The private taxis are managed by the hotels and resorts, but the public ones are owned and operated by the drivers themselves.

Conchos, or *carros*, are another common transportation option in the bigger cities. They have the letters of the routes they serve printed on the sides of their doors, and they operate along a given route, picking up passengers along the way, officially up to six to a car (though they often squeeze in as many as possible). You can flag one down as it passes and hop on, then call out your stop when you want to be dropped off.

Accessibility to the United States

The Santo Domingo airport (SDQ) is the closest international airport to Las Terrenas, with direct flights from the United

States. You can fly from or connect through Miami, Fort Lauderdale, Orlando, New York, Newark, Atlanta, and Boston. Punta Cana's airport (PUJ) is four hours from Las Terrenas (while the drive time from SDQ is just two hours), but it offers direct flights from Charlotte; Philadelphia; Washington, D.C.; and Baltimore. The flight time from Santo Domingo to New York is about four hours; to Miami it's two hours and twenty minutes; to Atlanta it's three hours and forty minutes.

Language

The language is Spanish. However, the island is home to sizable communities of both French- and English-speaking expats, and many locals, especially in the cities, have learned to speak English to communicate with the island's tourists. If you'd like, nevertheless, to invest in learning the local lingo, as I've explained, the most expedient method is a language immersion program. Two good options are C-E-I-C (www.ceic-spanish -school.com), in Santo Domingo, and the Instituto Intercultural del Caribe (www.edase.com), with branches in Sosua and Santo Domingo.

Culture, Recreation, and Entertainment

The big attractions of the Dominican Republic are its sea, sand, and sun. Don't think about retiring here if you don't like the beach. The island's Caribbean waters are ideal for diving, snorkeling, boating, fishing, and parasailing. Inland, the island is mountainous, with volcanoes, waterfalls, and rivers. The cities offer Las Vegas–style revues, discos, bars, and casinos, catering to the tourist trade.

Residency

The Dominican Republic offers what it calls a Fast Track program for residency. You can qualify for Fast Track residency with either $1,500 of pension income or $2,000 of other passive income per month or by investing $200,000 in the country (typically in real estate). If you don't qualify for the Fast Track, you can still obtain residency in the Dominican Republic under the country's "ordinary program," which takes many months longer to process but simply requires you to show "enough" financial ability and stability that the state is convinced you would not be a burden.

Environment

Make no mistake. The Dominican Republic is a developing country. This means you'll see garbage alongside the roads and smoke spewing from the backs of buses. You'll also see pristine beaches well maintained for the tourist industry. The locals understand the benefits of cleaning up the country, and education programs are evolving.

Taxes

➤ Personal income tax: marginal rates from 0 to 25 percent

➤ Personal property or wealth tax: none

➤ Sales tax: 18 percent

➤ Property tax: 1 percent on the recorded value above 7,019,383 Dominican Republic pesos (about US$149,000)

➤ Property transfer tax: 3 percent

➤ Capital gains tax: taxed at income tax rates after an adjustment on the gain for inflation during the holding period

Special Benefits for Foreign Retirees

Most visas in the Dominican Republic now cover you under the recently enacted Law 171-07. This new foreign resident benefits legislation means that you, as a foreign retiree, are now entitled to an exemption from property tax on the first piece of real estate you buy and a 50 percent exemption from property tax thereafter; a 50 percent exemption from the mortgage registration tax; an exemption from tax on dividends and interest payments, both foreign and from within the Dominican Republic; a 50 percent exemption from capital gains tax; an exemption from tax on the importation of household goods and office equipment; and an exemption from tax on the importation of one car or from value-added tax (VAT, or sales tax) on the local purchase of a car.

Education and Schools

The established expat communities on the island mean the Dominican Republic boasts several international-standard schooling options, including, in Santo Domingo, the American School (http://americanschool.edu.do/assd/index.html) and the Carol Morgan School, one of the most reputable (and expensive) in the country (www.cms.edu.do); in Santiago, the Santiago Christian School (www.scs.edu.do); and in Puerto Plata, the International School of Sosua (www.issosua.com).

In Las Terrenas, the relatively new Las Terrenas International School (http://ltischool.weebly.com/) teaches in English and Spanish. The École Française Théodore Chassériau de Las Terrenas teaches in French, but the children learn Spanish and English as well. The French school currently goes through ninth grade only.

At Home in Las Terrenas

The Dominican Republic is more than an all-inclusive resort destination. Yes, this country sees lots of tourists every year, thanks to its miles of sandy beaches, but it's also a top Caribbean choice for the would-be foreign expat and retiree.

Dominicans are friendly and hospitable. That sounds cliché, but these people are truly warm and welcoming. They're also smart enough to understand that the island's tourism industry, its most important, lives or dies on the experience of every visitor. If you have an enjoyable vacation, you tell your friends about it when you get home and you plan to return someday. The islanders do their best to make sure every visitor's experience is a great one. This extends to long-term visitors (that is, expats and retirees) as well.

Las Terrenas is not just another sandy Caribbean beach town. This island outpost is more cosmopolitan than you'd imagine, thanks to forty years of cultural and commercial nurturing on

the part of French and Italian settlers. This means fresh baguettes, restaurants whose menus include things like prosciutto
and melon and cold prosecco, kisses on both cheeks in greeting,
waitstaff who are alert and attentive, and other similar real-world
niceties not normally associated with life on the Caribbean Sea.

Ecuador

Focus On: Cuenca

- ➤ Cost of living: *****
- ➤ Cost of housing: *****
- ➤ Climate: *****
- ➤ Health care: ***
- ➤ Infrastructure: **
- ➤ Accessibility to the United States: ***
- ➤ Language: **
- ➤ Culture, recreation, and entertainment: ***
- ➤ Residency: ***
- ➤ Environment: ****
- ➤ Taxes: ***
- ➤ Special benefits for foreign retirees: *
- ➤ Education and schools: ***

Estimated Monthly Costs Living in Cuenca: $1,135 (Ecuador uses the U.S. dollar as its currency)

Cost of Housing

Ecuador is one of the most affordable places in the world to
buy or rent a home. In Cuenca, you could purchase a two-bedroom
apartment for as little as $50,000 or a two-bedroom house for less

than $100,000, and you'll find plenty of appealing options in the $150,000 range. You could rent a two-bedroom apartment in Cuenca for less than $300 a month or a two- to three-bedroom house in the center of the city for as little as $600 a month.

Climate

Ecuador lies on the equator, meaning temperatures are constant year-round, as is the length of each day. In Ecuador, you can count on twelve hours of daylight 365 days a year. In the mountains, temperatures are cool and comfortable, springlike, twelve months a year (in the range of 50 degrees Fahrenheit in the evenings to 70 degrees in the daytime). It's warmer, of course, by 10 to 20 degrees, on the coast.

Health Care

Health care is excellent in Ecuador's cities, particularly Quito and Cuenca, which boast hospitals with state-of-the-art equipment and specialists in all fields. Care often meets high standards and is also surprisingly affordable. A visit to the doctor can cost just $20; a specialist charges $25. An added bonus: Ecuadorian doctors spend thirty to forty-five minutes with each patient. As a general rule, health care costs are 20 to 25 percent of those in the United States, and local in-country health insurance is available for a fraction of the cost of health insurance in the States.

Quality dental work performed by highly skilled dentists is also widely available and inexpensive. You can have a complete set of dentures made for $1,200, including office visits, fittings, impressions, and lab work.

Infrastructure

Infrastructure is this country's biggest downside. While the infrastructure in general has improved over the past decade, it's still less developed than that of most other countries in South America. That said, the infrastructure is generally good and reliable in and around Cuenca, which is one reason this city is my top lifestyle pick for this country.

Ecuador has two main international airports, José Joaquín de Olmedo International Airport in Guayaquil and Mariscal Sucre International Airport in Quito. You'll have to connect through one or the other to arrive by plane in Cuenca. The national carriers are Tame and Aerogal.

Domestic flights operate from both Quito and Guayaquil to Cuenca. Buses are the far more affordable option for traveling within the country; they cost the equivalent of about $1 per hour of travel and run twenty-four hours a day. Taxis are plentiful all hours of the day and night, and the fare should be about $1.50 for most rides around town and $3 for the ride from the airport to downtown. I say "should be" because even though taxis have meters, drivers don't use them. Always ask how much the trip will be before you get in.

Autoferros are an option in the rural areas and between small towns. These are essentially buses converted to run on old train tracks. They are super cheap, but there are no seat classes, all passengers ride wherever they can find a place, and there's a good chance you'll be traveling with livestock.

Accessibility to the United States

You can fly direct from Quito to Miami, Fort Lauderdale, Atlanta, Houston, New York, and Dallas. Guayaquil offers flights from New York and Miami. The flight from Quito to Miami is about four hours ten minutes.

While Quito is relatively accessible, Cuenca is less so. Unfortunately, with the exception of Tame flights from JFK, U.S. flights arrive too late to connect to an in-country flight to Cuenca, necessitating an overnight stay in Quito. When you are going in the other direction, you don't have any connecting flight option and have no choice but to stay overnight in Quito. Cuenca is not a place to base yourself if you intend regular out-of-Ecuador travel. The general inaccessibility would wear you out over time.

Language

The official language of Ecuador is Spanish, used in virtually all business, government, and municipal transactions in Cuenca.

Government institutions often accommodate the Incan language of Quechua as well, but don't count on English.

That said, Cuenca is a place where you could get by without learning to speak Spanish, but you'd be confining yourself to (and making yourself dependent on) a small circle of English speakers and your fellow expats, while missing out on much of the rich cultural experience that the Spanish-speaking expats living here enjoy every day.

The Spanish spoken in Cuenca is crisp, clear, and relatively formal, making this city a great place to study the language, and Spanish study is a thriving business in Cuenca, home to international students year-round. I recommend the Simon Bolivar Spanish School (www.simon-bolivar.com), with branches in both Quito and Cuenca, which offers weeklong programs, including four hours of study daily for $200.

Culture, Recreation, and Entertainment

Quito and Cuenca have museums, concert halls, theaters, plazas, and markets in addition to bars, discos, and nightclubs. Most of Ecuador, though, is more undeveloped and rugged, and the attractions are more of the natural than the cultural variety, including hot springs, volcanoes, national parks, and waterfalls. The country's mountains are spectacular, offering endless opportunities for trekking and climbing (though hiking at these elevations is not a good idea if you have asthma or a heart condition).

Residency

You have two good options for residency in Ecuador—a *rentista* visa or an investment visa. The *rentista* visa requires $800 a month of permanent income. This can be from a pension, but investment income works, too. For each dependent (your spouse, for example) you'll need to be able to prove another $100 a month at least.

Ecuador offers a number of investor visa choices. The lowest minimum investment option is $25,000, which can be invested in a certificate of deposit in a bank in Ecuador, in a piece of property in Ecuador, or in an Ecuadorian company.

The onerous requirement of residency in Ecuador is that you

cannot be outside the country for more than ninety days during either of your first two years as a resident. This can be a deal-breaker if you're not up for committing to more or less full-time living in the country for at least two years.

Environment

Ecuador is a developing country with a relatively high population density. The big cities (Quito and Guayaquil) are congested and suffer from sometimes serious levels of air pollution. Cuenca is smaller, with less traffic and lower levels of air pollution, but this would not be a good choice for someone with breathing difficulties.

Taxes

➤ Personal income tax: marginal rates from 0 to 35 percent

➤ Personal property or wealth tax: none

➤ Sales tax: 12 percent

➤ Property tax: varies by municipality but typically less than 0.5 percent

➤ Property transfer tax: 1 percent

➤ Capital gains tax: none

Note that Ecuador charges a 5 percent tax on funds of more than $1,000 sent out of the country. This means that if you sell your house for $100,000 and proceed to wire those funds out of the country, you'll pay $5,000 in tax. If you transfer $2,000 back home for your granddaughter's birthday present, you'll pay tax of $100. The bottom line is, you shouldn't move any more money into Ecuador than you'll need to cover in-country costs and expenses.

Special Benefits for Foreign Retirees

Foreign retirees in Ecuador are eligible for discounts of 50 percent off all public transportation; 50 percent off national and international airfares; 50 percent off all cultural, sports, artistic, and recreational events; 50 percent off electricity, water, and telephone service; a special discount on property tax; relief from Ecuadorian income tax; a discount on the vehicle tax; a discount on judicial fees; and a refund of value-added tax (VAT, or sales tax). Best of all, you never have to stand in line; seniors always go to the front.

Education and Schools

Ecuador offers good options for bilingual education, including, in Quito, the American School of Quito (www.fcaq.k12.ec) and the British School Quito (www.britishschoolquito.edu.ec). However, Cuenca doesn't offer any good options for bilingual schools where the instruction is in English. It does have one International Baccalaureate (IB) school where the instruction is in Spanish, the Colegio Alemán Stiehle (www.casc.edu.ec). I wouldn't recommend Cuenca as a top choice overall if you're moving with school-aged children. You have better choices.

At Home in Cuenca

You begin to appreciate that Cuenca is a special city as you make your approach from the air. Passing through the surrounding Andean peaks, you're able to make out the more than fifty church steeples poking up from a sea of red-clay-tile roofs. Don't worry. Your plane may come within meters of these old colonial rooftops, but I've never known of one that collided with them.

Cuenca is a lovely and historic town (it predates the arrival of the Incas) in a majestic setting that's also a remarkably healthy place to live. The air is clear and fresh, and the sun shines strong all year long. Cuenca's large center, with its wealth of colonial homes with interior courtyards, thick adobe walls, and iron-railed terraces looking down onto the street, punctuated regularly by plazas and squares, is made for walking. Travelers come from the world over to enjoy these 250 square blocks of history; to study in Cuenca's world-class language schools; and to experience a rare glimpse of unadulterated life in an Andean colonial city.

Expats—especially expat retirees—make their way to this city for all these reasons, of course, but the retiree wants more than history and charm. He also seeks out Cuenca for its cost of living, which remains among the most affordable of any country in Latin America, even with the growing numbers of foreign retirees and expats; its real estate prices, which are extremely affordable for a city with such a rich quality of life; its thriving expat community and warm and welcoming people who make you feel like you really belong; and Ecuador's competitive program of retiree benefits.

A friend who lived in Cuenca for several years puts it like this: "I have traveled to just about every country in Latin America. In my opinion, the country of Ecuador is the best deal out there when it comes to an overseas retirement destination, and Cuenca is the best that Ecuador has to offer. If you're retiring on a budget, Cuenca should be at the top of your list."

Cuenca's Spanish colonial environment is one of the most genuine in Latin America, and the old-world Spanish-Andean culture has changed little over the past three hundred years. The beautifully restored original cathedral has occupied the main square since 1557 and has been facing the city's "new" cathedral (across the square) since the mid-1800s. The indigenous influence is strong in Cuenca. Many locals wear traditional dress, and bright and colorful indigenous markets dot the city, conducting business as they have for centuries. But don't worry. The city may appear frozen in time, but in fact it offers the modern conveniences you need. While it may be interesting to watch an Indian woman chopping a carcass apart with a hatchet in the market, it's comforting to know that a modern supermarket, with fresh meats, fish, and many of the familiar brands you may be looking for, is just around the corner. The year-round fresh fruit market offers exotic and familiar tropical fruits for pennies.

After-hours in Cuenca, you've got music, theater, dance clubs, shows, and a professional symphony orchestra that is free to all. Perhaps best of all is the never-ending stream of local festivals, each with its colorful celebrations, fireworks, and food and drink kiosks, every one a chance to join thousands of people on the streets having a good time.

When my friend moved to Cuenca more than fifteen years ago, he was one of three English speakers in the city. He told me recently of a cocktail party he attended where he met perhaps fifty other English speakers in a single evening. And they all, he reported, were delighted with their new lives in Cuenca.

Despite this growing community of expats, Cuenca is still a "go-local" choice. If you're looking for a planned community of fellow foreign retirees, Cuenca is probably not for you. This is not a place where the expats cluster in gated communities. Such communities don't exist here. The retirees choosing Cuenca and happy with their decision are the type who like to integrate.

France

Focus On: Paris

- ➤ Cost of living: ***
- ➤ Cost of housing: * (** for renting)
- ➤ Climate: ***
- ➤ Health care: *****
- ➤ Infrastructure: *****
- ➤ Accessibility to the United States: *****
- ➤ Language: ***
- ➤ Culture, recreation, and entertainment: *****
- ➤ Residency: ***
- ➤ Environment: ***
- ➤ Taxes: *
- ➤ Special benefits for foreign retirees: *
- ➤ Education and schools: *****

Estimated Monthly Costs Living in Paris: 2,735 euros

Focus On: Languedoc

- ➤ Cost of living: ****
- ➤ Cost of housing: ****
- ➤ Climate: ****
- ➤ Health care: *****
- ➤ Infrastructure: *****
- ➤ Accessibility to the United States: ****
- ➤ Language: ***
- ➤ Culture, recreation, and entertainment: ****
- ➤ Residency: ***
- ➤ Environment: ****
- ➤ Taxes: *
- ➤ Special benefits for foreign retirees: *
- ➤ Education and schools: ****

Estimated Monthly Costs Living in Languedoc: 1,355 euros

Cost of Housing

In Paris's seventh arrondissement, in the historic center of the city and one of its most expensive districts, the average selling price per square foot is about $15,000, meaning a 1,000-square-foot apartment sells for about $1.5 million. On the other hand, in the fifteenth and seventeenth arrondissements, central but still very appealing districts for expat living, the average price per square foot is about $10,000, meaning a 1,000-square-foot apartment sells for about $1 million. Fifty square meters would cost half as much in each case. Apartments in Paris (and all Europe), certainly apartments in the older historic districts, are typically small. Most single people and many couples live in one-bedroom apartments of about 500 to 600 square feet.

You could rent a one-bedroom apartment in the seventh for

as little as $1,500 per month or a one-bedroom apartment in the fifteenth for as little as $1,000 per month. Both sales and rentals, of course, are far more affordable in Languedoc. You could purchase a four-bedroom, 2,000-square-foot house near Cessenon-sur-Orb for $200,000 or rent a two-bedroom, 700-square-foot apartment for $500 to $700 a month.

Climate

Paris sees four distinct seasons each year. Summers can be hot; it snows lightly and occasionally in winter; autumn is pleasant; and springtime in this city is everything you've heard—blissful.

The textbook description of the climate in Languedoc is Mediterranean—that is, hot and dry in the summer, wet in the winter, and cool and clear in the spring and fall. Tourist brochures indicate that the area boasts three hundred days of sunshine a year. In reality, this area is geographically very varied, so this general description does not apply everywhere. The coastline is generally sunnier and warmer than inland regions, the valleys moister, and the mountains cooler. The coastal areas rarely freeze in winter, because of the influence of the Mediterranean, and summers can see the temperature rise above 86 degrees Fahrenheit. Inland areas are a few degrees warmer in summer and cooler in winter. This is a windy region in parts, particularly in the east, where the mistral blows, and the far west, where the tramontane whips down the valleys.

Health Care

The health care in France is the best in the world, and if you're a legal resident, it's also highly subsidized by the government, even free. Even if you're not eligible for subsidized health care, costs are low. A general doctor consultation in Paris is about $60 to $80.

Paris boasts the American Hospital of Paris, which is accredited by the U.S. Joint Commission International, where the staff all speak English. In the city you can also find any kind of alternative practitioners you might be looking for.

In the French countryside, including in Languedoc, health

care is very personal. If you fall ill, hurt yourself, or have any other emergency, you call the fire department (*les pompiers*). That's not so out of the ordinary, but what happens next is: A siren wails, summoning the firemen to their posts. It's reminiscent of sirens in wartime, warning the population of danger. Fortunately, it doesn't happen often, but when the alarm is sounded the fire department's trained paramedics come to your assistance and then organize whatever further service is required. If your concern is minor, a village doctor is summoned. If it's more critical, you are taken to a hospital in Béziers or on to Montpellier (Montpellier University boasts the oldest and one of the largest medical faculties in Europe). If you have a minor problem but are unable to drive, a private taxi-ambulance takes you to the hospital. One English expat told me that his recent experience of surgery in Béziers was faultless. The staff was helpful, the facilities immaculate. "When I returned home, we called the village nurse, and she came to the house the next morning to change the dressings and check that everything was okay," he explained.

Infrastructure

France also boasts some of the world's best infrastructure, and Paris is a key international travel hub. From Charles de Gaulle (CDG) you can get anywhere on the planet; Orly is the city's second international airport, servicing mostly Europe's discount carriers. Both airports are an easy taxi drive or train ride to the city, and both offer service throughout France as well as to Europe, North America, Africa, the Caribbean, and the Middle East; CDG also flies to Asia. The national air carrier is Air France.

Carcassonne Salvaza Airport, the main airport in Languedoc, offers service within the country and throughout Europe. Montpellier Méditerranée Airport is minutes away from Montpellier and flies within France and elsewhere in Europe (with low-cost direct flights from the UK, Holland, Switzerland, Denmark, and Morocco). Béziers Cap d'Agde Airport, also in Languedoc, flies within the country and to Britain. None of these airports offers direct service to North America. From the United States, you can connect to the Languedoc region via Paris or London.

The best way to get around Paris is by using its Métro, which is fast, clean, reliable, and cheap and can take you anywhere in the city. The RER train, an extension of the Métro, runs from central Paris to the suburbs and elsewhere outside the city. For RER travel, you must buy a different, more expensive, though still very affordable ticket.

The bus system in Paris is the same price as the Métro (you use the same tickets for both) and also comfortable, clean, and efficient. Even if you don't typically enjoy traveling by bus, you'll appreciate Paris's local bus system. It's a convenient way to get around, even a good option for sightseeing. The routes and schedules are indicated clearly at every stop, and the buses stick to them.

You can also get around Paris by taxi. This is the most expensive option but convenient. You'll see taxi stands around the city, or you can hail one on the street. It's possible to call a taxi in advance to pick you up, though you'll be required to open a credit account with the taxi company. Note that when you call a taxi to meet you, the meter starts running from the time the taxi leaves the station. You can also travel along the Seine through central Paris on a *bateau mouche*. These boats are a good way to see the city from the river, but they are more for tourists than for day-to-day transportation.

Depending where you're going and what you're carrying with you, the quickest, cheapest, and most fun way to get around Paris can be the city's Vélib', the citywide bike rental system, and the Autolib, a citywide electric car rental system. Both systems have locations all around the city where bikes or cars can be picked up and parked. Before your first use, you register with your credit card and then arrange the rental. When you're done with your bike or car, return it to any location near where you end up. It's all automated and super user-friendly.

Domestic flights are plentiful, reliable, and affordable, but the best way to travel within France is by train. The country's national train service, SNCF, is extensive, quick, and reliable, plus you can continue by rail from France throughout Europe. A good website for researching European train travel is www.raileurope.com, where you can buy a rail pass in advance. For the best prices, purchase your tickets before arriving in Europe.

As in Paris, Languedoc's public bus service is efficient, inexpensive, and clean. Taxis are easy to come by and less expensive than in Paris. The roads in the Languedoc region, as in all France, are in very good condition and clearly marked. Traveling on the interstates (*autoroutes*) is straightforward and quick, though the frequent tolls (*péage*) can make highway travel expensive. Sometimes you take a ticket, then pay farther along the route as you exit (credit cards are accepted at windows marked with a CB sign, which stands for Carte Bleue, the French vernacular for "credit card"); sometimes you pay as you go. The frequent roadside rest and gas stations are called *aires*.

Accessibility to the United States

You can fly direct to Paris from New York; Newark; Washington, D.C.; Philadelphia; Charlotte; Atlanta; Miami; Houston; Chicago; Los Angeles; Seattle; and San Francisco. The flight time from Paris to New York is eight hours; to Miami it's ten hours and fifteen minutes; to Los Angeles it's eleven hours and thirty minutes.

Language

You can get by in Paris with little to no French, but it will limit your experience of the city. Plus a little effort to learn the language goes a long way with the French. I heartily recommend, therefore, that you invest two or three weeks at least in an immersion program at Accord École de Langues (www.accord-langues.com) in Paris, near l'Opéra. One week of study, including twenty hours, is about 330 euros. Another option in Paris is Alliance Française (www.alliancefr.org), where twenty hours of study a week for one to three weeks is about $300 per week. In Languedoc, Real Adventures (www.realadventures.com/g607 _languedoc-roussillon-france-vacations.htm?mRegionType =Educational%3A+Language+Schools) offers full-immersion programs starting at about $300 per week.

Culture, Recreation, and Entertainment

Paris is the most culturally rich and diverse city in the world, home to important museums, monuments, churches, and other historic sites, as well as luxe shopping, five-star dining, and every manner of nighttime diversion you could imagine.

In Languedoc, the diversions are recreational as well as cultural—hiking, climbing, and horseback riding. The region is home to more than its share of festivals, with food and farming the main focus. In Cessenon-sur-Orb, for example, there is the Fête du Cochon (the Festival of Pigs), held the first weekend in February, when the town square is taken over by stallholders selling their local wares, including olive oil, wine, cheeses, and handmade baskets. A traditional jazz band wanders through the crowds, and despite its being midwinter, there is a party atmosphere. Later in the evening, tables are set up in the village hall for a grand feast of roast pig. Year-round, news and happenings are broadcast over the village's loudspeaker, and perhaps once a day, a ding-dong sound comes from the village hall, and one of the ladies announces the news, such as that "today at six P.M. there will be dancing in the village hall followed by a meal at Le Helder."

Residency

If you're not looking to work in France, you can obtain residency in this country relatively easily simply by showing that you can support yourself. The challenge is French bureaucracy. As in most countries, you're probably better off engaging an immigration attorney to help cut through the red tape. That said, the test for proving "sufficient resources" is straightforward. You'll need to show 9,600 euros per year as a single person applying and 14,904 euros per year as a couple to qualify.

One of the most important things to understand about the process for residency in France is that you must begin it from wherever you're living now. Before making your residency application, you must have previously obtained (before arriving in France) a long-stay visa. A short-stay visa does not lead to residency.

Environment

Pollution in the cities, particularly in Paris, is less of a problem than it has been at times in the past, and Paris continues to add to its fleet of renewable energy buses. France has fewer Blue Flag–designated (that is, eco-certified) beaches than Portugal, for example, but it has them. Recycling is the norm everywhere, especially in Paris, where large depositories for glass bottles, for example (all that wine!), are everywhere, and every apartment building and business puts out separate bins for garbage versus recyclables.

Taxes

➤ Personal income tax: marginal rates from 0 to 45 percent

➤ Personal property or wealth tax: 0.5 to 1.5 percent on your total assets for a total asset value of more than 1,300,000 euros; residents pay this wealth tax on their worldwide assets, nonresidents on their assets in France only

➤ Sales tax: 20 percent

➤ Property tax: Varies by municipality but is nominal, less than 0.25 percent; a second *taxe d'habitation* is also charged of the resident of a dwelling. This is paid by the owner if he's occupying his property or by the renter, but it, too, is nominal.

➤ Property transfer tax: 5.8 percent

➤ Capital gains tax: This is phased out for real estate starting in the sixth year of ownership and reduced to 0 percent after twenty-two years of ownership. Along with the capital gains tax is a second tax for social charges, which is phased out over thirty years of ownership. The calculation is so complicated that the Notaire Society of France (Notaires de France) provides a calculation simulator on their website here: https://www.notaires.fr/en/capital-gains-tax-property-0.

Special Benefits for Foreign Retirees

Seniors in France, foreign or not, enjoy discounts at movie theaters and museums.

Education and Schools

Both Paris and Languedoc are among the top choices world-wide for places to raise and educate a child. You have great bilingual schooling options in Paris, including the International School of Paris (www.isparis.edu), the American School of Paris (www.asparis.org), and the École Internationale Bilingue (www.eab.fr). Near Montpellier is the Ecole Privée Bilingue Internationale (www.ecole-privee-bilingue-internationale-montpellier.fr).

At Home in Paris

Paris is the most beautiful, most romantic city in the world. It's also a place where your cost of living can be hugely variable and highly controllable.

In Paris, you can live happily car-free, walking nearly anywhere you'd want to go. The butcher, the baker, the grocer, the wine shop, a half-dozen busy cafés, and as many lovely parks and gardens are all less than fifteen minutes' walk from almost any point in central Paris. And, when you want to venture beyond your quartier, the Métro will transport you from restaurant to nightclub, from museum to café for less than $2 (when you buy your tickets in a ten-pack).

France boasts perhaps the world's best infrastructure, and it's a bargain. Cable TV, Internet, and telephone, as well as the Métro, the bus, and the RER train system . . . all are likely less costly than comparable services where you're living now.

Our phone plan in Paris costs less than 40 euros per month and allows unlimited free calls anytime to anywhere throughout Europe and to anywhere in the United States. That's hard to beat.

My point is not that you should plan to move to Paris to reduce your cost of living. It is possible, in fact, to do just that, but that's not the typical agenda where Paris or France is concerned. My point is that you shouldn't deny or delay your dreams of *la vie française* because you're worried you can't afford them. We lived in Paris for four years, with two children, and I'm here to tell you that we were able to control our costs within a very reasonable budget.

For me, Paris . . . indeed, all of France . . . is as good as life gets. And right now, this country, including its City of Light, is on sale for us dollar-holders. Our U.S. dollars go further in France today than they have in many years. It's an irresistible window of opportunity.

At Home in Languedoc

The "other" South of France, the Languedoc region, lies between Provence-Alpes-Côte d'Azur to the east, the Midi-Pyrénées to the west, and the Auvergne to the north, while Spain is only a few hours' drive to the south. This region may not be the cheapest place to retire in the world, but it is in many ways one of the most appealing. Languedoc is historic, colorful, eclectic, always changing, authentically French, and at the same time, very open to retirees. Villages here date from prehistoric times, but the feel of this part of France is medieval. The living here is simple and traditional while still offering all the services and amenities of the twenty-first century, including good schooling for children ages three to eighteen.

Languedoc has a fascinating history, even including its own ancient language, Occitan, still taught in some schools today. The region was once independent from France and ruled by Raymond IV, Count of Toulouse. And it was here in the Languedoc Province that the Cathar religion (a sect of Catholicism) first appeared in the eleventh century and flourished into the twelfth and thirteenth centuries.

Italy

Focus On: Abruzzo

- ➤ Cost of living: ***
- ➤ Cost of housing: ****
- ➤ Climate: ***
- ➤ Health care: ****

➤ Infrastructure: ****

➤ Accessibility to the United States: *****

➤ Language: ***

➤ Culture, recreation, and entertainment: ****

➤ Residency: ***

➤ Environment: ****

➤ Taxes: *

➤ Special benefits for foreign retirees: *

➤ Education and schools: ****

Estimated Monthly Costs Living in Abruzzo: 1,279 euros

Cost of Housing

Abruzzo is one of the most enchanting yet affordable regions of Italy. It rivals the best of Tuscany without the price tags. You could purchase a small one-bedroom apartment for as little as $75,000 or a two-bedroom country house for as little as $150,000. You could rent a three-bedroom apartment for as little as $700 per month.

One interesting opportunity in Abruzzo could be to buy a small farmhouse to renovate on a piece of land where you could grow your own food. This is one of the best places in Europe to embrace a self-sufficient lifestyle.

Climate

Like France, Italy enjoys four distinct seasons. Summers can be hot (temperatures can reach as high as 90 degrees Fahrenheit), though winters are typically mild (rarely do temperatures reach freezing; the average winter temperature is 40 to 50 degrees). Fall can be warmer than you might expect (temperatures still can climb into the 80s); spring is pleasant and comfortable (temperatures average 50 to 70 degrees).

Abruzzo runs from the mountains to the sea, meaning you can move around until you find your preferred temperature.

Health Care

Italy follows France as well when it comes to health care, offering the world's second-best, according to the World Health Organization (by contrast, the United States ranks thirty-seventh in WHO's world health standards survey). That said, in Italy, opt for private care over public. Although public facilities are adequate for emergencies, public hospitals tend to be overcrowded and underfunded.

Like France and most of Europe, Italy has a national health plan (Servizio Sanitario Nazionale) that provides hospital and medical benefits for legal residents who qualify (eligibility can depend not only on your residency status, but also on your nationality and work status). You probably won't qualify. Still, medical costs are more affordable than you might think. A visit to the doctor is about $30, and an overnight stay in a hospital is about $200 a day.

Infrastructure

Abruzzo is serviced by the Abruzzo International Airport in Pescara, which offers service throughout Italy and Europe. Naples International offers more options, again within Italy and throughout Europe. There are two international airports in Rome, Leonardo da Vinci–Fiumicino and Giovan Battista Pastine Airport, but Battista Pastine offers flights only elsewhere within Europe (no domestic service). The national air carrier is Alitalia.

Trenitalia, Italy's national train service, is the top option for travel within the country. There are six main types of trains in Italy, some intercity, some traveling across the country. Generally, all are comfortable, clean, and quick.

Some places in Italy can be reached only by boat; ferry service is offered regularly to these islands and other similarly inaccessible areas. Some mainland routes are easier reached by bus than train. The path from Florence to Siena, for example, is more efficiently served by bus. Smaller towns that do not have train stations do have bus stops, so bus travel is also a good option for getting more off the beaten path, though bus schedules are less dependable than train schedules; when traveling by bus in this country, be prepared to be flexible. Taxis are available in all cities and towns but can be expensive.

Accessibility to the United States

Pescara, the provincial capital of Abruzzo, is about a two-and-a-half-hour drive from Rome's Leonardo da Vinci–Fiumicino Airport, which offers direct flights to Russia, South America, Canada, Asia, and the United States, specifically Boston; Chicago; Atlanta; Washington, D.C.; Philadelphia; Charlotte; Miami; Los Angeles; Dallas; and New York. The flight time from Rome to New York is about eight hours and thirty minutes; to Chicago it's nine hours and fifteen minutes; to Miami it's about nine hours.

Language

Abruzzo isn't the tourist draw Tuscany is. One practical consequence of this is that you'll find fewer English speakers in this part of Italy. You'll need to hone your Italian language skills. The Athena International Italian Language School in Abruzzo (www.athena-it.com) offers group-study language programs for $225 per week. Private classes are about $40 per hour.

Culture, Recreation, and Entertainment

Like France, Italy offers nearly every cultural and recreational diversion you could imagine, from museums, monuments, ancient churches, classic architectural structures, and ruins to thermal spas, hiking, boating, scuba, snorkeling, fishing, horseback riding, skiing, and golf. Italy's cities are international meccas for shopping, dining, and wine tasting and offer top options worldwide for opera, ballet, and theater. Abruzzo, specifically, offers great diversity of outdoor and rural activities, including skiing. Plus, from Abruzzo it's less than three hours to Rome when you're in the mood for big-city distractions.

Residency

As in France and most of the EU, the requirement for residency in Italy is straightforward. You simply prove that you can support yourself. Italy doesn't indicate a specific amount of income required to meet this standard, but you'll need to show at least enough not to qualify for the country's public health system.

One important thing to note about establishing residency in Italy is that the country requires Americans who obtain residency to sign an integration agreement within twelve months of moving there. By signing the agreement, you commit to earning enough points over two years to show your willingness to embrace and become part of Italian culture. You'll be required to pass language and other tests during that period. If you don't accumulate the required thirty points, you could be kicked out.

Environment

Northern Italy suffers some of the worst air pollution levels anywhere in Europe. Southern Italy and the coast enjoy cleaner air, and the region around Abruzzo is perhaps the least polluted in the country. The country's recycling industry is number one on the Continent.

Taxes

➤ Personal income tax: marginal rates from 23 to 43 percent (unlike in most countries, you are taxed from your first euro of income)

➤ Personal property or wealth tax: Tax resident individuals holding assets outside of the country are taxed annually on the value—0.2 percent for financial assets and 0.76 percent on real estate.

➤ Sales tax: 22 percent

➤ Property tax: 0.4 to 0.7 percent

➤ Property transfer tax: 2 to 9 percent

➤ Capital gains tax: 26 percent; no capital gains taxes on real estate owned for five years or more

Special Benefits for Foreign Retirees

Seniors in Italy, foreign or not, enjoy discounts at restaurants, and many places, including supermarkets, offer express lines for seniors.

Education and Schools

Canadian College Italy offers English language education for high school grades 10 through 12 at their campus in Lanciano (about an hour south of Pescara) (www.canadiancollegeitaly .com). Other top bilingual education options in Italy include the bilingual International School of Venice (www.isvenice.com), the Ambrit Rome International (www.ambrit-rome.com), the Britannia International School in Rome (https://britanniainter nationalschool.com), and the American Overseas School of Rome (www.aosr.org).

At Home in Abruzzo

The Abruzzo region is the most overlooked and undervalued in central Italy; you can buy here for 30 to 70 percent less than in Tuscany or Umbria. But Abruzzo isn't only affordable. It is also at least as appealing as either of Italy's more famous regions, with both mountains and seacoast, meaning that, at certain times of year, you can ski in the morning and swim in the afternoon. Plus, daily flights on Ryanair make the region super accessible from elsewhere in Europe in summer via the airport at Pescara. Or fly to Rome; Abruzzo is less than three hours away.

Abruzzo is a top choice for old-world living on the Continent. Near the sixteenth-century thermal-spring town of Caramanico, for example, you could live in a centuries-old *majella* stone house (this is the stone from the nearby mountains that the region is known for) nestled in an extraordinary natural setting but only minutes from a charming medieval town where day-to-day life continues as it has for centuries.

Malaysia

Focus On: Kuala Lumpur

➤ Cost of living: ***½

➤ Cost of housing: ***½

➤ Climate: ***

➤ Health care: ***

➤ Infrastructure: ****

➤ Accessibility to the United States: ***

➤ Language: ****

➤ Culture, recreation, and entertainment: ***½

➤ Residency: ***½

➤ Environment: **

➤ Taxes: *****

➤ Special benefits for foreign retirees: ****

➤ Education and schools: ****

Estimated Monthly Costs Living in Kuala Lumpur: 6,286 ringgit

Cost of Housing

Malaysia is one of the few countries in Asia where foreigners can legally own real estate in their own names, although this right comes with a minimum purchase requirement of 1 million ringgit (about US$235,000 as of this writing) in most states and of 2 million ringgit in the state of Selangor, where Kuala Lumpur is located. While you can find good apartments in the best neighborhoods for sale for a quarter of that amount, if your budget doesn't allow for the 2 million ringgit minimum, you'll need to look at renting. (Note that under the country's Malaysia My Second Home [MM2H] residency program, the minimum is reduced to 1 million ringgit in some areas of Selangor.) You could rent a furnished two-bedroom apartment in Kuala Lumpur for as little as $500 to $600 a month. Rentals typically come fully furnished.

Climate

Malaysia's temperatures qualify as steamy, with average highs right at 90 degrees Fahrenheit year-round. Rainfall is also consistent throughout the year, though May through July is the slightly drier season. Monsoons hit Peninsular Malaysia every year; there are two seasons for this—October through January and March/April.

Health Care

The Malaysian government is committed to making high-quality health care available to the entire population. That said, don't count on quality health care in the country's most remote regions. In the cities, and certainly in Kuala Lumpur, however, the medical care standards are top-notch. As a result, Malaysia is developing a reputation as a medical tourism destination, especially for cardiology, dentistry, gastroenterology, screenings, general surgery, orthopedics, ophthalmology, and plastic surgery. The costs of all kinds of medical care are a fraction of what you'd expect to pay for comparable services and procedures in the United States. A visit to an English-speaking general practitioner in Kuala Lumpur costs about $5, while an English-speaking, Europe- or U.S.-educated specialist charges $25 to $30, including free follow-up visits. A complete dental examination is about $30; a crown costs less than $300.

Infrastructure

The international airport in Kuala Lumpur provides direct service throughout Asia and to Australia, Frankfurt, London, and Amsterdam. The flight time from Kuala Lumpur to London is thirteen hours; to Melbourne, Australia, it's eight hours and ten minutes; to Amsterdam it's thirteen hours and ten minutes. The national air carrier is Malaysia Airlines.

Malaysia boasts a highly developed transportation network. All cities are serviced by modern bus and train routes, and more than twenty-five airlines fly to all airports throughout the country, making air travel a convenient way to get around. It is also possible to travel by rail within and to Peninsular Malaysia from Thailand and Singapore; Malayan Railways connects all major towns on the peninsula with first-, second-, and economy-class air-conditioned service. Many popular island destinations are linked to the mainland with regular ferry service. Other smaller islands are accessible by charter fishing boat.

Buses are an inexpensive way to travel around the country. Most buses in Kuala Lumpur are air-conditioned, but this is not necessarily true in the smaller towns. City buses charge fares based on the distance covered; interstate buses have fixed rates.

Taxis in major cities are usually fitted with meters. Interstate and smaller-town taxis charge flat rates (as opposed to a per-mile-traveled fee), which you should negotiate before getting into the taxi.

Accessibility to the United States

Typically, access from North America to Malaysia is through China. Indirect flights are available from San Francisco, New York, Houston, Florida, San Diego, Pittsburgh, and Chicago.

Language

Kuala Lumpur is a melting pot where all aspects of life are varied and diverse. English is spoken and understood by almost everyone, though, and serves as a bridge language among the many different ethnic groups. Many families speak the language of their country of origin at home but English in public settings. English is also the language of business, most newspapers, television, and movies. Realistically, you aren't going to learn to speak Malay, and in fact, as I've explained, you don't need to. Still, studying the language could be fun. Malay Language Course in Kuala Lumpur (www.elec.edu.my/course/malay-language-course) offers intensive five- to six-week courses that include a hundred hours of language instruction for $430.

Culture, Recreation, and Entertainment

Malaysian cities offer great diversity of entertainment, including a national opera and symphony, a national theater, and bars and clubs with floor shows and live music. In addition, there are museums and galleries, ancient ruins and temples, volcanoes and waterfalls, parks and gardens, thermal springs and nature reserves. You can trek, climb, boat, scuba, snorkel, and ski.

Residency

Unlike other countries in Southeast Asia, Malaysia actively encourages foreign residents to relocate here. Qualify for the Malaysia My Second Home (MM2H) program, and you're eligible for an excellent package of incentives. You can apply at any age. When accepted, you receive a multiple-entry visa good for up to ten years allowing you and your spouse, children, and parents to reside in Malaysia. Under certain conditions, MM2H status even allows you to hold part-time employment or to start a business in the country.

As an MM2H resident in Malaysia, all your foreign-source income, including pension, interest, and dividend income, as well as foreign-earned income, is exempt from Malaysian taxes. Note, though, that income from employment or business within Malaysia is taxable.

In addition, with MM2H residency status, you can:

➤ Purchase residential real estate with a lower minimum price—1 million ringgit in parts of Selangor and as low as 350,000 ringgit in some states. You can make more than one real estate purchase if you want, then combine the purchase amounts to meet the minimum, and you can receive rental income from your properties. You can finance up to 80 percent of the value of the property through a Malaysian bank.

➤ Import one automobile duty-free (as long as it was purchased before you made your application for MM2H status) or buy a locally assembled automobile free of import duty, excise duty, and sales tax (to qualify for this exemption, you must make the purchase within one year of your MM2H status).

➤ Obtain a Malaysian driver's license.

If you are under the age of fifty, you qualify for MM2H status by showing that you have liquid assets of at least 500,000 ringgit (about $116,500 as of this writing) and an offshore income of at least 10,000 ringgit (about $2,350) per month. Additionally, you will need to open a fixed-deposit account of at least 300,000 ringgit ($70,000) at a Malaysian bank. This deposit will earn interest, exempt from Malaysian taxes.

If you are over the age of fifty, you must show financial proof of only 350,000 ringgit in assets (about $81,600) and an offshore income of at least 10,000 ringgit a month. If you are retired, you must show proof of a monthly pension. You have the choice of opening a fixed-deposit account of at least 150,000 ringgit (about $35,000) or of showing proof of a government pension income of 10,000 ringgit a month.

Environment

Air pollution is a problem in this densely populated and urbanized area and results at times in a haze over the city. Levels are at their worst during the open burning season, May through July.

Noise pollution is another reality of life in Kuala Lumpur, thanks to traffic, construction, industrial machinery, and the light rail.

Taxes

➤ Personal income tax: Marginal rates from 0 to 28 percent. As a resident you are taxed only on income derived from within Malaysia, meaning even income you remit to Malaysia is not taxed as long as it was earned outside the country.

➤ Personal property or wealth tax: none

➤ Sales tax: 6 percent

➤ Property tax: none

➤ Property transfer tax: 1 percent on the first 100,000 ringit; 2 percent on the value from 100,000 ringgit to 500,000 ringgit; 3 percent on the value over 500,000 ringgit (a property valued at 600,000 ringgit would incur a transfer tax of 12,000 ringgit, for example)

➤ Capital gains tax: For citizens and permanent residents the rate is 30 percent for real estate sold within three years of purchase; 20 percent for real estate sold in year four; 15 percent for real estate sold in year five; and 0 percent for real estate sold after the property has been held for five years or longer. For everyone else, the capital gains tax is 30 percent if you sell the property before owning it for at least five years, and 5 percent once that anniversary has been reached.

Special Benefits for Foreign Retirees

See above.

Education and Schools

Top choices in Penang include the Dalat International School (www.dalat.org) and, in Kuala Lumpur, the International School of Kuala Lumpur (www.iskl.edu.my), the Mont'Kiara International School (for elementary; www.mkis.edu.my), the Alice Smith School (www.alice-smith.edu.my), the Fairview International School (www.fairview.edu.my/fv_livc), and the Garden International School (www.gardenschool.edu.my).

At Home in Kuala Lumpur

Located just north of the equator, Malaysia is a tropical country divided into two parts, Peninsular Malaysia and Malaysian Borneo. Most people live near the west coast of Peninsular Malaysia, an attractive and ecologically diverse strip of land that borders Thailand to the north and Singapore to the south. Vibrant towns and cities, separated by long stretches of sandy beaches, make up the coastline on either side of the peninsula, while the rugged and less populated interior is given over to cool jungle highlands, coffee and tea plantations, mountains, rivers, and caves. Malaysia's largest city, Kuala Lumpur, with a population of around 1.76 million, sits in the west-central part of the peninsula.

Of all countries in Southeast Asia, Malaysia is probably the most culturally diverse. It prides itself on moderation and tolerance. Fifty percent of the population belongs to the ethnic group called Malay, who are technically Muslim and practice a moderate form of Islam. Malay women are liberated by Islamic standards; they drive cars, hold jobs, and enjoy equal rights with their male counterparts. The country's ethnic diversity leads to diversity in every aspect of life. Out of necessity and prudence, the government promotes religious harmony and tolerance, and clothing and customs are as varied as the population, as is the cuisine. Restaurants offer menus that are Malaysian or Chinese, Indian or Thai, Japanese or Korean.

The Malaysian government is on a mission to reach "first-world" status by 2020, and it has made remarkable progress toward this goal. Modern divided highways serve the length of the Malaysian mainland, and almost all roads in Peninsular Malaysia are paved. Malaysian Borneo is less developed, with many areas of the interior accessible only by boat or plane, although one major highway runs the length of Sarawak, through Brunei, and into Sabah.

All the cities have airports, as do many of the smaller, more remote villages in Borneo. Cell phone coverage is reliable and inexpensive and extends even into the smallest villages. In Kuala Lumpur and increasingly in other Malaysian cities, tap water is potable. The government has eradicated malaria throughout the entire Malaysian peninsula, and for the most part in Malaysian Borneo as well.

Malaysia is a country of contrasts. The ultramodern city center in Kuala Lumpur, with its many skyscrapers, overlooks Kampung Baru, a traditional Malay village and the city's oldest neighborhood. Kampung Baru has somehow managed to survive completely untouched by modernity less than half a mile away from the downtown area. Beneath the shadows of the Petronas Towers and the Public Bank skyscraper, Muslim families raise vegetables, hold open house on their front lawns, and tend to chickens roaming freely on the quiet streets.

Mexico

Focus On: Mazatlán

- ➤ Cost of living: ***
- ➤ Cost of housing: ***
- ➤ Climate: ****
- ➤ Health care: ***½
- ➤ Infrastructure: ****
- ➤ Accessibility to the United States: *****
- ➤ Language: ****
- ➤ Culture, recreation, and entertainment: ***½
- ➤ Residency: ***
- ➤ Environment: ****
- ➤ Taxes: ***
- ➤ Special benefits for foreign retirees: *
- ➤ Education and schools: **

Estimated Monthly Costs Living in Mazatlán: 26,950 Mexican pesos

Focus On: Playa del Carmen

- ➤ Cost of living: ***
- ➤ Cost of housing: ***
- ➤ Climate: ****
- ➤ Health care: ***½

➤ Infrastructure: *****

➤ Accessibility to the United States: *****

➤ Language: ****

➤ Culture, recreation, and entertainment: ****

➤ Residency: ****

➤ Environment: ****

➤ Taxes: ***

➤ Special benefits for foreign retirees: *

➤ Education and schools: **

Estimated Monthly Costs Living in Playa del Carmen: 33,180 Mexican pesos

Cost of Housing

Mazatlán offers a wide selection of housing options from apartments on the *malecón* with easy access to the beach and ocean views to houses inland with price tags as small as $50,000. In the areas where most expats prefer to settle, you could buy an apartment for $125,000 or a house for $200,000.

Real estate prices are generally higher in Playa del Carmen than in Mazatlán, but you can find small apartments starting at less than $125,000. Houses are less common in Playa; the available stock starts at about $250,000. Of course proximity to the beach plays a role in housing prices in both cities.

Climate

Mazatlán highs run right at 90 degrees Fahrenheit for about half the year and in the high 70s to mid-80s the other half. Summer nights cool off to the high 70s while winter lows fall to the high 50s. Summer monsoons start in June and continue through September. Temperatures in Playa del Carmen are more consistent throughout the year, running from the mid-80s up to 90 degrees except in December and January, when highs are close to 80. Lows range from the mid-60s to the mid-70s. The rainy season in Playa coincides with hurricane season—June through November. Hurricanes are something you should factor into your planning when considering anywhere along Mexico's Yucatán Peninsula, including Playa del Carmen. At home along this coast, you'll encounter them.

Health Care

In general, health care in Mexico is good; in many places in this country, it's excellent. Most doctors and dentists received at least part of their training in the States, and many U.S. doctors have trained in Mexico. Every medium to large Mexican city has at least one first-rate hospital, and costs, not only for hospital care but for medical care in general and for prescription drugs, can be as little as half what you'd expect to pay in the United States for comparable services. A doctor's visit, even a house call (yes, Mexican doctors still sometimes make house calls), can cost $25. An overnight hospital stay can be as little as $35. Prescriptions are $4 to $5 on average. Anyone living with a permanent residency visa in Mexico can qualify for IMSS (state social security) health insurance, which costs about $300 per year.

Infrastructure

Mexico is a big country with international airports in every region, dozens in total; the most convenient for travel to and from the United States are in Acapulco, Cabo San Lucas, Cancún, Guadalajara, León, Mazatlán, Mexico City, Morelia, Oaxaca, Puerto Vallarta, and Veracruz. The national air carrier is Aeroméxico.

All of Mexico's international airports also offer service within the country, and plane travel can be the most efficient way to get from city to city. Buses are the most affordable way to travel between cities. First-class buses can be as comfortable as planes; "chicken buses," as the local buses are called, on the other hand, are short on comfort but long on adventure. Fellow passengers can be of the web- or four-footed varieties. Taxis are available everywhere, including radio taxis (identifiable by the antennas on top), which are dispatched by radio and reliable for prearranged pickup.

Accessibility to the United States

The Mazatlán International airport has direct flights from Los Angeles, Phoenix, Houston, Dallas, and Minneapolis. However, the best part about basing your new life overseas in this city can be that you can come and go from it by car. Mazatlán is a sixteen-hour drive from Phoenix and a fourteen-and-a-half-hour drive from El Paso.

Access to Playa del Carmen is via the Cancún airport, which has direct flights from dozens of U.S. cities, many thanks to Southwest Airlines. From Cancún it's an hour's drive to Playa.

Language

Both Mazatlán and Playa del Carmen are resort and tourist areas, meaning many locals speak English and you can get by without learning much Spanish if you really want to. However, your experience of the area will be greatly improved if you learn even some Spanish. The Mazatlán Language School (http://mazatlanlanguageschool.com) offers weekly group classes from $142 per week, with immersion programs from $215. The Playa del Carmen Spanish Institute (www.cancunspanish.com) offers programs with a minimum of two weeks starting at $300 for the two weeks.

AmeriSpan (www.amerispan.com/country/Mexico/12) offers Spanish courses in several countries including Mexico and currently offers program options in Playa del Carmen as well as Guanajuato, Mexico City, and Oaxaca.

Culture, Recreation, and Entertainment

Just off Mazatlán's Centro Histórico main plaza is El Teatro Ángela Peralta, a beautifully restored theater dating to 1874 that today hosts concerts of all types (classical, opera, and symphony included), conventions (from motorcycle rallies to Day of the Dead festivities), dance exhibitions (modern, ballet, folkloric—you name it), tours, performances, and special events. Art galleries and museums dot the streets, and parks punctuate the grid system.

This city offers everything a truly first-world city should offer by way of cultural entertainment; even the self-identifying snob will be well satiated here. Mazatlán's Malecón is a great choice for upscale full-amenity living, right on the beachfront, with one of the city's best gyms and one of its largest malls, plus lots of cafés and restaurants and the area's best wine shop.

From the south end of the Malecón sector, you can walk to Centro Histórico. Best of all, you're on the area's best and longest beach, bordered by the longest boardwalk in the Americas, replete with eating, drinking, and shopping opportunities. Few other places in the world can you live in a city with these kinds of cultural offerings with a beautiful, swimmable beach on your doorstep.

Playa del Carmen is a beach party town. This is not a place to come for cultural or cerebral distractions but for fun in the sun. Water sports by day, beachside cantinas at night . . . that's Playa.

Residency

Mexican residency is granted to those with sufficient foreign income to support themselves. The bar isn't high. You need to show $1,500 per month from earned or pension income or $2,600 per month from investment income. The additional required income for a dependent is considerably higher in Mexico than in most countries, though, at $520 per dependent per month.

Your application for residency must originate at a Mexican consulate in your country of citizenship, meaning you must start the process before leaving home. Once you have obtained a provisional visa from the Mexican consulate in your current home country, you can finalize the process in Mexico. You'll be issued a renewable provisional visa. After four years, you can apply for permanent residency. You can bypass that process and skip ahead to permanent resident status by showing a higher income (of at least $2,500 per month).

Environment

Air quality in Mazatlán is not bad given the size of the city. The prevailing breeze coming in from the ocean regularly clears out the stale air. A diesel-powered generator south of town used to spew volumes of black smoke, but it's been converted to natural gas, which has gone a long way to improving the city's air quality.

Water throughout Mexico is treated to first-world standards, but as in many places, the water that exits the plant isn't the water that comes out of the tap. Before reaching your home, it has to travel through miles of pipe, the condition of which can't be guaranteed. Mexicans and gringos alike play it safe by drinking bottled water.

Litter is a problem in both Mazatlán and Playa del Carmen, as it is throughout Latin America and the developing world.

Taxes

➤ Personal income tax: marginal rates from 1.92 to 35 percent

➤ Personal property or wealth tax: none

➤ Sales tax: 16 percent (0 percent on food and medicine)

➤ Property tax: 0.5 to 1.2 percent

➤ Property transfer tax: 2 to 3 percent

➤ Capital gains tax: 10 percent on financial instruments; marginal income tax rates are charged otherwise, including on gains from the sale of real estate

Special Benefits for Foreign Retirees

Retirees resident in Mexico, foreign or not, are eligible for discounts from age sixty through INAPAM, a government program coordinating discounts from a variety of businesses (https://www.gob.mx/inapam/acciones-y-programas/tarjeta-inapam-conoce-los-requisitos-para-obtener-la-tarjeta-inapam).

Education and Schools

Mazatlán has several bilingual schools to choose from, including Instituto Anglo Moderno (www.anglomoderno.edu.mx), Instituto Cultural de Occidente (www.ico.edu.mx), and Colegio Andes de Mazatlán (www.colegioandes.net).

In Playa del Carmen, you'll find Colegio Inglés (www.colegioinglesplaya.com) and Colegio Weston (www.colegio weston.com) among others.

At Home in Mazatlán

Mazatlán is one of the few places in the world where you can walk for miles on an uncrowded beach within the city limits. Real city, beautiful beaches, and walkable colonial center . . . popular expat choice and authentic Mexican resort town that manages to feel homey . . . It's hard to pin Mazatlán down.

Located about midway along Mexico's Pacific coast, Mazatlán has been out of favor among tourists and expats for decades but is making a comeback. The renaissance has been focused on the city's historic center, which has undergone an impressive facelift and now rivals Mazatlán's twenty miles of beach in drawing attention. The focal point for this renaissance is Plaza Machado, which is now surrounded by busy outdoor cafés and international restaurants. Forming the eastern border of the plaza is Calle Carnaval, which is pedestrians-only at the square.

Mazatlán lies about 720 miles south of the Arizona border, making it a thirteen-hour straight shot down Highway 15D. What a luxury to be able to throw everything you need in the car and drive to your new life overseas without worrying about what the airlines will or won't let you bring with you. If you'd rather fly, Mazatlán is a two-hour nonstop flight from Phoenix. Nonstop service is offered to many cities in both the States and Canada. Mazatlán is at once a real Mexican city of about half a million people, a resort town, and home to a sizable American and Canadian expat community. You can choose to associate primarily with fellow expats, speaking mostly English and easing your way into your new life in Mazatlán aided by people like you who've already made the move. Or you can choose to live in a Mexican setting, speaking mostly Spanish and immersing yourself in Mexico's culture.

Centro Histórico is the place to base yourself if you want more Mexico, less resort. The areas around Plaza Machado and Olas Altas beach are populated by tourists and expats, but the rest of Centro Histórico is old-fashioned Mexico. Walk two blocks north and two blocks east from Plaza Machado and you're in the middle of a bustling downtown that is genuine Latin America, with hundreds of small shops, banks, businesses, parks, and locals going about their daily business.

Centro Histórico is also the right choice if you want to be able to walk everywhere you need to go and avoid the expense of owning a car. The real and unique appeal of life in Centro Histórico is that it's city living . . . on the beach. Along the city's edge are twenty miles of well-maintained sand beaches lining warm, swimmable waters. Much of this beachfront is bordered by a wide boardwalk that's busy early until late with people strolling, jogging, and biking.

The beach nearest to the Centro Histórico, about four blocks west of Plaza Machado, is called Olas Altas. Don't be put off by the name (which means high waves); the water here is sheltered and calm. The beach is a crescent-shaped, sandy cove about a quarter mile in length. Along this shoreline are cafés and restaurants popular among both locals and expats looking for a good cup of coffee and fresh pastry by the ocean each morning.

Plus, Mazatlán is the shrimp capital of Mexico, and Sinaloa, the state where Mazatlán is located, is where the bulk of this country's produce is grown. As a result, this is a foodie paradise, with many dining options, from five-star to street vendor, all a bargain.

At Home in Playa del Carmen

Playa del Carmen (Playa to the locals) is a little beach town that sits about an hour south of Cancún on Mexico's Riviera Maya. Once a sleepy fishing village, the port was inadvertently put on the map by Jacques Cousteau in 1954 when he filmed an underwater documentary of the Great Maya Reef just offshore of

Cozumel Island, which is about twelve miles offshore of Playa del Carmen.

Today Playa is home to more than 10,000 foreigners—expats make up 7 percent of the city's total population—including Europeans, Americans, Canadians, Argentinians, Venezuelans, and others. It's an eclectic mix of beach lovers of all ages, including young couples, families with small children, and retired folks. This is also a welcoming destination for the LGBT community, with several gay bars around town.

At the center of it all is La Quinta Avenida (5th Avenue), the pedestrianized street that runs parallel to the beach one block in. All along 5th Avenue, music rolls out of the open storefronts... Led Zeppelin, then Jimmy Buffett, then salsa . . . then Amy Winehouse.

Around ten P.M., as most of the older crowd heads home after a long day in the sun and a few cocktails with dinner, rock and roll gives way to club music. The younger generation fills the streets, and they're just getting started for the evening. The party here lasts until the wee hours. Next morning, though, the streets are clean, and brunch is served at all the sidewalk cafés bright and carly.

Thinking more practically, you'd have no trouble finding anything you'd want or need for day-to-day living in Playa. This little town has twelve supermarkets and two Walmarts.

Nicaragua

Focus On: Granada

➤ Cost of living: ****

➤ Cost of housing: ****

➤ Climate: ***½

➤ Health care: **½

➤ Infrastructure: ***

➤ Accessibility to the United States: *****

➤ Language: **

➤ Culture, recreation, and entertainment: **½

➤ Residency: *****

➤ Environment: **

➤ Taxes: ****

➤ Special benefits for foreign retirees: **

➤ Education and schools: ***

Estimated Monthly Costs Living in Granada: 63,510 córdobas

Cost of Housing

You could buy a three-bedroom colonial house ready to move into (though probably finished to a Nicaraguan standard) for $200,000 or a five-bedroom house (renovated more to a U.S. standard) for $250,000. Whatever you're interested in buying, you won't have trouble finding someone to help you shop. Little Granada is overrun with agencies specializing in the sale and rental of real estate to the foreign market.

Climate

Nicaragua has wet (May through December) and dry seasons (January through April). The transformation at the start of the wet (or rainy) season is dramatic throughout this region (including in Costa Rica and Panama), but nowhere more so than in Nicaragua. Within two weeks of the first rainfall, the country goes from dusty to lush, the hillsides from brown to brilliant green. Highs throughout the year in Granada break 90 degrees Fahrenheit, so if you don't like it hot, Granada may not be for you.

Health Care

Beyond Managua, the health care in Nicaragua is basic; however, in the capital (less than an hour from Granada), the quality of medical care available exceeds expectations and can be top-notch, especially at the Hospital Metropolitano Vivian Pellas, which boasts not only state-of-the-art facilities and highly (often U.S.-) trained English-speaking doctors and staff, but also a kind of personalized attention and care that is increasingly difficult to find in the United States. Before Hospital Metropolitano Vivian Pellas opened, residents in this country had no choice but to travel to Costa Rica or the States for private hospital care of an acceptable standard. Still, as a retiree in Nicaragua, you may want to invest in medical evacuation coverage as part of your health insurance plan. For open-heart surgery, for example, you'd want to be airlifted to Houston or Miami.

The Hospital Metropolitano's staff of three hundred includes specialists (most English-speaking) in gynecology, cardiology, orthopedics, pediatrics, internal medicine, surgery, neurology, urology, anesthesiology, and ophthalmology. Facilities include a modern emergency room, pain clinic, maternity ward, burn unit, pharmacy, and lab. A private room is $110 a day.

A friend who has been living in Latin America since 2001 points out that one important reason medical costs are so much more affordable in Nicaragua (and elsewhere in the region) than in the United States is because physicians and hospitals in this part of the world don't have the hours of paperwork or the insurance headaches that physicians in the States have to deal with.

Infrastructure

Augusto C. Sandino International Airport/Managua International Airport, about fifteen minutes outside central Managua and an hour from Granada, is the main airport in Nicaragua. Expanded and updated over the past decade, it is today a modern user-friendly airport. The Costa Esmeralda international airport was built recently near Rivas to service the growing resort developments along the nearby coast, but currently only has scheduled flights from Liberia airport in Costa Rica.

Nicaragua has improved and added several new paved highways in recent years in an effort to expand and improve its infrastructure, but the country is still largely undeveloped. That said, the infrastructure in and around Granada is good and reliable.

Domestic flights are available to get you to the Caribbean coast, as driving really isn't an option.

The country is compact enough, though, that hiring a taxi or a private driver can be a reasonable option for travel from Managua to Granada, León, down south to San Juan del Sur on the Pacific coast, or anywhere else you'd want to go. I don't recommend driving in Nicaragua yourself until you're well familiar and comfortable with getting around this country. The two primary means of transportation among the locals are bicycles and their own two feet, meaning that the roadsides, including along the highways (which have no shoulders), are crowded with people, including children, walking and riding their bikes.

The most common and affordable way to get around Nicaragua is by bus. Bus travel is generally reliable, except sometimes on Sundays, but it's also hot, crowded, bumpy, and dirty. International bus service is an option for travel from Nicaragua to Costa Rica and Panama. Taxis are easy to come by in Managua, Granada, León, San Juan del Sur, and other cities, and fares are cheap. A within-the-city ride in Managua, León, or Granada costs a dollar or two. In Granada, you can travel around town by horse and carriage for the same cost as a taxi ride.

Accessibility to the United States

You can fly direct from Managua to Miami, Houston, Atlanta, Dallas, and Fort Lauderdale. The flight time from Managua to Miami is about two hours and twenty-five minutes; to Atlanta it's about three hours; to Houston it's two hours and forty minutes.

Language

Nicaragua Spanish Language Schools (www.nicaraguaspan ishlanguageschools.com) has six locations in Nicaragua and offers an intensive twenty-hour-a-week program for as little as $200. Colibri Spanish School (colibrispanishschool.com/en) offers twenty-hour-a-week programs in Matagalpa for $220 a week.

Culture, Recreation, and Entertainment

The attractions in Nicaragua are more recreational than cultural. This is a land of lakes (including the crater Lake Apoyo and Lake Nicaragua, the only freshwater lake in the world with sharks living in it) and volcanoes (with seven still active). Nicaragua also boasts two long and beautiful coastlines, and the surf off the southern end of the Pacific coast is considered among the world's best by surfers in the know; an international surfing community has taken hold here. Nicaragua is horse country, and every region hosts regular *hípicos*, or horse fairs. Nightlife centers around local bars and clubs, sometimes with live music. Try some Flor de Caña, Nicaragua's own rum. I'm a rum aficionado, and I consider it among the world's best.

Fueled by Flor de Caña rum and the local Toña beer, Nicaraguans like their fiestas. In Granada in August is the Tope de Toro, a bull-running event, and the grand parade of the Desfile Hípico, the largest and most elaborate horse show in the country. Nicaraguans take their horseflesh seriously, and it is a mark of honor and prestige to be allowed to ride in this parade. Dress well. If you pass muster, you could be invited to observe the event from the balcony of the Spanish embassy, overlooking the parade route.

In December in Granada are the Purísima (Immaculate Conception of Mary) celebrations, revolving around a Franciscan statue of Mary found and retrieved from Lake Nicaragua in 1721. The icon is said to have protected the city for over a century, but, alas, couldn't save the populace from the depredations of the pirate William Walker in 1855, when the rogue torched the town. The fact that the statue, hidden in the cathedral, escaped the flames is remembered as a local miracle.

Residency

Nicaragua's *pensionado* program features the lowest pension income requirement of any country offering such a visa option. You can qualify with as little as $600 of guaranteed pension income a month. You'll need to show an additional $150 a month for each dependent. If you don't have a pension, you can qualify with $750 a month of passive income. Residency through investment is also an option. You can qualify for an investor visa with an investment in real estate of at least $35,000.

Environment

Nicaragua has the second-lowest GDP per capita in the Americas. The focus in this country isn't on recycling but on day-to-day survival. Don't drink the water anywhere in the country. Most of the waterways are polluted, especially Lake Managua, which is unfit not only for drinking but also for swimming and fishing (though the locals do all those things in these waters). As is the case throughout Central America, litter and garbage are real and visible problems. Grassroots cleanup initiatives are at work, supported by both locals and the country's expat community.

Taxes

➤ Personal income tax: marginal rates from 0 to 30 percent; residents are taxed on Nicaragua-sourced income only

➤ Personal property or wealth tax: none

➤ Sales tax: 15 percent

➤ Property tax: 1 percent of assessed value

➤ Property transfer tax: 1 percent

➤ Capital gains tax: 10 percent

Special Benefits for Foreign Retirees

In June 2009, Nicaragua became a far more interesting overseas retirement option when it enacted changes to its residency and retirement laws that increased the tax exemptions and other benefits for foreign retirees. Specifically, the recently enacted program means foreign residents can bring up to $20,000 worth of household goods and personal belongings into the country duty-free; pay no duty when importing a car valued up to $25,000;

and pay no taxes on out-of-country earnings. The minimum age for eligibility is forty-five.

Education and Schools

Options for international-standard bilingual education include the American Nicaraguan School (www.ans.edu.ni), the Lincoln International Academy (www.lincoln.edu.ni), the Nicaragua Christian Academy (www.nca.edu.ni), the Notre Dame School (www.notredame.edu.ni), and the Saint Dominic School (www.saintdominicschool.edu.ni), all in Managua. However, I would not recommend Nicaragua as a choice for raising children beyond elementary school age. You have better options.

At Home in Granada

When asked about her chances for defeating the Sandinistas in Nicaragua's first presidential election following the Contra War, Violeta Chamorro replied, "Forget about the Sandinistas. They're obsolete." That was September 1989.

To the surprise of sitting president Daniel Ortega and all Nicaragua, Mrs. Chamorro won the election in February 1990. The Sandinista Ortega stepped down graciously, and Doña Violeta began the work of rebuilding her country. I visited Nicaragua for the first time three years later. Managua, thanks to the earthquake of 1972, the revolution, and the civil war, was a near-disaster zone. There was no reason to stick around. Frankly, this is only slightly less true today. You must fly into Managua, for it is home to this country's only international airport, but this city is not what you've come to Nicaragua to find.

Politics have too long distracted people from recognizing what Nicaragua has to offer. Take Doña Violeta's advice and forget about Ortega and the Sandinistas. Two decades ago, they tried to make a new Nicaragua. Fortunately for you and me, the old Nicaragua, the largest but least-visited nation in Central America, lives on. This Nicaragua is a beautiful country with loads of sunshine and two long coasts, one of white sand, one with wildly crashing surf. It is a land of lakes and volcanoes, of cloud forests and tropical jungles, of cattle ranches and Spanish colonial cities, of rare orchids and white-faced capuchin monkeys. It is also a very affordable, welcoming, and safe place to call home.

That is not to say that the Sandinistas, the party or the people, have disappeared. The most famous Sandinista of all, Daniel Ortega, sits again, right now, in the seat of the country's presidency. Through 2006, when Ortega was reelected, Nicaragua seemed on the fast track to a big, bright future. But in 2007, with Ortega scheduled to retake office and the U.S. real estate market beginning to tumble, investors panicked and pulled back from this country. The world continues to be skeptical of Nicaragua's leader and the country's future, but the truth is, Ortega hasn't done anything to set off any alarm bells. He has played nice with the United States; he has worked to clean up title on 3,800 properties held by Nicaraguans (questionable history of ownership of land in this country has been a key investor issue); and he has continued to support foreign investors' rights.

Like the investors, tourists also took Nicaragua off their list back in 2007, but they have returned. Tourism figures today are well ahead of the best figures from prior to Ortega's reelection. The city of Granada is this country's number one tourist draw. Nobody visits Nicaragua without visiting colonial Granada. I'm a big fan of the postcard-esque, charming town, just inland from Lake Nicaragua and at the foot of a sleeping volcano named Mombacho. It's one of the most historic and, I feel, most romantic cities in all the region. But because Granada is such a tourist draw, there's no avoiding the sightseers or their trappings, which are noticeably more present every time I pass through.

A Spanish-colonial city can be a great lifestyle choice, and Granada is perhaps the queen among all Spanish-colonial city options in the Americas. This is one of the best preserved and best restored examples of the legacy of the Spanish left behind in this part of the world. At the heart of the city, radiating from the central square, is a great variety of classic and charming Spanish-colonial homes with high ceilings, painted tiles, and private center courtyards.

Granada today is home to one of the world's biggest expat and foreign retiree communities, accounting for the city's wealth of upscale restaurants and shops. The city is completely walkable; everything you need is close at hand.

Despite all the tourists and the sizable expat community, Granada remains authentically Nicaraguan in many ways. You still see old oxcarts lumbering through the streets, restaurants serve local specialties, and street vendors offer pottery handmade according to traditions that date back centuries and that have been passed down from generation to generation. The city is a unique blend of native Nicaraguan city life and expat amenities. You won't be a pioneer here; the expat way is well paved. For some, this is a plus . . . for others, not so much.

Panama

Focus On: Panama City

- ➤ Cost of living: ***
- ➤ Cost of housing: ***
- ➤ Climate: ***
- ➤ Health care: ***½
- ➤ Infrastructure: ****
- ➤ Accessibility to the United States: *****
- ➤ Language: ***½
- ➤ Culture, recreation, and entertainment: ***½
- ➤ Residency: *****
- ➤ Environment: ***
- ➤ Taxes: *****
- ➤ Special benefits for foreign retirees: *****
- ➤ Education and schools: *****

Estimated Monthly Costs Living in Panama City: $2,420 (Panama uses the U.S. dollar)

Focus On: El Valle de Antón

- ➤ Cost of living: ****
- ➤ Cost of housing: ****
- ➤ Climate: ***½
- ➤ Health care: **½ (need to go to Panama City for anything major)
- ➤ Infrastructure: ****
- ➤ Accessibility to the United States: ****½
- ➤ Language: ***
- ➤ Culture, recreation, and entertainment: ***
- ➤ Residency: *****
- ➤ Environment: ****
- ➤ Taxes: *****
- ➤ Special benefits for foreign retirees: *****
- ➤ Education and schools: * (need to be in Panama City)

Estimated Monthly Costs Living in El Valle de Antón: $1,676

Cost of Housing

The cost of owning and of renting in Panama City has increased dramatically in the past ten years.

The city is an international hub for business and banking, and all the foreign employees of all the international companies operating here are increasingly paid international-level salaries. This continues to drive up real estate costs in the most desired areas. Punta Paitilla, Punta Pacífica, and Avenida Balboa, fronted by the park and pedestrian areas of the Cinta Costera, are the city's most sought-after and most expensive addresses. In the fast-growing suburbs of Costa del Este and Panamá Pacífico, popular among Panama's young urban professional crowd as well as families with young children, prices can be even higher.

For more reasonable prices, look to neighborhoods like San Francisco and El Cangrejo.

Panama City is a market unto itself. In the interior of the country, in El Valle, you could buy a three-bedroom house for $200,000 or rent one for as little as $300 or $400 a month.

Climate

Panama has a rainy season (May through November), referred to locally as winter, and a dry season (December through April), known as summer. Panama City high temperatures are in the low 90s in the dry season and the mid-80s in the rainy season. Nightly lows are in the low 70s year-round.

Like the rest of the country, El Valle has two seasons, wet and dry, but it's noticeably wetter here than at sea level. The kind of rain common in this highlands region is comparable to an Irish mist, but you'll also see plenty of downpours.

Health Care

Panama boasts the best standard of medical care in the region (Central America), with two world-class hospitals in Panama City, Punta Paitilla Medical Center and the newer Hospital Punta Pacífica, the latter affiliated with Johns Hopkins Medicine International in the United States. Even outside the capital, though, except in the most remote regions, you have access to good-standard care. The city of David in the inland Chiriquí Province, for example, is home to a great medical center with modern facilities and equipment. Many Panamanian doctors are U.S. trained, and the standards at the top hospitals compare favorably with those in the United States.

Private health insurance is available and much less expensive than insurance in the United States; depending on your age, you could arrange a policy for as little as $80 per month. Prices for prescription drugs are low as well, because manufacturers set prices for the market. Plus, many drugs that require a prescription in the States are available over the counter in Panama, including antibiotics and antidepressants.

Infrastructure

Generally speaking, Panama's infrastructure, especially in Panama City but throughout the rest of the country as well, is superior to that in any other country in this region. Even in the remote and mountainous interior, roads are paved, bridges are new and well maintained, and you find things like streetlights and fire hydrants, normally lacking in this part of the world.

That said, even Panama City experiences power and water outages, so be prepared. All high-rise buildings in the city have backup generators and water supplies. If you rent or buy a stand-alone house in the city or in El Valle, your budget should allow for a generator and water storage.

Panama's Tocumen International Airport, about thirty minutes from downtown Panama City, is the busiest in Central America and is being continually expanded. Panama's national carrier is Copa Airlines, but many airlines fly regularly from the United States and Canada.

David, in the west of the country, has an international airport, but the only international flights are to Costa Rica. A new international airport has been built in Río Hato to service the nearby beach resorts and hotels. However, to date, no regularly scheduled flights are operating, only charters bringing in guests for the resorts.

There are airports as well in Bocas del Toro, Colón Province, and Chiriquí Province, but these are small, with single runways, and they're typically used for small aircraft traveling domestically and to and from Costa Rica.

The most common forms of transportation in Panama, both in Panama City and throughout the rest of the country, are taxi and bus. Panama City also boasts the only metro system in the region. Currently one line has been completed and the next two are under way.

In Panama City, taxis are plentiful but sometimes impossible to hail. When you give the driver your destination, it's not uncommon for him to reply, "*No voy,*" meaning, "Nope, not going there." It is illegal for taxi drivers to refuse to take you to a destination, but that doesn't stop most of them from doing just that. Uber makes for a reliable and maybe safer option in Panama

City. Uber is not much more expensive than what a taxi should be for comparable travel and is probably cheaper than what most taxis try to charge the unsuspecting and inexperienced. Hotels are also a good place to find a taxi, but if you ask a hotel to provide a taxi for you, the ride will cost four or five times what it would cost with a street taxi.

A taxi to or from the airport should cost you a standard $30. For any other destination, either ask the driver up front what the fare will be or find out in advance from a local what the ride should cost and hand that much to the taxi driver as you get out of the cab without even asking about the cost. It is not uncommon for taxi drivers to pick up other fares while you are in the car. It is their way of getting the biggest bang for their miles.

This can extend the duration of your drive and could represent a safety issue, so if you are not comfortable with having someone else in the taxi, just let the driver know as soon as you get in.

In Panama's interior towns, taxis are far easier to come by, and a ride anywhere within the town shouldn't cost more than $1.50.

Buses travel to and from cities several times a day, and even first-class fares are very cheap. You can travel long distances for $20 or less.

Accessibility to the United States

You can fly direct from Panama City's Tocumen International Airport to New York; Atlanta; Chicago; Boston; Las Vegas; Miami; Dallas; Los Angeles; Washington, D.C.; and Houston. Copa adds new U.S. destinations regularly. The flight time from Panama to Miami is about three hours; to New York it's five hours; to Los Angeles it's six hours and twenty minutes.

Language

You can get by in Panama City speaking only English, but I don't recommend it. In El Valle, still very much a local Panamanian community, you'll need at least basic Spanish.

The Spanish Panama School (www.spanishpanama.com) in

the Panama City neighborhood of El Cangrejo is a good choice for Spanish-language instruction (sixty hours of class study is $500; total immersion is $575 per week). El Paraiso Spanish Language School in Bocas del Toro (www.elparaisoschool.com), on the Caribbean side of the country, offers weekly programs, including twenty group classes for $205 or fifteen private classes for $235. I wouldn't recommend Bocas as a place to live, but it could be a fun place to spend a few weeks improving your Spanish.

Culture, Recreation, and Entertainment

Panama City boasts legitimately top-notch restaurants with international-standard menus and wine lists and white-glove service. In addition, Panama City has dozens of fun, off-the-radar dives you wouldn't think to try unless someone pointed you in their direction. Panama City after dark is about the nightclubs (especially along Calle Uruguay and in currently trendy Casco Viejo), the casinos, and the gentlemen's clubs; the serious Panama City nightlife doesn't get going until past midnight.

Parque Omar is Panama City's Central Park, comprised of acres of green space in the center of downtown, with areas for soccer, basketball, tennis, and picnicking, a jogging track, and a public pool. The best place to spend Saturday and Sunday mornings is the Amador Causeway. Designed as a huge breakwater to protect the entrance to the Panama Canal and the Port of Balboa, the Causeway was built with rock excavated during the digging of the Culebra Cut. It's a giant fill project. On one side is the best possible view of modern Panama City, the high-rises, the new towers under construction, the cranes, the skyward-reaching glass, steel, and concrete of a city trying so hard to move beyond developing-world status; off the other side, the islands of the Bay of Panama, the Panama Canal, and the Pacific Ocean beyond. At the far end of the Causeway are restaurants and shops. About midway is the Biodiversity Museum designed by Frank Gehry. There's also a cruise port, a marina, a convention center, hotels, and the Smithsonian Tropical Research Institute.

Central Panama City has been made much greener, thanks to the decade-in-the-making Avenida Balboa expansion project, which took the city's main thoroughfare from six lanes to ten but added an impressive *malecón* and park area along the Bay of Panama in the process. Residents of Panama City appreciate their new center-city recreation area, and you find people jogging, biking, walking, shooting hoops, and using the free workout equipment here every day at all hours.

Beyond Panama City are two coasts and some of the world's best fishing, boating, snorkeling, diving, and surfing, as well as jungle and mountain highlands for hiking, biking, and bird-watching.

Residency

Panama offers what I'd say qualifies as the world's easiest residency option. Referred to as the Friendly Nations program by immigration attorneys and expats, all you need to qualify for this residency permit is a passport from one of fifty countries on the country's "friendly nations" list. U.S. and Canadian passport holders qualify, as do those holding passports from most Western countries. While qualifying is super easy, you do have to jump through some hoops to be issued your visa. There is no monthly minimum income requirement, but you must deposit $5,000 in a local bank account (not forever) and either buy a piece of property (of any value; I've known people to qualify by purchasing property for as little as $10,000) or set up a Panama corporation (the cost for this should be no more than $1,500).

Panama also offers one of the world's best-known and most benefit-heavy *pensionado* residency options, which you can qualify for by showing pension income of at least $1,000 per month (plus $250 per month per dependent).

In addition, Panama offers at least a dozen other residency options. If you want to live in this country full time, speak with an attorney about all the options so you can choose the one that suits your situation best.

Environment

Panama City is a boomtown with lots of cars and buses generating lots of fumes and construction everywhere. The city has recently installed new wastewater treatment plants in some areas, but effluent still flows into the bay from some sources, so swimming in the beaches located in and near the city isn't recommended (though the locals do). As everywhere in Central America, garbage and litter are a problem, though not as dramatically visible a problem as in Nicaragua, for example.

El Valle, in the country's mountainous interior, doesn't struggle with the air or the noise pollution of Panama City. In fact, this town is known for its clean air. Because the population density is low, garbage is also much less dramatic a concern than in the capital.

Taxes

➤ Personal income tax: marginal rates from 0 to 25 percent; residents are taxed on Panama-sourced income only, and interest earned from local banks isn't taxed in Panama

➤ Personal property or wealth tax: none

➤ Sales tax: 7 percent

➤ Property tax: At one time a twenty-year exemption was in place for new construction; then a tiered exemption replaced that program. You can still find buildings with some years remaining on their twenty-year exemptions; this is something to ask about for any property you are considering purchasing. After the exemption has expired, property taxes are 1 percent of the property value.

➤ Property transfer tax: 2 percent, paid by the seller

➤ Capital gains tax: 10 percent

Special Benefits for Foreign Retirees

Panama offers a long list of discounts available to any resident meeting the age requirement—fifty-five for women and sixty for men—including 30 percent off public transport, 25 percent off airfares, up to 50 percent off of published hotel fares, 25 percent savings in restaurants (15 percent for fast food), 20 percent off prescriptions, and 25 percent off your monthly electric bill up to 600 kilowatt-hours.

In addition, *pensionado* visa holders can import personal goods and a car duty-free or can purchase a new car locally and deduct the (big) import duty from the sales price.

Education and Schools

Panama City could be a great choice if you're looking for a place to start your own business while raising a family. Panama's capital is home to more than a dozen good choices for international-standard bilingual (Spanish-English) schooling, including the Balboa Academy (www.balboaacademy.org), the Colegio Europeo Panamá (www.colegioeuropeo.edu.pa), the Crossroads Christian Academy (www.ccapanama.org), the Academia Interamericana de Panamá (www.aip.edu.pa), the Colegio De La Salle Panamá (www.lasalle.edu.pa), the Colegio St. Mary (www.stmarypa.com), and the Lincoln Academy (www.thelincolnacademy.edu.pa). In addition, Panama City offers a good option for educating your child in French, the Lycée Français Paul Gauguin (www .lfpanama.com).

At Home in Panama City

Panama City is a boomtown. While for years it has been recognized as one of the world's top retirement havens, I would not call this city today retiree-friendly. This is a place to come not to relax and savor life but to start a business and make some money. Investors and entrepreneurs, big and small, from the world over, continue to descend on Panama City, bringing with them ever-greater appetites for everything from housing and health care to cars, Internet, restaurants, and shopping malls. The city's infrastructure, though the best in the region by far and improving and expanding all the time, is more stressed with every passing month.

Panama City is a land of opportunity, not only for investors and business builders, but also for anyone looking for gainful employment. Panama's Friendly Nations visa program makes it not only possible but easy for anyone holding a passport to any of the fifty countries on the list to show up and find a job. As a result, Panama City is home to an eclectic and fast-expanding community of global digital nomads.

This is an exciting time to be in this city reinventing itself in real time. Again, though, Panama City is not an ideal choice for retirement, not only because the pace and way of life aren't what most people imagine for retirement but also because the cost of living in this city is no longer retiree-compatible. Panama City has set the goal of becoming the next Dubai. Dubai is not a cheap place to live, and neither, anymore, is Panama City.

At Home in El Valle de Antón

El Valle, on the other hand, could be a great place to live as a retiree.

El Valle enjoys a unique geographic distinction. This is the only settlement in the world contained within and surrounded by the walls of a volcano. Plenty of towns and cities have been built on the outsides of volcanoes, but nowhere else did people choose to build their homes on the inside. El Valle is also the oldest continuously inhabited volcanic settlement in the world (inside or out); its recorded history goes back 10,000 years.

About ninety minutes from Panama City, El Valle is a world away from the chaotic metropolis. As you travel up the hill from the Pan-American Highway, you pass through microclimates until you reach lush El Valle. This is a place where you could stick a twig in the ground and expect it to grow and flower.

El Valle is also known for its mineralized springs, healing mud baths, and generally healthy environment, and many health tourists traveling to Panama City for medical tourism come to El Valle to recuperate after their procedures.

El Valle is a mountain town but just thirty minutes away from Panama's City Beaches, the country's most developed coastal stretch, with an established expat community and all the services and amenities to support it, including U.S.-style grocery stores, shopping malls, restaurants, hardware stores, banks, dry cleaners, etc.

Meantime, a half hour away up in the hills, El Valle is sticking to its roots as a Panamanian mountain village. To live in El Valle is to step back in time. The pace of life is slow, and the community is close-knit. Farmers might have a truck to bring their goods to market . . . or they might load up their donkey. Instead of motor vehicles, most residents get around on bicycles, sometimes with a family of five loaded up all together.

Portugal

Focus On: Algarve

➤ Cost of living: ****½

➤ Cost of housing: ****½

➤ Climate: *****

➤ Health care: *****

➤ Infrastructure: ****

➤ Accessibility to the United States: ***½

➤ Language: ****

➤ Culture, recreation, and entertainment: ****

➤ Residency: *****

➤ Environment: ***½

➤ Taxes: *****

➤ Special benefits for foreign retirees: *

➤ Education and schools: ***

Estimated Monthly Costs Living in Algarve: 1,565 euros

Focus On: Lisbon

➤ Cost of living: ***½

➤ Cost of housing: ***½

➤ Climate: ****

➤ Health care: *****

➤ Infrastructure: ****½

➤ Accessibility to the United States: ****

➤ Language: ***½

➤ Culture, recreation, and entertainment: *****

➤ Residency: *****

➤ Environment: ***

➤ Taxes: *****

➤ Special benefits for foreign retirees: *

➤ Education and schools: ****

Estimated Monthly Costs Living in Lisbon: 2,382 euros

Cost of Housing

Real estate prices in Portugal bottomed out in 2015. Since then, values in both the Algarve and Lisbon have seen decent appreciation year over year. In fact, the per-square-meter prices in some Lisbon neighborhoods have reached levels to rival those of other major European capital cities. That said, you can still find excellent values in much of Lisbon and its suburbs, especially considering the quality of life on offer, if you spend time on the ground.

The Algarve is a big and diverse region with many different localized real estate markets. Small town, big town, resort town, close to the water, inland . . . each situation demands a different price. You can still, as of this writing, find a small apartment for sale in the Algarve for less than 100,000 euros, but it's not the buyer's market that it once was.

Climate

Portugal's mild year-round weather is one of its biggest selling points.

Thanks to its 3,300 hours of sunshine per year, more sunny days than almost anywhere else in Europe, the Algarve has a long-standing reputation as a top summer destination among European sunseekers and a top winter retreat for those looking to escape northern Europe's coldest months.

Temperatures are generally higher in the south (the Algarve), but nowhere in the country would you experience any great extremes. Algarve summers can see 90 degrees, but the wind and the water help keep you cool. Winter nights get cold enough to warrant heating, but you won't see snow in either the Algarve or Lisbon. If you like four seasons but no extreme temperature changes, Portugal could be ideal for you.

Health Care

Like the rest of Europe, Portugal has a socialized health care system. Unlike most of the rest of Europe, however, Portugal allows you to access it when you become a legal resident, even if you haven't paid into the system. That said, as an expat in Portugal, you'd probably want to avail yourself of the private health care infrastructure, meaning you either pay as you go for care or invest in a health insurance policy.

Portugal ranks twelfth on the World Health Organization's world health report. Virtually every doctor in Portugal speaks English, even those working in the public system.

Infrastructure

Portugal's road infrastructure has benefited from the country's membership in the EU. Highways are modern and well maintained. While the statistics indicate that Portugal has a higher population density than neighboring Spain, the roads in the Algarve tell a different story. You run into traffic during the high season, especially in the late afternoons when people are returning home from the beaches, but it'd be hard to find a traffic jam in this part of Portugal any time of year.

Even Lisbon is mostly free of traffic congestion. The city can be navigated by bus or metro or, in the historic center, on foot.

Internet speeds and cell phone coverage are all first-rate. This is a very wired country.

From the Lisbon airport you can fly direct to all the major cities of Europe and to many secondary cities, as well. The Algarve has an international airport in Faro with flights to the UK, Ireland, Germany, France, Belgium, and the Netherlands . . . all the places where the tourists come from.

Accessibility to the United States

You can fly direct to Lisbon from Boston, Miami, New York, Philadelphia, and Washington, D.C. To get to the Algarve from Lisbon, connect to the airport at Faro or drive (it's two and a half hours).

Language

Portuguese falls into the same language category as Spanish, French, and Italian but is generally considered more difficult to learn. You'll be able to get by with little to no Portuguese, especially in the Algarve, thanks to the abundance of English-speaking locals and the big British expat community (Brits have been retiring and relocating to the Algarve in big numbers since World War II), but I'd recommend learning at least a little Portuguese. It will make your time in the country more fulfilling.

In Portimão, in the Algarve, try Centro de Línguas, Cultura e Comunicação (www.clcc.pt), which offers a variety of programs for beginners.

Culture, Recreation, and Entertainment

The Algarve is known for its hundred miles of Atlantic coastline punctuated by jagged rock formations, lagoons, and extensive sandy beaches, eighty-six of which have earned coveted Blue Flag status from the European Blue Flag Association. The water off these shores is azure, and the cliff-top vistas are spectacular. Beachcombing, swimming, sunning, and boating are among the pleasant ways to pass your time in this part of the world.

In addition, Portugal has been named Europe's Best Golf

Destination, and its Algarve is home to forty top courses, including some of the recognized best in Europe.

What you may not expect is that this region also boasts art galleries, a symphony, an opera, a theater, and an impressive library. The Algarve is much more than its beach.

Lisbon, as you would expect of a European capital, is rich with culture. Music plays an important role in the day-to-day life of this city's residents, and every year Lisbon hosts several summer music festivals.

Meantime, Lisbon is one of the few European cities surrounded by white sandy beaches, including fifty-four Blue Flag beaches within easy reach.

Residency

You can establish residency in Portugal by buying a piece of property in the country or by showing enough income to support yourself. The Golden Visa program allows you to gain residency by investing between 280,000 and 500,000 euros in real estate, depending on where in the country you buy and the age of the property. Older properties in certain targeted regions can qualify at the 280,000-euro level; if you want to buy new in Lisbon, you'll have to invest at least 500,000 euros.

The alternative is to show pension or investment income that totals at least twice the monthly minimum wage (about $1,250 at today's exchange rate)—the thinking being that with guaranteed income of more than twice the local minimum wage you won't become a burden on the state.

Remember, this is for residency in Europe. That monthly income figure competes with those of the best-known residency programs in Latin America.

Environment

While the Algarve's streets, coasts, and air are clean and eighty-six of its beaches have been awarded Blue Flags, the region's inner waterways suffer from pollution. The Ria Formosa is the source of income for many Algarve fishermen, but local environmental groups have continued to express concern about the lagoon system. A new water treatment plant that should address the problem is under construction in Faro.

Lisbon and surrounding areas experienced major development and a population boom beginning in the 1980s that resulted in a super-dense urban area that struggled with waste removal and soil and water pollution. While the situation has been improving over the past thirty years, it hasn't been completely resolved.

All that said, Lisbon overall is a pretty, clean, and green city. You don't see litter on the streets, the air quality is very good for an urban center, and fifty-four of the nearby beaches have been awarded Blue Flags for excellence in cleanliness, safety, amenities, and meeting certain environmental standards.

Taxes

➤ Personal income tax: six tax bands ranging from 0 to 48 percent

➤ Personal property or wealth tax: none

➤ Sales tax: 23 percent

➤ Property tax: 0.3 to 0.8 percent

➤ Property transfer tax: 0 to 8 percent marginal rates, with a 6 percent maximum total tax

➤ Capital gains tax: 28 percent; only 50 percent of gains from real estate are taxed, but they are taxed at marginal income tax rates

Special Benefits for Foreign Residents

Portugal offers what the powers that be have given the unfortunate name of the non-habitual resident (NHR) tax regime. This program is available to any new resident who hasn't been tax-resident in Portugal during the previous five years. The NHR makes it possible for you to pay no or virtually no income tax in Portugal on income from outside of Portugal for ten years.

The program isn't limited to retirees and also offers a reduced tax on income for specific professions working in Portugal.

Education and Schools

Most expats choose to send their children to private schools. Both Lisbon and the Algarve offer many private bilingual schooling options. Costs range, depending on the school and the grade, from 4,000 to 8,000 euros a year. Some of these offer elementary-level education only, but some are affiliated with the internationally recognized International Baccalaureate (IB) system.

At Home in the Algarve

Located at Europe's westernmost tip and boasting a hundred miles of Atlantic coastline, Algarve could be Europe's most famous secret. This region boasts Europe's best beaches, Europe's best golf courses, some of Europe's friendliest folk, and western Europe's lowest cost of living. It's also Europe's newest tax haven.

The Algarve has been an increasingly popular destination for foreign retirees since the end of World War II, when a first wave of former British officers fell under its spell. Attracted by a sunny climate many had become used to from service in Asia and the Middle East, they also appreciated its low cost of living, which stretched their pensions.

In the 1960s, the charms of the Algarve were discovered by the Beatles and their groupies, who moved into the Algarve fishing port of Albufeira, still the home of the most authentic fish and chips on the south coast.

Thanks to this long history of dealing with the British empire, the Portuguese have been learning English almost since they've had schools. There are plenty of non-British foreigners in the Algarve, too, from Germany, Eastern Europe, Scandinavia, and even the Far East (and they all speak English, as well).

Silves and Lagoa are two top options in the region that offer history, Old World charm, and spectacular beaches. Silves, nestled in verdant valleys on the banks of the Arade River and surrounded by fields of citrus, offers a warm microclimate. It's like summertime all year long. In addition to orange and lemon trees, all around are the olive, carob, and fig trees the region is also known for. Silves's coastal town is Armação de Pêra, with an expansive white sandy beach.

Lagoa, with a capital town of the same name, is a much smaller municipality located close to the ocean and boasting seventeen top beaches, specifically around the fishing towns of Carvoeiro and Ferragudo.

The Algarve, a land of cobblestoned streets and whitewashed houses with lace-patterned chimneys surrounded by fig, olive, almond, and carob trees, is the best of an old-school, Old World lifestyle at a very affordable cost. Here you can enjoy all that a continental lifestyle has to offer, from medieval towns and fishing villages to open-air markets and local wine, even if your budget is what would typically be considered more compatible with life in the New World.

At Home in Lisbon

Blessed with warm sunny weather year-round (roughly 300 days of sunshine a year), ringed by the Atlantic Ocean on one side and protected by the calm deep blue waters of the Tagus River (the longest river on the Iberian Peninsula) on the other, Lisbon is a sophisticated historic city that also serves up a clean, swimmable beach.

With a vibrant downtown of small, walkable neighborhoods, the "White City," as it is known, thanks to the way the ocher stone used throughout reflects the sun, is also home to some of the most modern buildings and luxury villas of our era. As a result, Lisbon offers lifestyle choices for all tastes and budgets and is home to a big and well-established community of expats from around the world.

Lisbon isn't Paris, but as in Paris, every time you leave your home here, you'll encounter something new and surprising. This is the oldest city in western Europe, with 300,000 years of history, but continually reinventing itself and increasingly vying for attention on the Euro-stage. Lisbon is one of the Old World's best-kept secrets.

Thailand

Focus On: Chiang Mai

➤ Cost of living: *****

➤ Cost of housing: *****

➤ Climate: ***

➤ Health care: *****

➤ Infrastructure: ***½

➤ Accessibility to the United States: **

➤ Language: **

➤ Culture, recreation, and entertainment: ***½

➤ Residency: ***

➤ Environment: ***

➤ Taxes: ***½

➤ Special benefits for foreign retirees: *

➤ Education and schools: ***

Estimated Monthly Costs Living in Chiang Mai: 43,750 baht

Cost of Housing

You can buy a comfortable expat-standard house in Chiang Mai for as little as $100,000; however, while foreigners can hold fee-simple title to construction in Thailand (that is, a house), they can't hold title to land. This means that when you buy a house, you're literally buying the house, not the piece of land it sits on, unless you put some kind of workaround in place with a Thai partner. This can be risky. On the other hand, foreigners can own up to 49 percent of the constructed area of a condo building through fee-simple title. Nevertheless, it is much safer and simpler to rent. You can rent a small furnished house or apartment in Chiang Mai for as little as $250 per month, and you'll find an abundance of larger options in the range of $600 to $1,000 a month.

Climate

Chiang Mai enjoys the mildest climate of any region in Thailand. The rainy season is May through October; November through February is considered the "cool" season, when daytime temperatures drop to the mid-80s and nighttime lows can break into the high 50s. The hottest time of year is March through April, when highs jump into the 90s.

Health Care

Thailand has evolved over the past decade to become a world leader in medical care, one of the top choices worldwide for medical tourism. The treatment is an unbelievable value as well. Expats are often (sometimes embarrassingly) eager to share stories of the medical care they've received. Commonly, they point out that their procedure averaged 20 to 80 percent less than comparable care would have cost in North America or Europe, and the quality of care that they received was far superior.

Chiang Mai offers residents excellent and easily accessible health care, and many of the city's hospitals are internationally accredited, with plenty of English-speaking staff. The health care options here are second in Thailand only to big-sister Bangkok. With at least nine large hospitals and dozens of clinics, smaller hospitals, and specialty treatment centers scattered around the city, you'd never have to wait long for care. The private Chiangmai Ram Hospital has been quality approved by the Joint Commission International (JCI) and offers everything from a specialist cardiac balloon center to an oncology unit. Sriphat Medical Centre and Maharaj Nakorn Hospital, Lanna Hospital, Rajavej Hospital, McCormick Hospital, and Bangkok Hospital Chiang Mai are all also highly recommended by Chiang Mai expats.

Infrastructure

Bangkok has two airports, Suvarnabhumi Airport (BKK) and Don Mueang International Airport (DMK). DMK has only domestic flights and regional flights. BKK is about a half hour outside the city and has flights throughout Asia and to Australia, Africa, and some destinations in Europe, including London, Paris, Vienna, Amsterdam, Rome, Frankfurt, Helsinki, and Zurich. Flight time from Bangkok to Paris is ten hours and forty-five minutes; to London it's twelve hours; to Amsterdam it's fourteen hours; to Rome it's eleven hours. The national carrier is Thai Airways International.

Chiang Mai International Airport flies throughout Asia but has no direct service to Europe. The flight time from Chiang Mai to Bangkok is one hour and ten minutes, and flights leave more than once an hour.

Buses are probably the most common means of transportation in Thailand, both in Bangkok and for long distances around the country. The long-distance buses are modern, even luxurious; the city buses are smaller and less comfortable. Prices are incredibly low. The city buses, though, can be a challenge; schedules and routes are not readily available, and often these buses don't run on regular schedules anyway.

There are overwhelming numbers of taxis and motorcycle taxis in Bangkok, as well as a metro and an elevated rail system (called the Skytrain). This last offers very limited service, but if it is going your way, it's by far the fastest and cleanest way to travel. *Tuk-tuks* are three-wheeled motor taxis that are good for traveling short distances in Bangkok and other cities. They aren't metered like taxis, so make sure you negotiate a price before you get in. *Samlors* are three-wheeled bicycle rickshaws that have been banned, but you'll still see them in many areas of the country.

Trains travel from city to city; this is a cheap and comfortable but slow way to get around the country. Some routes offer trains with different speeds, and most offer a choice among three classes of service: third class with wooden benches, second class with reclining seats and often air-conditioning, and first class with air-conditioned cabins.

Ferry service is available to many destinations, including some international. Any destination near a river can be accessed by boat, and this is a cheap and relaxing way to get around.

Note that they drive on the left in Thailand, which you can get used to. However, if you've never driven on the left before, Thailand may not be the best place to learn. Roads in the towns and cities are narrow, and you never know what to expect around the next corner.

Accessibility to the United States

You can't fly direct from Thailand to North America but must connect through Europe or Asia. Chiang Mai isn't a place to base yourself if you want to be able to hop back to the States to visit family often.

Language

Thailand is a place where, realistically, you aren't going to pick up the local language—and yes, you'll be able to get by with English. Still, a Thai immersion program could be a great way to launch your adventures in this country. The language school Effective Thai in Chiang Mai (www.effectivethai.com) offers fifty lessons for less than $400.

Culture, Recreation, and Entertainment

Thai cities are famous worldwide for their thriving nightlife and Amsterdam-esque red-light districts. Bangkok, Phuket, and other places are home to hundreds of girlie bars, nightclubs, and floor shows. Bangkok, though, also has a national opera, a symphony, and theaters, plus museums, galleries, and parks.

Chiang Mai is a cosmopolitan city known for its food, restaurants, and markets showcasing traditional and contemporary Thai crafts. Home to a sizable and established expat community, Chiang Mai boasts regular expat meet-up and hobby groups but not much real "city culture."

This is an excellent base for hiking and mountain biking, and the region around Chiang Mai includes more than 300 wats, including 121 within the city limits, many offering classes to Westerners interested in learning about Buddhism or meditation or massage techniques.

Residency

For years most foreign retirees in Thailand simply did the border run to renew their tourist visas every ninety days. This was so prevalent that businesses cropped up offering a border-run service. They would take your passport to the border and have it stamped for you, saving you the trip. This is still possible but not advisable. Thailand (like most countries in today's world) has cracked down on this "workaround" to establishing legal residency.

Thailand offers a retiree residency program known as the non-immigrant O-A (long-stay) visa that must be renewed every year. To qualify you must be fifty or older and either deposit 800,000 baht in a Thai bank account for at least two months prior to making your application or show at least 65,000 Thai baht in monthly income.

Another option for Thai residency is the country's Thailand Elite program. This is straightforward but expensive. You simply select the length of the residency term you want—five, ten, or twenty years—and then pay the government a fee of $3,000 per year up front plus an additional fee of $600 annually.

Environment

Each year, as the end of the dry season approaches, local farmers in Chiang Mai use the slash-and-burn method to prepare for the next growing season. The result is serious air pollution, so serious that most people who are able to leave do leave for a few months. For this reason, few expats choose to remain in Chiang Mai twelve months a year.

Taxes

➤ Personal income tax: marginal rates from 0 to 35 percent; residents are taxed on a remittance basis, including pension income; dividends and interest are taxed at the source at 15 percent

➤ Personal property or wealth tax: none

➤ Sales tax: 10 percent

➤ Property tax: none on owner-occupied dwellings

➤ Property transfer tax: 2 percent paid by the buyer; 0.5 percent paid by the seller

➤ Capital gains tax: capital gains are taxed at marginal income rates; for real estate, you can take a deduction for each year you hold the property up to a maximum deduction of 50 percent after eight years

Special Benefits for Foreign Retirees

None.

Education and Schools

Bilingual schooling options in Bangkok include the International School Bangkok (www.isb.ac.th) and the Bromsgrove International School Thailand (www.bromsgrove.ac.th). Options in Chiang Mai include the American Pacific International School (www.apis.ac.th) and the Nakornpayap International School (www.nis.ac.th).

At Home in Chiang Mai

Thailand is arguably one of the cheapest places on earth to live well. Our friends Paul and Vicki, on-and-off residents of the country for more than three decades, have long been teasing and tempting me with tales of $1 pad Thai lunches and $11-a-night hotels (including breakfast and free Wi-Fi). They've gotten my attention, not only because I want to see a comfortable and pleasant $11-a-night hotel for myself, but also because the way of life they describe sounds both exotic and idyllic, full of adventure and discovery and, at the same time, completely at peace.

Vicki wrote recently to explain that her doctor in Thailand says she needs more exercise. So she and Paul are taking morning speed walks through the back lanes of Chiang Mai's inner city. As she explains, "We leave around seven A.M., when it's still cool and there's little traffic. At that hour, we often see the last few Buddhist monks, in their flowing orange robes and bare feet, finishing up their morning 'begging' rounds. Actually, the monks are not begging at all. They're allowing households to make merit and receive a blessing by offering the monks cooked food in single-serving-sized plastic bags.

"On our walk, we pass two schools on a narrow lane. Private police control traffic at the school entrances. To help keep traffic moving at the first stop, a nursery school, the cops open car doors and gently lift the sleepy little children out of the cars. They then hand them off to the staff of the school.

"At the second school, grade school students arrive on the backs of their parents' motorcycles or in cars, hired vans, or small red semipublic buses. No one walks to school here. We see the kids wearing different uniforms on different days, and we figure that Friday must be 'tradition day.' On Fridays, girls wear long sarongs and dressy white blouses.

"After weaving through the school traffic, we pick up our walking tempo. We stay attentive to cars, motorbikes, bicycles, and dogs that share the lanes with us. I also pay attention to our lovely surroundings. We pass several temples. The sun plays on the golden ornaments and brings the glazed tiles to sparkling life.

"We pass mini-mansions and small, ancient teak houses. We pass empty green fields and well-tended gardens with bright, tropical flowers. We pass small food stalls selling favorite Thai breakfast treats. Rice and spicy meat. Vegetable curries. Sweet milky iced coffee or hot, sweet soy milk, served with fried doughy squares.

"After about ten minutes walking, we arrive at Suan Buak Hat Park, the only public park within the old city walls and moat. On a typical weekday morning, we see speed walkers, joggers, and amblers chatting on cell phones. We all loop around the small park several times on a well-worn cement path. We pass ponds, bridges, pavilions, a children's playground . . . but mostly we pass through lush, tropical green: grass, trees, bushes, and plants. Even the ponds look green, reflecting the surroundings. Gardeners work everywhere, keeping the park in shape.

"In the open area, locals play badminton, and, on the weekends, students play soccer. Some days, a dignified-looking woman leads elderly Thais through a series of elegant movements with brightly colored hand fans.

"After various loops in the park, Paul and I head back. We stop for a Thai breakfast: noodles and vegetable soup or a combination plate of rice or noodles with vegetable stir-fry and spicy curry. Then we return home and get ready for the day."

Life in Chiang Mai is both traditional and increasingly influenced by the growing and active expat community in this region of Thailand. Living here, you could fill your calendar completely with expat activities if you wanted to. You could sing in a choir, act in a play, volunteer in one of several service organizations, participate in a writing club, learn what's going on at the Newcomers Club, dine with other women at the monthly women's dinner club, and on and on. You could meet Thais in Rotary or Toastmasters. There are a couple of mega fund-raising parties each year for local charities. For more physical activity, there are hatha yoga classes, tennis groups, and hiking clubs.

Best of all, you could meet people from all around the world, people like you looking for new lives in an exotic, beautiful, welcoming, and almost unbelievably affordable part of the world.

Uruguay

Focus On: La Barra

➤ Cost of living: ****

➤ Cost of housing: ****

➤ Climate: ****

➤ Health care: ****

➤ Infrastructure: ****

➤ Accessibility to the United States: **½

➤ Language: ****

➤ Culture, recreation, and entertainment: ***

➤ Residency: *****

➤ Environment: ****

➤ Taxes: ****

➤ Special benefits for foreign retirees: ****

➤ Education and schools: ***

Estimated Monthly Costs Living in La Barra: 38,000 Uruguayan pesos

Cost of Housing

You could purchase a three-bedroom house in La Barra for as little as $100,000, or you could spend millions. Organizing a year-long rental, on the other hand, isn't nearly as straightforward a proposition, because owners don't want to give up the extremely high rents they can charge for the months of January and February (between $5,000 to $30,000 per month, depending on the house). With an annual lease, you'll be asked to pay rent to take into account the inflated rates that can be commanded during this two-month period. This is one of the reasons Uruguay can make sense as a part-time retirement destination. Don't try to rent for twelve months at a time but for four to six months, for example. Putting January and February aside, you could rent for as little as $600 a month.

Or invest in a $150,000 home here yourself, live in it up to ten months a year, then rent it out for January and February. You could earn enough in rent from those two months alone to cover your mortgage and other related property expenses for the entire year. The rental market distortion here creates a remarkable opportunity.

Climate

Uruguay has four distinct seasons, and its 41-inch rainfall is spread evenly throughout the year, without any wet or dry season (although rain is uncommon in the midsummer months of January and February).

The average daytime high is about 82 degrees Fahrenheit in midsummer; the average low is around 65. Midwinter, highs run around 60, with lows near 42. Frost is rare, and it never snows. Few people use air-conditioning in the summer, thanks to the cool evenings and ocean breezes, but you'll use the heat in wintertime.

Health Care

Basic care in Uruguay's public hospitals is free; in private hospitals, you'll be charged for all services, but rates are low. Some private hospitals in Uruguay offer a kind of health coverage that covers in- and outpatient services at that hospital. Note that this is not the same as health insurance and that your benefits extend to only the particular hospital where you've arranged coverage. You would not be covered for care outside Uruguay or, indeed, anywhere else in the country. Still, if you're a full-time resident, these programs can be remarkably appealing, costing as little as $50 per month and providing very comprehensive coverage (again, at the one hospital only).

An in-country insurance package can also be a great deal, even if you're in Uruguay only part of the year. The least expensive plan starts at just $49 per month with La Asistencial, a network that operates eleven facilities in the area. With this basic plan, you'd be in a semiprivate room if hospitalized, and inpatient drugs would be covered. The copayment for doctor visits ranges from $3.50 for a doctor visit to $13 for a visit to the emergency room. You'd be responsible for 75 percent of the cost of outpatient drugs.

At the other end of the scale is the $129-per-month program, which entitles you to a private room, VIP treatment both in the hospital and at the doctor's office, ambulance service, and medicines at a flat-rate copayment of $5. Both plans cover you for emergency service while traveling outside Uruguay. Note that the rates I'm quoting are the highest published rates available for those over fifty-five years old. If you're younger, your premiums should cost less. There is no minimum term; you could join for just part of the year if that suits you better.

From La Barra, the nearest free clinic is in Maldonado, about twenty minutes away. But the paid system is such a good deal (especially when compared with costs in the United States) that most foreigners opt for private facilities. Going this route, La Barra is served by an efficient, modern (though small) clinic called Policlínica La Barra, which is fine for general illnesses, prescriptions, or routine doctor visits (and part of the La Asistencial insurance network I mentioned above). If you need surgery, however, you'd likely opt for one of its affiliated hospitals in Punta del Este or San Carlos, both about fifteen minutes away. Entering the emergency room without insurance, you can expect to pay about $75 for the ER service, the doctor visit, and related lab work.

Infrastructure

Carrasco International Airport, about thirty minutes from Montevideo, is the main airport for Uruguay, and the largest. About fifteen minutes outside Punta del Este is the Capitán de Corbeta Carlos A. Curbelo International Airport, servicing the country's Gold Coast, the coastal resort region about an hour northeast of Montevideo. El Jagüel is the nearest international airport to La Barra; however, frankly, it goes almost nowhere, and flights to the regional destinations it does serve (for example, Buenos Aires) cost more than they would if you flew from Carrasco in Montevideo.

You can fly from Montevideo to Punta del Este or take the bus. Comfortable express buses run among all cities around the country. Inner-city buses have vague routes but are cheap. Taxis are easy to hail in the cities.

Accessibility to the United States

You can fly direct from Miami to Montevideo on American Airlines (the flight time is nine hours); otherwise, you must connect through Buenos Aires, Argentina, which is a half hour flight from Montevideo or Punta del Este.

Language

Centro de Enseñanza de Español La Herradura offers Spanish classes in Montevideo and Punta del Este (www .spanish-herradura.com). Spanish immersion group classes run $215 per week and private lessons (two a day) $290 a week.

Culture, Recreation, and Entertainment

Montevideo is a small cosmopolitan city, but it boasts theater, concerts, ballet, museums, fine dining, casinos, and nightclubs, though all on a limited scale. Inland is hiking, horse riding, polo, and golf. The eighteen-hole, par-72 La Barra Golf Club in Manantiales is playable year-round.

Wintertime (June through August) in La Barra is bustling. In summer, it's madness. The city fills to capacity with people coming from all over the world to enjoy the region's world-class beaches.

Residency

Uruguay is one of the easiest places in the world to establish residency. You simply need to show proof of "enough" income to support yourself. No set minimum is required. Those I know who've gone through the residency process in this country describe it as a delightful experience. "The people processing my paperwork," one friend told me, "were less like bureaucrats and more like friends inviting me in for a coffee."

Environment

Nearly 95 percent of this country's electricity comes from clean energy sources, and in general this is a clean, green, and environmentally conscious place to be. Runoff from the country's big meat-packing and tanning industries has led to water pollution in some areas. Otherwise, again, Uruguay is one of the least polluted countries in the world.

Taxes

➤ Personal income tax: marginal rates from 0 to 36 percent; non-Uruguayan interest and dividend income is taxed at 12 percent with tax credit given if income is taxed in the source country

➤ Personal property or wealth tax: 0.7 to 2.5 percent

➤ Sales tax: 22 percent

➤ Property tax: 0.25 to 1.2 percent

➤ Property transfer tax: 4 percent split between the buyer and the seller

➤ Capital gains tax: 12 percent

Special Benefits for Foreign Retirees

As a foreign resident, you'll be able to import your household goods duty-free.

Education and Schools

Uruguay has a long history of bilingual schools, so the options are plentiful. In Montevideo, top international-standard bilingual education options include British Schools (www.british .edu.uy), the Colegio Stella Maris (www.stellamaris.edu.uy), the Escucla Integral Hebreo Uruguaya (www.escuelaintegral.edu .uy), Saint Brendan's School (www.stbrendan.edu.uy), and the Woodlands School (www.woodlands.edu.uy).

Nearer to La Barra in Punta del Este are St. Clare's College (www.scc.edu.uy), Woodside School (www.woodsideschool.edu .uy), and International College (www.ic.edu.uy).

At Home in La Barra

Despite being a former Spanish colony, Uruguay is home to a cultural mix of people that shows little Spanish influence aside from the language. There are virtually no indigenous people left in Uruguay and, because slavery was never legal here, few people of African descent.

The Uruguayan government is a stable democracy, and the country enjoys a solid banking system whose secrecy laws have drawn offshore investors from the world over. The legal system is based on civil law, and the judiciary is fair and stable. Uruguay has one of the lowest crime rates in Latin America, as well as one of the lowest poverty levels and highest standards of living, along with the longest life expectancy.

La Barra sits on Uruguay's Atlantic coast, almost halfway between Montevideo and the border with Brazil. It's located in the department of Maldonado, and the 96-mile drive to the capital city takes about two hours. The picture of La Barra as you approach along the coastal highway from Montevideo is arresting. Sitting on a peninsula rising out of the clear blue South Atlantic waters, La Barra is a small town of neat white houses boasting beautiful beaches, great restaurants, quiet wooded neighborhoods, and more nightlife than you would imagine for a place this size. For some reason, seaside La Barra has been overshadowed by its more famous neighbors, yet it has the best of everything you could want in a seaside retirement destination.

There are plenty of little beach towns along Uruguay's coast, but La Barra is special. It is a small, walkable town, yet it offers all the luxuries, services, comforts, and conveniences of twenty-first-century living. Furthermore, La Barra is clean, well maintained, and safe. Like all Uruguay, it enjoys first-world infrastructure with good public facilities, drinkable water, and well-maintained beaches.

La Barra is one of the few places in this country that offers an opportunity for true beachfront living. In most of Uruguay, a beachfront road known as the *rambla* separates the beaches from the closest private properties. In La Barra, you'll find several areas with houses and low-rise apartments right on the water. You'll also find excellent restaurants where you can look out at the water while dining on the day's fresh-caught seafood specialties, or if you prefer, traditional Old World cooking, even sushi.

In addition, there are fine art galleries, antiques shops, and countless boutiques. La Barra even has one of Uruguay's few Harley shops, as well as a number of five-star hotels and a new luxury casino. When you drive down La Barra's main street, you have to slow down to take in the odd collection of eclectic buildings and shops. It's chaotic, colorful, and random. You pass the hardware store, then a high-end art gallery. One antiques shop looks like someone is cleaning out his barn, while the next offers expensive collectors' items to wealthy tourists. A fine northern Italian restaurant sits comfortably across the street from a burger shop with sidewalk tables.

PART IV

SETTLING IN

You're in paradise. Now what?
Here's a guide to establishing yourself and settling in.

Renting, Renovating, or Building Your New Home

How to Rent a Home Overseas

When we arrived in Waterford, Ireland, some twenty years ago, luggage and then nine-year-old daughter in tow, we intended to invest in a new home straightaway. We were eager to launch our new life on the Auld Sod, and I had a clear picture of what that life was to look like. I wanted a big old Georgian-style house with land around it for chickens and a garden, plus stables where Kaitlin could keep a pony.

We checked into the Granville Hotel in the center of town, walked around the corner to visit the estate agents at O'Shea O'Toole, and described what we were in the market to buy. As I've explained, we didn't understand at first that the Irish property market better resembles those in Central America than that in the United States. There's no multiple listing service, the agents don't split commissions, and to find out what's available for sale, you've got to visit every agent in town. When we landed in Waterford, these secrets of real estate shopping Irish-style were unknown to us. We were blissfully naive.

Mr. O'Shea cured us of this affliction quickly. The man insisted

that there were but two houses available in all of County Waterford that might suit us. How could that be, we asked ourselves in
bewilderment after every conversation with him. Finally it occurred to us to try another agent. We got in touch with estate
agent John Rohan, who likewise told us of two houses available
that might be interesting to us, but, we discovered, these were not
the same two houses as those Mr. O'Shea had shown us. Mr.
Palmer, down the street, showed us three houses, none the same
as those we'd seen with Mr. O'Shea or Mr. Rohan. Then Desmond
Purcell told us about three old Georgian-style houses for sale, one
of which was the same as one of the houses that Mr. O'Shea had
shown us weeks before—but in Mr. Purcell's listing book, the
price tag was 10,000 pounds greater.

This was going to take a while, we finally had to admit. We
realized we'd have to abandon our plan to buy right away. We
couldn't afford to remain guests of the Granville Hotel indefinitely, so we began looking for a house to rent.

In Ireland, we discovered, as in most places where you're likely
to be in the market for a short-term rental, the best system for
finding one, especially if budget is a concern, is by word of mouth.
You can search on the Internet, but as with property for sale, the
rentals you find this way are typically the most expensive, certainly if you search English-language sites. Your chances of getting a better deal are increased if you reference sites in the local
language. Still, going this route, you're going to find only those
properties for rent by locals with the wherewithal to advertise
them online.

You can also source rentals through the local print classifieds.
This can be an effective method, a way to penetrate the local
market and to gain access to local pricing, if you read and speak
the local language fluently. Understanding Spanish well enough
to read a rental property listing in a local newspaper in Medellín, Colombia, for example, isn't enough. You've got to be able
to speak Spanish well enough to have a conversation by telephone with the owner to arrange a viewing appointment. Then
you've got to feel comfortable enough in your Spanish to meet
with him or her in person, at the property, to ask your questions,
to negotiate the price and other particulars, and ultimately, to
review the rental agreement (which will be in Spanish if that's

the language of the country where you're shopping). I've known many people who've successfully sourced rentals this way and been happy with the results, but I, for example, couldn't do it without help, not in a market where the language is Spanish. Mine isn't good enough.

The most efficient and effective strategy, therefore, certainly if you're not fluent in the local lingo, is to ask around. You can begin this process before you arrive in your new home, but finding a suitable rental in the right location for you at a good price can be a difficult thing to accomplish from afar.

Two months in advance of the date we planned to move from Paris to Panama City, I tried to launch our search for a rental in the Panamanian capital. I sent off emails to friends, business contacts, and property agents in the city. Everyone replied to say, in effect: Searching long-distance for an apartment or a house to rent in this market is nearly impossible. Much better to wait until you're here in person. Probably any time you invest before you're on the ground will prove wasted.

This was 2008. The Panama City rental market at the time was an extreme example. It qualified as one of the most active short-term rental markets in the world. The would-be renter had to be ready to act. If you hesitated (showed up to a viewing without your local bank checkbook, for example, and therefore unable to write a local check for the deposit on the spot), you risked losing out. Few markets are this competitive. But there's another, more universal reason it's not easy to try to shop for a rental apartment in one country while you're sitting at home in another.

Say you ask around from the comfort of your armchair. One of your sources replies to tell you about a rental in such and such neighborhood available for such and such price. It sounds great in the email, the best value you've come across. But is it a place you'd want to live? Making that determination without having seen the place yourself is dangerous. Maybe you'd trust your best friend or your significant other to scout and secure a rental on your behalf, but I've known even that to backfire. It's not the end of the world, of course. Eventually the lease term will expire, freeing you to move wherever you like. Maybe you could even negotiate with the landlord to get released from your rental contract early. However, in some countries, this is not easily accomplished, and regardless, the negotiation is a hassle you don't want during what should be the honeymoon period in your new home in paradise. Better to set your own two eyes on a place before you hand over the security deposit and the first and last months' rent (as you'll likely have to do, though sometimes these terms are open for discussion).

It may sound like a nonstrategy, but the best approach is simply to make a reservation at a hotel located in the area where you think you'd like to live. Plan to stay up to four or five weeks. It may not take you this long to find a place to live more permanently, but don't be discouraged if it does. We were guests of the Granville Hotel in Waterford, Ireland, for a full eight weeks (we negotiated a discounted long-term rate with the manager) before we finally found the rental cottage that became our first home in that city. Easing into a place this way gives you a chance to get the lay of the land and to take your time considering your options.

Perpetual travelers Paul and Vicki face this challenge of finding a rental in a new place as often as two or three times a year, and this is the strategy they employ. "Paul and I prefer to begin our search after we have landed in our city of choice," Vicki explains. "However, before we arrive, we gather as much information as we can about rentals through friends, travel guides, and the Internet. We check into a moderately priced hotel, then head out to the neighborhoods that sounded appealing to us in our research. We check bulletin boards in grocery stores, cafés, English-language churches, and Laundromats. We read the local papers and chat with anyone who might have a lead. In small towns, we visit the local tourist office.

"We keep an open mind while at the same time remembering what's important to us. In a tropical climate like Chiang Mai, Thailand, we want a place with an outdoor sitting area. In big cities like Paris, we want to be close to public transportation and grocery shopping. In small towns like Chapala, Mexico, or Boquete, Panama, we want to be in the center of town, living like the middle-class locals. We always choose places where we can walk to shopping, restaurants, libraries, bus stops, etc.

"We deal only with owners. When a deposit is required, we amortize it over the number of months we intend to rent to give us what could be the real cost of the place if our deposit isn't returned. Normally, this isn't a problem, but remember, in a developing country, you have no easy resource for help getting your security deposit returned if the landlord decides he'd rather keep it in the end.

"Where eating out is cheap (as in Southeast Asia), we live without a kitchen. Sometimes we decide that our best bet is to stay in a hostel with kitchen privileges, a guesthouse, or a simple apartment hotel, rather than a furnished apartment. We often find what we need in a few days. We move in. I set up my nightstand and make a cup of coffee, even if it's instant with an immersion heater, as long as it's in my own cup. I sit down, savor the coffee, look out the window at my new view, and relish the moment. I'm home."

In Waterford, where we spent two months in the Granville Hotel before we found a suitable rental cottage, our challenge was particularly great because we were trying to find not only a house to rent but also an office. We began making inquiries about available rentals at the front desk of our hotel, of fellow shoppers standing in line at the grocery store, of fellow parents at our daughter's school, in the bank, and of every taxi driver we encountered.

Finally, someone in a corner shop gave us the address of a small office he thought might be available for rental. By this time we were nearly desperate, so, new lead in hand, we headed across town immediately, without an appointment (for we had no phone number, only the address), to knock on the door of the office in question. Is our information correct? we inquired of the nice Irish lady Claire who greeted us inside. Is this office for rent? Indeed it was. We negotiated a price and terms on the spot and asked if we could return the next day to begin setting up shop. In addition, on our way out the door, I asked, as an afterthought, "Would you happen to know of a two-bedroom house for rent?"

Indeed, Claire did. She wrote down another address for us. Again we walked out the door, went directly down the street to the taxi queue, and took off in a cab straightaway to see the residence for ourselves. The landlord, it turned out, was at home in his own house on the same property. He showed us the place, the view of the river, and the garage where we could store belongings that wouldn't fit in the little cottage. We were delighted with our riverside discovery, which boasted "all mod cons," as the Irish would say, or all modern conveniences. We negotiated price and terms for renting on the spot. We sealed the deal, our second of the morning, like the first, with a handshake.

Our new rental cottage was ideal.

It was a comfortable size for the three of us and comfortably furnished, and it was situated in a pleasant location on the river and within walking distance of town, Kaitlin's school, and our new office. Living here, though, only reinforced our original dream. Waterford City life wasn't what we'd come to Ireland to find, and we were more certain of this with every passing week. It took several months of searching, but at last we found the two-hundred-year-old Georgian house on seven acres a half hour outside the city that we eventually purchased, renovated, lived in for six years, and remember so fondly today.

How to Undertake a Renovation in a Foreign Country

Are you thinking that, after renting for a while in your new home overseas, you might like to invest in a home of your own, maybe a charming old historic one in need of some tender loving care? I sympathize.

I'm a romantic. More than what's in front of me, I see what what's in front of me has the potential to become. This can be a dangerous habit when it comes to buying real estate in a foreign country. Take our home in Ireland, for example. It was a two-hundred-year-old stone farmhouse that had been vacant for more than four years. The previous owner had been an elderly woman who'd lived in the house alone for decades while it fell slowly to ruin around her. After her death, the rate of deterioration accelerated. When I walked in for the first time, though, I didn't see the mold growing on the walls or the rot eating away at the wooden doorframes. I saw classic Georgian symmetry complemented by high ceilings, ornate moldings, a grand central staircase, original wood plank floors, and built-in shutters on all the oversized windows that opened, in every direction, to views of rolling green fields embroidered with low stone walls and centuries-old hedgerows. The best of Irish country life, just what we'd come to Ireland to find. Sure, the place needed a little work, but what a great project, to restore this stately structure to its original Georgian splendor.

Irish banks don't require a formal inspection of any piece of property they lend you money to buy. Still, we thought we ought to have one. We asked our estate agent to recommend an inspector, whose eventual report puzzled us. Rather than detailing required upgrades to the electrical wiring or gaps among the slate tiles on the roof, the report suggested that the "decor could be modernized." We didn't disagree, but was it odd that the inspector found little else to comment on, we wondered. We took this as an encouraging sign and bought the place.

Friends recommended a general contractor, Noel, to help with the modernizing we wanted to carry out. We met Noel at the house one cold, drizzly Irish morning and began showing him around. "We'd like to build in cabinets here," I explained, "and bookcases at the top of the stairs. We want to replace the tub in the master bathroom and the shower in the guest room and then paint and paper throughout."

Noel nodded but kept silent. He continued on along the hallways from room to room, with us following behind. Finally Noel declared: "I'd say you need a damp guy."

"Excuse me," I replied. "A damp guy?"

"I know a good one."

"Okay. Would you put us in touch?"

A few days later, on another cold, drizzly Irish morning, we stood outside the heavy front door to the old stone house waiting for Noel's damp guy, who approached, finally, well hunched over and carrying a screwdriver in his hand. He tipped his woolen cap to me, then headed toward the living room, where he began poking his screwdriver into each piece of wood he passed. The window casings, the shutters, the skirting boards at the bases of the walls, the frames of the doors to the patio . . . the little Irishman poked and poked, his look growing graver after each thrust. From the living room to the dining room, through the kitchen and up the stairs, Noel's damp guy made his way through the entire house, poking and frowning as he went.

"Rising damp," he declared solemnly. "All throughout."

We didn't know what rising damp was, but we were pretty sure from the look on the damp guy's face that its presence wasn't good news.

The damp guy turned to leave. "Uh, wait, sir, please," I stuttered. "What should we do?"

"Got to treat it," he replied as he walked out the door. I called Noel.

Rising damp, it turns out, is a common phenomenon throughout the Emerald Isle, where damp from the constantly wet soil seeps into the foundation of a house and then rises up the walls until gravity gets the better of it. Left untreated, damp will rise, we learned, about six feet before the force of gravity halts its progress. In our house, it'd been left untreated for a very long time, meaning, Noel explained, we had to blast away the interior plaster back to the stone from the base of every wall to a height of six feet. The exposed stone would be injected with a chemical to treat the mold, then sealed, then the wall would be repaired using plaster treated to withstand further damp.

Blast they did, Noel's crew, with jackhammers, for days and days, until every plaster wall had been made dust. At first I'd visit every second day or so to check on the work. After a while I couldn't face the mess and resorted to phone calls with Noel, who reported his men's progress to me, as they blasted, then treated, then sealed, then . . .

No, no, not so fast. Just when I thought the demolition was complete, and the time had arrived finally to begin rebuilding, Noel explained that the next step in treating a bad case of rising damp (ours was one of the worst he'd seen) was to tear out all the wood. Every piece, every panel, from the floorboards to the baseboards, from the window casings to the doors and the shutters—it all had to be ripped out, treated, then replaced. If the rot was too bad, a new piece had to be made to fit.

Week after week, we watched as the charming Georgian country house we'd bought was reduced to rubble inside. Meantime, I discovered that I was pregnant, and our sense of urgency about the planned move into bigger country quarters increased. What we thought would be three or four weeks of carpentry, painting, and wallpapering turned into what we've come to refer to as our first "total gut job," a project that in the end took nearly two years to complete. I insisted we move in before the baby, our son, Jack, was born, which meant we spent our first month in our first house overseas holed up in the master bedroom, the one dust-free room, without a real kitchen and with but one working bathroom.

That's what it means to undertake a renovation in a foreign country. We so enjoyed the experience that we undertook another one when we moved to Paris several years later. How bad could this be? we thought. There's no rising damp in Paris.

No, but in a three-hundred-year-old building, like the one where our Paris apartment is located, there are other problems. This time we intended to add a bathroom and paint but ended up redoing the plumbing, the heating, and the wiring throughout the entire apartment. A project expected to take two months took eight and cost two and a half times as much as we'd budgeted.

In all, over the past twenty years, I've been involved in ten renovation projects in eight countries. Here's what I've learned: It always takes longer and costs more than you think it will. Lief and I now count on twice as long and two times as much. That way, sometimes, we're pleasantly surprised by the actual outcome.

I've also learned that it's madness to undertake a renovation long-distance. That's not to say I haven't managed a renovation in one country from another, several times, or that I wouldn't do it again. I'm saying only that the idea qualifies as nuts. If you decide to pursue it nevertheless, as I have, budget for the cost of your travel for site inspections at critical points and engage someone you trust in-country to visit the property regularly, at least weekly and certainly before you make the final payment to the contractor. Have your on-site representative send you regular reports, including photographs.

This was my strategy for the apartment I restored in Medellín, Colombia. I was living at the time in Panama City, which is a quick 45-minute flight away. I made the trip at least monthly for the eighteen months of that project. Still, I invested in on-the-ground help as well, someone who was able to visit the site weekly and whenever else I asked. My local friend met with my contractor when I couldn't, sent me photos between my visits, and helped to make sure all final punch-list items were addressed to my satisfaction. That renovation took twice as long and cost twice as much as we'd projected. In other words, it went precisely according to plan. Seriously, I'm sure it would have taken longer and cost more if not for my friend on the scene.

The gentleman who renovated the 150-year-old Spanish colonial house in Casco Viejo that we rented as our first home in Panama didn't follow this strategy. He was living in New York while the work was taking place in Panama City, and he opted not to engage an independent overseer, not even to review the finished work before signing off with the contractor. I can sympathize with his reasoning. He invested a great deal in the renovation, including high-end fixtures in the kitchen and the bathrooms, hardwood floors, and shutters on every window. It's a beautiful three-story house that probably cost him considerably more to restore to the current standard than he ever imagined possible. Frustrated by the cost overruns, he told us, he opted not to engage a third party to inspect the property upon completion, and he didn't return to the country himself to sign off on a final punch list.

We were the first people to inhabit the house after the renovation. Our first week living there, we discovered more than a dozen punch-list items that any U.S. inspector would have cited but that here, in the land of mañanas and fiestas, went unnoticed— including no hot water in the guest bathroom, because the hot water pipe was clogged with plaster dust; no hot water in the first-floor powder room, because the sink was never plumbed for it; a lighting fixture positioned in the ceiling of the master bedroom in such a way that the door to the room could not be closed; no doorframe around the bathroom door for the second bedroom; and most difficult for us to correct, improper wiring from the street to the house, meaning the installation of telephone and Internet was at first thought to be impossible. These are the things that can happen when you oversee a renovation in one country from a base in another.

The third thing I've learned about undertaking a renovation in a foreign country is that you're better off working with professionals. I've managed renovations using off-the-books laborers

(Romanians in Paris, Colombians in Panama). Working this way saves money but adds additional risk and management burden. I would do it again, though, on a case-by-case basis.

I've also once undertaken a renovation with a nonprofessional contractor. This not only adds risk and hassle but doesn't save money in the end, I'd argue, because if the top guy doesn't know what he's doing, you're going to have to pay for his mistakes. This I would never do again. My most successful experiences have been when I've engaged a general contractor with long experience renovating specifically the kind of property in question, be it a 200-year-old Georgian country house in Ireland or a 150-year-old French-colonial building in Panama City's old town.

How to Build Your Dream Home in Paradise

Perhaps your dream is to build your own retirement home overseas. This was the case with my friend Ann.

Ann had dreamed her whole life of living in the Caribbean. Finally Ann and her husband, Mike, were able to realize their aquamarine fantasies when they launched a new life on Ambergris Caye off the coast of Belize. Even though they weren't ready to take up full-time residence on the island right away, they were committed to their long-term future here and ready to set about creating their dream home at the beach. Ann and Mike bought a lot and drew up house plans.

Their situation was complicated because Ann had just taken a new high-powered job with a big international company, meaning she'd be traveling a lot and fully occupied. At the same time, Ann and Mike realized that building a house in another country long-distance would be about as crazy as renovating a house in another country long-distance. Their solution was for Mike to move to San Pedro Town on Ambergris Caye full time, while Ann stayed back in San Francisco, where they'd been living and where she was continuing her climb up the corporate ladder.

"Mike made regular trips back to the States," Ann explains. "He wanted to check in with me, but these were also buying trips. He'd come home to purchase whatever he needed but couldn't find in Belize. It wasn't easy living apart, but we agreed it was critical that Mike be in San Pedro full time to make sure that the construction work was done according to our plans.

"Made primarily of concrete block, the house (we named it Mi Casa) is built to last," Ann continues. "Its structure and integrity were tested early when Hurricane Keith swept through San Pedro in October 2001. Mike watched as a section of our not-yet-completed roof floated away down the street. The local insurance company paid up, quickly and efficiently. And more important, of course, Mike came through without a scratch.

"Building a house in a foreign country is stressful enough. Our situation was made more stressful by our separation. Whenever I came to visit, I was yearning for a tranquil vacation. What I got was regular seven A.M. wake-up calls from workers drilling and sawing. Some mornings I was driven nearly to tears by the noise and the commotion. Several of the crew slept on cardboard beds at the site. They rose with the sun and hit the ground running. They were ready to work from sunup to sundown. This was great, of course . . . unless you were seeking escape from the corporate fast track, as I was.

"Frankly, I didn't have much time to swing in the hammocks back in those days. Part of each of my 'vacation' visits was spent hunting for local furnishings and decor. We did make time during each visit, though, for a few days at a dive resort on a remote island. This was my chance to indulge my appreciation for Belize's exotic underwater landscape and sea creatures, the things that had attracted us to this part of the world in the first place.

"For his fiftieth birthday, I treated Mike to a few days at the Caves Branch jungle resort. We floated on inner tubes down a river that carried us through caves where mysterious Mayan rituals were performed centuries ago. We slept in a simple but lovely cabana. Only a screen separated us from the jaguars that prowled the surrounding jungle. These adventure trips helped to compensate for the chaos of construction at Mi Casa.

"If you were to ask me today for a single piece of advice on building a home in another country, it'd be this: Make sure to allow yourself time to enjoy your new home while you're building your new house. Don't be overwhelmed by the work of what you're doing. Give yourself time to play and to enjoy what this new part of the world has to offer."

Here are nine other things to keep in mind when building a house overseas:

1. Be sure you have the time, money, and fortitude to complete the project. Frankly, purchasing a condo or house can be a much easier way to invest in a home in another country. Building one yourself is a lot of work.

2. Understand that any home-building project is going to exceed your budgets for both schedule and cost. Count on it.

3. If you can't be on-site full time, you need a plan to protect your investment. You need both security and eyes on the contractor.

4. And in regard to the contractor, take the time to investigate his track record and reputation before pulling the trigger. Your contract is only as good as the person with whom you enter into it. In addition, insist that your contractor present you with a detailed itemized bill based on the architectural plans that includes everything from windows and doors to iron railings and zinc-plated screws.

5. Don't skimp on the architectural plans. You get what you pay for. We worked with one of the most expensive architects in Panama to draft the plans for the house we built on this country's Pacific coast. We could have saved a few thousand dollars at least by using someone else, but we've seen how wrong things can go when the plans aren't fully thought through and painstakingly detailed. When you are working in a foreign country with workers of varying levels of education, experience, and expertise, it's a risk to leave anything open to interpretation. The crew on the ground has no choice but to improvise. I promise you that their improvisation will not meet your expectations.

6. As much as possible, use local materials. These are more affordable than the alternative (importing everything) and more familiar to the local workers.

7. Consider the context. If you're building at the coast, as we did in Panama, remember the toll that sun and sea air take. We chose to finish the local hardwoods we're using in the construction with wax, and we're prepared to have to reapply the wax finish regularly. We understand this is not a one-and-done kind of thing. It will be a constant part of the maintenance of the property. We invested in oversized rain gutters because during the winter (rainy) season on this coast, the rain can fall in torrents. And we installed extra insulation beneath our red-clay-tile roof to help control air-conditioning costs over time.

8. Don't pay in full up front for anything. You know this. It's common sense. However, we've gotten into trouble when we've listened to workers' hard-luck stories. Pay something to get the work in question under way, something more at agreed-upon progress benchmarks, and the final amount after all punch-list items have been addressed. Don't be tempted to compromise on that plan.

9. Be sure the construction supervisor can communicate with the workers in their language. In Belize, for example, the primary language is English, but many of the construction workers are Spanish speakers from Central America and Mexico.

Setting Up: Furnishing Your Home and Finding Household Help

How to Furnish Your New Home

Accomplishing the tasks associated with settling into your new home—things like shopping for furniture and appliances—can seem like a great big hassle. Or you can see these getting-settled chores as an opportunity to get to know your new neighborhood and your new neighbors. It helps if you take this sunnier perspective, because, frankly, in some places in the world, finding items like washing machines and dryers, lighting fixtures (which, even when renting, you may be required to supply yourself), refrigerators, and dining room tables and chairs can be a pain in the neck. And expensive, especially if you prefer imported over local—as I do when it comes to washing machines and dryers, for example. In my book, it's worth nearly any expense to ship Maytag machines from the States to wherever we set up housekeeping. The time and hassle savings over years of use outweigh the initial investment.

When we made our first international move and took up residence in Waterford, Ireland, we were wholly unprepared for the frustrations and complications of establishing a new household in a new country. We spent weeks running around in circles, trying to find the best places and the best deals on televisions, telephones, appliances, and kitchenware. Whenever I'd complain about our struggles to friends and family back home, they'd respond with silence. How could it be so time-consuming and so much trouble to buy a refrigerator and a TV?

It's so time-consuming and so much trouble because the language is different (this wasn't the case, strictly speaking, in Ireland, though we still struggled with lost-in-translation confusions trying to shop for things like bathroom fixtures and cabinetry); because shops in some parts of the world sometimes close for lunch, call it a day by five in the afternoon, and aren't open on weekends; because in "mañana" countries, deliveries never arrive at the hour or even necessarily on the day they're promised; and because you're trying to accomplish a great deal in a consolidated period without any existing infrastructure of support or trusted contacts.

In the United States, this kind of shopping is increasingly done online. This is the case in Europe, too, but not in Central America and the Caribbean, for example, where online outlets are more limited and less user-friendly.

If you move into a new home in the States, even if you move to a new state, you bring your old household with you. When you move overseas, this isn't necessarily the case. Unless you decide to ship all your furniture and personal belongings, you're faced with outfitting a bare-walls apartment or house, sometimes, again, including the stove, the oven, the lighting fixtures, even, for example, the doorbell. Back wherever you're coming from, you have established sources for these things, favorite places where you've shopped maybe for years. In your new home, you're at a loss. Your best resources are your fellow expats, and this is where any investment you've made in joining local expat societies or becoming part of online country chat groups begins to pay off.

About eight months after we'd been living in Panama City full time, a friend from San Diego, Chris, decided to move to the Hub of the Americas, too. We helped him with his apartment rental search; then for the first several weeks after he'd moved in, we came to look forward to his near-daily telephone calls. Chris called one day to ask where to go for the best deal on a flat-screen television and another to find out where I'd bought our living room sofa. Where's the best place to shop for lighting fixtures? he wanted to know, and at seven A.M. his first Saturday living in his new apartment, he called to find out if I knew anyone who could install window blinds on short notice. He still didn't have any on his bedroom windows, and the sun in this part of the world, he was discovering to his dismay, rises reliably and bright at five thirty every day.

Chris called to ask where to buy an espresso maker and where to shop for kitchenware in general. He called wondering where to buy an Apple TV, if any store in Panama City sells Ralph Lauren bed linens, and on and on. We were happy to help, of course, and Chris's regular calls reminded me just how much goes into setting up a new household in a new country.

As you work through the process of furnishing and equipping your new home, keep your expectations of yourself in check. This isn't a race. Again, use the experience as a chance to get to know your new community. And understand that wherever you're setting up your new household, certain things are going to seem unacceptable to you, and some things you're looking for won't be available at all. In Ireland, the bath towels, even the most expensive ones, were thin and prickly, so we brought new towels back with us after each visit stateside. In Paris, I could never find a decent floor mop, so I finally bought one of those in the States and flew it across the ocean as well.

In Central America, your furniture options are limited to very high-end and local. In Panama City, Managua, Buenos Aires, Montevideo, and Quito, for example, you can find quality antiques and nice reproductions, but the prices can be shockingly high. Outside these capital cities, your home furnishing options in Latin America in general are more limited. The best choice often can be to find a local furniture maker. Beautiful, made-to-order wooden tables, chairs, bookcases, and cabinets can come very cheap in this part of the world. In Ecuador and Nicaragua, for example, whole towns are given over to particular trades such as handmade furniture, with dozens of family craftsmen following centuries-old traditions and techniques that have been handed down for generations. Take screenshots of pieces you like from the Pottery Barn website, for example, to show to a local woodworker in one of these places and ask how much for him to make something similar. You could finish and furnish an entire house this way for a fraction of the cost of importing or even buying new locally.

Beds are a challenge and have become a running joke in our family. Our children have grown accustomed to odd-sized beds dressed with ill-fitting linens. The mattresses we bought in Ireland didn't quite fit the beds we'd shipped over from the States. The beds we brought with us from Ireland didn't fit in the bedrooms in the apartment we purchased in Paris. The beds we transported to Panama required custom-made mattresses, and the antique headboard I bought upon arrival in Panama City is today, finally, after a series of failed attempts, attached to an appropriately sized frame (though the sheets, from the States, remain too big). My advice: Buy your beds and your bedding locally once you've arrived in the country. Don't try to bring these things with you from elsewhere.

One final tip: When furnishing your new home, try to consolidate household purchases as much as possible. Many shops throughout Latin America, including retail furniture and kitchen stores, will give you a discount (as much as 20 percent) when you buy in quantity.

How to Find Household Help

Our first year in Waterford, we needed plasterers, plumbers, electricians, carpenters, and landscapers, plus someone to help us take care of the pony we'd bought for our daughter and someone to come in once a week to help with household chores. In Paris, when we undertook the renovation of our apartment, we needed someone to build cabinets and bookcases, someone to lay tiles in the kitchen and the bathrooms, someone to rewire the place, someone to install the new bathroom fixtures, and someone to plaster and paint the walls. In both these cities, unlike in the more developing world, it's possible to source these kinds of services online, but that's not how we found any of the tradespeople or vendors we worked with. I tried the local classified route, both print and online, with little success. I'd call a plumber and make an appointment for him to come by to review the work to be done and to prepare an estimate of the cost. He wouldn't show. I'd call back to reschedule. He wouldn't return my call. In France, my limited language skills made every telephone contact a challenge.

So I began asking around, anyone and everyone. To the mother of Jack's friend when she dropped her son off for a playdate: "Would you happen to know a good plumber?" To Jack's teacher at day care in Waterford: "Do you have a painter you've worked with in the past?" To our upstairs neighbor in the apartment building in Paris: "Who cleans the chimneys of your fireplaces each fall?" This is how to source local labor—on the strength of word-of-mouth recommendations. Not every one works out, but your chances of connecting with reliable help are greatly increased with a personal referral.

When we moved to Panama City, we forgot this bit of wisdom and hired our first maid through an agency. Stephanie came with a long résumé and the strong endorsement of the agency. After her first week, I found her so unhelpful that I started taking on her chores myself. Then she began showing up late and calling in sick. Then one day she didn't call, and she didn't show up at all. I took this as an opportunity to part company. When I bemoaned the situation to a friend later in the week, my friend replied matter-of-factly, "What did you expect? You can't hire a maid through an agency. I have a good one. I'll ask her if she has a friend or a family member looking for work. That's how you find a maid."

Our friend's maid had a friend, Olga, who was our maid in Panama for six years. Olga kept the house spotless, ironed the sheets (though I've told her again and again that this wasn't necessary and certainly I never did it myself), prepared dinner for us each evening, and was there when Jack returned home from school each afternoon. Olga became part of the family, and, whenever someone mentioned that she was looking for help, I replied, "I'll ask Olga." Several of Olga's friends eventually were employed helping friends of mine to keep house.

Establishing an Administrative Infrastructure

How to Open a Local Bank Account

One practical key to a successful new life overseas is being able to manage your administrative and financial lives virtually. This way, you don't have to worry about not being able to access an account to get cash, to move money, or to pay a bill. You want these critical functions to be hassle-free, not a distraction in your new life in paradise.

Let's begin with a bank account. Probably you'll need two—one back home in the place where you're moving from and a new one in the place where you're moving to, out of which to pay local bills and expenses.

First, your existing account where you're living now. You probably already have Internet banking set up to check your account balances and maybe to pay your bills online. If not, that's the first step. Go to your bank's website and follow the instructions. If you find that your bank doesn't offer all the services you'll need online, switch banks. You don't want to relocate to another country without the ability to do your banking transactions online.

Specifically, you want to be able to move money (from one account to another or from one country to another, via wire or automated clearing house—ACH—transfer) and to pay bills remotely and electronically. These are the critical criteria, and again, if your current bank doesn't offer these services, find a new bank that does. How are you going to stop in at your bank in Des Moines to initiate a wire transfer if you're living in Medellín?

Now your new account in your new country . . .

The first thing to understand about this item on your Settling In to-do list is that, like everything else in your new home, it's not accomplished the way it would be accomplished in the United States.

In the States, to open a checking account at your neighborhood bank, you walk in, sit down with an account representative, answer a few questions, fill out some forms, and in no time, you've got a bank account. That's not how it works in the rest of the world in this post-FATCA, anti-money-laundering age.

The U.S. wars on terror, offshore havens, and banking, drugs, and money laundering have created stress on banks worldwide to comply with ever-more-onerous "know your client" standards, especially in the case of an American abroad. Furthermore, many countries (including Panama, for example) view opening a bank account not as a right but as a privilege.

Every country's requirements are different, and every bank processes the requirements in its own way. Bottom line, you're going to have to jump through hoops. Depending on the jurisdiction, the process can take weeks or longer.

Generally speaking, you'll need two banking references. If you have only one bank account currently, you might be able to substitute a letter from a credit card company for the second bank reference. You'll also need at least one professional reference—from an attorney or accountant, for example, in the country. The attorney helping with your residency visa (if you're applying for one) or the purchase of your home (if you're buying one) should be happy to help. You'll need two forms of photo identification, typically your passport and a second ID, such as a driver's license. You'll also be required to produce proof of address. Most banks want a utility bill in your name.

Armed with those documents, make an appointment to meet with a bank representative. Yes, you may need an appointment. Better is an introduction or personal referral from someone already doing business with the bank. During your meeting (it will seem more like a job interview or, at some banks in some countries, an interrogation), expect lots of questions. Why are you opening this account? How much money will you be depositing initially? Where is that money coming from? How much money do you expect to receive into the account on an ongoing basis? What will be the source of those funds? How much will you be withdrawing from the account each month?

The paperwork involved will be far greater than for opening a U.S. bank account. Expect reams of forms and required signatures, including a W-9 form, thanks to FATCA. This is all part of creating your file. Once your file (or *dossier*, as it's called in France) has been compiled, it must be reviewed. You'll be told this review process will take a week, but in many cases it can take much longer. Don't be afraid to contact the bank every day to check on the status of your file, lest they lose track of it.

Opening a corporate account is an even greater challenge. For this, you'll need considerably more documentation, and you may have to schedule a personal interview with each of the company's named officers and shareholders. Your file in this case will be reviewed by a committee. The committee's job is to ask for more documentation. No matter how much paperwork you've provided, it won't be enough. Week after week, you'll receive additional requests for further material—additional reference letters, corporate financial statements, financial information on the principals involved with the business, etc. Expect the entire process to take at least two to three months in most countries, even if you're proactive and following up regularly. It took us two years to open a corporate account for my business in Panama, even though we had had personal accounts with the bank for years.

How to Arrange for the Installation of Utilities and Internet

I realize I'm being redundant, but I'll make the point one more time: Like everything else in your new home, arranging for electricity, telephone, cable, and Internet may not be as straightforward an exercise as you might hope. France is one shining exception. I'd say it's easier to organize utilities in this country than anywhere else in the world. When we moved into our apartment in Paris, we made a single phone call to Orange, one of the local service providers, and two days later a "Live Box" arrived at our door, complete with easy-to-follow instructions for installation. We set up the box in a matter of minutes, and voilà, we had telephone, cable, and wireless Internet throughout the entire apartment. Orange support services even include an English-language hotline.

In Paris, we have arranged to pay all monthly utility bills by direct debit—not only Orange charges, but electricity and gas as well. In each case, we gave the utility provider authority to debit our local account on a particular day each month. We don't write a check, lick a stamp, or address an envelope with this setup.

In most of the rest of the world your experience arranging for your utility needs won't be anything nearly as straightforward or as pleasant. In the developing world, dealing with these things will sometimes seem to be the bane of your local existence. You'll need to keep your sense of humor, and sometimes you'll have to get creative in your efforts to stay connected with the rest of the world.

A friend living in Costa Rica tells a good story about his experiences to that end. "When we moved here four years ago," David explains, "we chose a home in the hills, in an area with no high-speed Internet access. We couldn't bear the idea of living with a dial-up connection, so we asked a friend living in the valley below to take out a subscription (for us) to a cable TV service that offered high-speed Internet as an upgrade. This wasn't cheap, as we had to pay for the cable TV (which we didn't use) in addition to the Internet service. Our friend took the signal from the cable modem and, through some clever technology, converted it and beamed it up the hill to a small receiver on the side of our house via microwave. This worked fine. The only downside was that we weren't able to be reimbursed by my wife's employer, as the service was not official and we couldn't provide receipts.

"Some time later, I saw a flyer advertising a new service from Racsa, the monopoly Internet service provider in Costa Rica, called WiMAX. I followed up with the WiMAX people, who sent someone out to check the suitability of our location. We passed the test, and for $800, we were able to install WiMAX high-speed Internet service. Great. Our monthly bills were less than before, and we were official, finally, so we could claim back part of the cost as a business expense. At Christmas, we moved. Internet in the new house was via a local cable TV company. In the dry season, it worked fine. But as soon as the rains started, our service pooped out. Water in the cable joints. We're applying again for the WiMAX service."

Getting a local cell phone can be another challenge. A pay-as-you-go cell phone can be the easiest option and all you need. In Panama you can buy one of these for less than $30 in any electronics store and the pay-as-you-go calling minutes from any pharmacy or grocery store. In Costa Rica, on the other hand, the only available service is by monthly subscription. Plus, tourists and temporary residents in this country can't subscribe to cell phone service (probably because other expats have skipped town without paying their bills). Unless or until you become a permanent resident, you'll have to enlist the help of a local friend willing to arrange a subscription in his name on your behalf.

When arranging in-country services like phone and Internet anywhere in the developing world, remember the mañana factor. Representatives scheduled to appear Tuesday may show up Thursday . . . or not at all. Services scheduled to be installed next week probably won't be. We were resident in our new home in Casco Viejo, Panama, for more than a month before Cable & Wireless finally succeeded in activating our phone and Internet services. We'd contacted them for the first time two weeks in advance of our move. As we were the first to take up residence in the recently renovated house, it was empty at the time. We encouraged the Cable & Wireless representative to meet us or the property manager at the house anytime to connect the appropriate wires and flip the appropriate switches. Having Internet installed and active from our first day living in the house was important to us, so we put ourselves at the Cable & Wireless guy's disposal. Six weeks later, still no phone, still no Internet, although at least six appointments had been scheduled. Either the cable company representative didn't show up on the appointed day and time or he showed up without the proper tools or, we finally realized, expertise to do what needed to be done. During these six weeks, we phoned Cable & Wireless daily and mentioned our woes to our friends and neighbors in passing regularly—not so much to complain as in the hope of finding someone with a good contact high up inside the company. Finally, a neighbor put us in touch with a manager friend of his at Cable & Wireless, who after two more weeks of back-and-forth was finally able to get us connected.

How to Pay Your Bills

Traveling around Panama City, you'll notice kiosks in shopping malls and grocery stores with long lines snaking away from them. Nothing's being sold, so what's going on? Local residents are paying for their utility services.

Throughout most of Latin America, you pay electricity, Internet, phone, and cable bills in person. Sometimes, as in Panama, you do this at a booth in a shopping mall; in other countries, you do it at your bank branch; some places (in Nicaragua, for example), payment must be made in person at each utility's office. The good news is that while payment must be made in person, you needn't necessarily be the person making the payment. Send a proxy, such as your maid or driver, for example. Lines and waiting times can be long.

In Portugal, the Multibanco ATMs are the place to pay your utility bills, among other expenses (including various taxes). If you see someone with a pile of papers in front of you, look for another machine, as they may be a while. However, in Europe in general, monthly bill paying can be put on autopilot, as we did in Paris. You can arrange to pay almost every bill by direct debit. It's convenient, as you don't have to remember to write a check or show up anywhere by any deadline to make a payment. On the other hand, you do have to remember to have enough money in your account to cover the payments on the dates they're to be debited. Bouncing a check in some countries is a far more serious infraction than it is in the United States, and everywhere in the world, it's costly. You'll pay a penalty to your own bank and to whoever tried to cash your check but couldn't. Bounce a check in France, and your account will almost certainly be closed, and it could take months (the worst case I've heard about was three years) to get it reopened. If you've set your bills to be paid by direct debit, make a habit of checking your local account balance online at least twice monthly, say on the first and the fifteenth, to make sure you have as much money in it as you think you do.

How to Satisfy Your Annual Tax Obligations

As I've explained, as an American abroad, you have two tax obligations. No matter where in the world you live or how long you reside there, you are still required to file a U.S. tax return each year. (The one exception is if you earn less than the minimum income filing threshold any year; this amount changes but is about $10,000.)

Generally speaking, therefore, as an American abroad, you must file a U.S. tax return every year no matter where you're residing. This does not mean, however, that you owe U.S. taxes. As I explained in Part I, by taking advantage of the foreign earned income exclusion (FEIE), you can be exempt from U.S. tax on your first $102,100 of earned income in 2017 (the amount is adjusted for inflation annually). Other deductions, exemptions, and double-taxation agreements can reduce tax owed on investment income. As an American abroad, you should not be liable for state tax or, if you're paying social welfare taxes in another jurisdiction, Social Security tax. Yes, this gets complicated, and it's easy to overpay because you're not aware of all the (completely legal) mitigating options available to you. This is why I strongly recommend you seek advice from a U.S. tax attorney or accountant with experience helping Americans abroad manage their U.S. tax burden. The average tax attorney or accountant doesn't qualify, because the average U.S. tax attorney or accountant doesn't understand the FEIE, much less any less standard exemption or deduction.

In our first year living in Ireland, Lief and I engaged the U.S. accountant who'd been doing my taxes for several years to prepare our first returns as Americans abroad. He was uncertain which forms to use and not sure how to account for the foreign earned income exclusion (or even how much of our salaries were exempt from U.S. tax). Lief, an accountant by training, was able to identify the miscalculations and correct for the missed opportunities for savings, but that first year's experience taught us that when it comes to international tax advice, not all accountants are created equal. Lief has prepared our U.S. returns every year since, not because he wants to, but because he was unable to find anyone else we trusted to do the job for us. Your situation may be more straightforward than ours. My point is that you likely are going to need new tax counsel once you launch your new life overseas.

In fact, you're going to need two tax advisers: one in the States and a second in the jurisdiction where you take up residence.

Again, you may not owe tax in your new country. You may not even have an obligation to file. For example, if you live in Panama but earn no income in the country, you have neither a tax liability nor a filing obligation. You want someone who is well familiar with the tax requirements for foreign residents to make these determinations for you, though. And critically, you want to begin the conversation about what your local tax obligations will be before you take up physical residence in the jurisdiction. Important opportunities to mitigate your obligations, whatever they are, can be reduced or eliminated if not addressed before you have a local address.

Note that you don't have to worry about any second, local tax burden whatsoever if you're physically present in your chosen overseas haven fewer than six months per year. Spending fewer than 183 days in a place means you are not considered resident for tax purposes. (Though remember that if you aren't a legal resident of another country for tax purposes and you spend 35 days or more in the States, you can't take advantage of the foreign earned income exclusion.)

If you're not physically present in the United States on April 15, the IRS grants you an automatic filing extension until June 15 (no form required). However, you should still file Form 4868 by April 15 to get a six-month filing extension to October 15.

On the U.S. Internal Revenue Service website, it's Publication 54 that you want to pay attention to. This is the IRS guide for U.S. citizens residing abroad. In it, you'll find more information that will help you manage your U.S. tax obligations once you've taken up residence overseas. Go to www.irs.gov to download a copy.

Getting Around: Owning a Vehicle and Obtaining a Driver's License

How to Buy and Keep a Car in a Foreign Country

Owning a car anywhere is a liability, an expense, and a hassle, so consider first whether you really need one. We spent more than four years in Paris happily car-free. This is a city easily navigated on foot. After living in Panama for a year, my husband and I are just beginning to think about investing in a vehicle. We've gotten to know our way around, and Lief says he's ready to get behind the wheel of a car on these crazy and chaotic Panama City streets. It'll be nice to have a car for weekend trips to the beach and the mountains. On the other hand, owning a car means registering and maintaining a car, and it also means getting a local Panamanian driver's license, which presents a separate challenge that I'll address later.

In Ireland, though, we recognized that we needed a car from the start. Ireland isn't a place you can navigate easily without your own means of transportation. We set aside our first Saturday to go car shopping, only to discover that every car dealership in town was closed. Car dealerships in Ireland kept weekday hours only. Our second surprise, when we returned the following Monday, was the prices. Super-high import duties make even standard cars in this country—Hondas and Toyotas, for example—expensive. We couldn't bring ourselves to spend 50 percent more for a new Accord than we would have in the States, so we decided to buy used instead.

This turned out to be a very fortunate decision. Ireland is one of the most challenging places in the world to be a driver. The narrow, winding country lanes are bordered on both sides by stone walls and dense hedgerows. Outside the country's biggest cities, there are no shoulders, no lane markings, and no streetlights. Around any bend could be a tractor or a Guinness truck, headed seemingly straight for you, as the road is rarely wide enough for two vehicles to pass each other. The farmer on his tractor or the Guinness deliveryman could be followed, over the next hill, by a mother walking her children to school or another farmer leading a flock of sheep from one field to another. You must navigate these obstacles all the while reminding yourself to stay to the left and, most days, trying to see through the rain and fog. During my first month behind the wheel in this country, I scraped three stone walls and two box hedges and got stuck in a ditch. This was all much easier for Lief to handle because our car wasn't fresh off the assembly line.

If your chosen overseas haven is likewise a place where you're going to want to own your own vehicle, you could bring your car with you from home. If you've acquired retiree (or *pensionado*) visa status in your new country, typically the duty associated with importing your car is waived. The only consideration, therefore, is whether the vehicle is appropriate.

Years ago, friends who retired from Canada to Nicaragua decided to bring their van with them. "It'll be great for sightseeing trips within the country," they explained. "We'll be able to load it up and take off for the beach or the mountains whenever we want."

When I spoke with them a few months after their move, they explained that they'd sold the van and bought a truck. A city van, they'd discovered quickly, was no match for this country's roads. By the time they decided to off-load the van, they'd already replaced all four tires and had the front end aligned twice. The van's suspension was shot. In a country like Nicaragua, where many of the roads you use on a regular basis are dirt, rutted, and flooded during the rainy season, you need a four-wheel-drive truck or SUV. Anything else is foolishness.

In Ireland, your U.S. car's steering wheel will be on the wrong side. You see right-hand-drive vehicles on the road in this country, but I think sitting on the wrong side makes navigating these byways even more difficult than it is ordinarily. Different car makes and models are more or less common in different parts of the world, meaning that for some cars in some places, it can be difficult to find either mechanics who know how to repair them or the parts that might be required to make the fixes.

If you want to own a car in your new home, it can be easier and more sensible to buy it there. The key is to be at least as careful during the purchase process as you would be at home. Don't buy the first car you see, and don't buy any car without having it inspected by a local mechanic you trust. Even if you speak the language, take a local shopping with you. Everything, including buying a car, has a protocol that's different from country to country. How much should you expect to be able to negotiate off the sticker price? What warranties or extras are standard? In Panama, used cars bought through a dealership should come with at least a one-month warranty. A local knows these standards.

In the United States, it is possible to shop for and even to purchase a car for the price you want to pay without leaving your home. In the rest of the world, this isn't the case. The car purchase process works like it used to work a couple of decades ago in the States. You've got to invest the time to visit different dealerships, comb the newspaper classified ads, and pound the pavement looking for *Se Vende* signs in car windows.

Before choosing a car, research repair costs. They can vary dramatically for different makes and models. In places like Panama and Nicaragua, repairs are generally much cheaper than in the United States, because labor costs are so much lower. You can have a flat tire repaired at a gas station in Panama for $2. On the other hand, the standard of typical repair work may not be what you expect. Mechanics, especially in the interior of countries like Panama, Nicaragua, and Belize, prefer to weld broken parts back together, for example, rather than replace them.

Know what you must carry in your car. In Panama, you're required to keep an emergency road kit, including flares, in your vehicle at all times, as well as the most current edition of the national driver's handbook (you see them for sale in pharmacies and at newsstands around the country). If you're pulled over for any reason, the traffic officer may ask to see these things.

You pay an annual fee for license plates and vehicle registration everywhere in the world, as you do in the States. However, as can be the case with other bills and expenses in some countries, these fees must be paid in person. Lee, a friend who lived in Ecuador for two years, explains: "In all my time in the country, I never owned a car, but once, I accompanied my roommate on vehicle registration renewal day, an event that takes place sometime during the first quarter of each year.

"The day begins early, as you jockey for position among a hundred other cars in an undersized lot. The hours tick by as two mechanics work their way among the vehicles, checking serial numbers, verifying that you haven't installed a stolen motor since last year.

"But that's just the start. Next, you stand in line to obtain verification that you have no unpaid tickets. Then you stand in line to verify that you haven't changed your address. Then you stand in line for an administrative review. If during any of these exchanges, some uncertainty arises, you typically have to start the process over another day. If, though, you get the A-OK from each of these reviews, then you're set. You get to come back the next day to pick up your new one-year registration. And to wait in line to have it laminated. People wondered how I got along without a car in Ecuador. I wondered why any sane person would keep one."

How to Get a Local Driver's License

You'll be able to drive in your new country for some period on your U.S. driver's license, typically three months to a year. Obtaining a local driver's license in your new country, therefore, isn't a top priority upon arrival, but don't forget to take care of this chore before your free pass to drive on your U.S. license expires. In Panama, you can drive on your U.S. license for three months. As of this writing, Lief has yet to find time to make the trip to the appropriate government agency to apply for his Panamanian license. As a result, he's been fined three times by traffic officers whose paths he's crossed.

Most countries allow you to exchange your U.S. license for a local one or simply to confirm that you have a U.S. license and then issue you a new one. You may have to have your U.S. license "authenticated" at the local U.S. consulate before the in-country authorities will accept it on exchange. It's better for you if the country allows you to keep your U.S. license (rather than exchanging it), as many rental car agencies want to see the same address on your driver's license as on the credit card you're using to pay for the rental.

In some countries, however, you're going to have to qualify for a local license according to the local requirements. Because they drive on the other side of the road, Ireland is one country where this is the case. To obtain an Irish driver's license, you must take both written and on-the-road driving tests. If you've been driving in the States for decades, this may seem silly, but don't be overly cavalier. Study and practice. Some rules of the road in Ireland may surprise you (who has right-of-way in a roundabout, for example), and some driver requirements are unique. Also, you can't just show up to take the test, as you can at the Department of Motor Vehicles in the States. You must apply for an appointment. The wait time for getting one can be as long as a year. Fortunately, Ireland is a country that allows you to drive on your U.S. license for up to a year after becoming a foreign resident.

Becoming Part of Your New Community: Learning the Language and Making Friends

We knew not a soul in Ireland when we moved to Waterford. Looking back now, I realize how much that slowed us down. It took us several years to accomplish in Ireland the things (setting up housekeeping, establishing an office, and finally, developing a circle of local friends) that we accomplished after only a year in Panama. In Panama, our transition from outsider to local (broadly speaking; no one mistakes us for Panamanians when they see us walking down the street, of course) has been seriously fast-tracked.

What's the difference? When we moved to Ireland, we'd visited that country but a handful of times, and for only a week or ten days at a stretch, before becoming residents. On the other hand, Lief and I had been spending time and doing business in Panama, visiting for as long as six weeks at a time, for more than twelve years before we made our move to Panama City. In that time, we'd bought real estate in this city, opened bank accounts, installed Wi-Fi, renovated buildings, hired staff, shopped for appliances. . . .

Before we arrived as full-time foreign residents, we already knew how to get around and where to go for help. We didn't have to place any of those "where do I go to find such and such?" calls that our friend Chris made during his first several weeks in

Panama. We knew from our own experience where to source the things we needed.

You aren't likely going to invest in a dozen years of planning visits to your chosen overseas haven. Indeed, I'd recommend against it. My point is that the better connected you are on the ground in your new home before you arrive, the easier it will be for you to navigate the initial transition from visitor to resident. It's all about who you know. Our friend Chris didn't come and go from Panama City for a dozen years before deciding to move here. Yet his getting-settled curve was slight, because he had our phone number on speed dial.

How can you get yourself connected on the ground in a new country? The Internet. It's not the place to search for a new home to buy or rent. It's not the place to look for an attorney or tax adviser or to shop international health insurance policies. But it is the place to make contact with expats and retirees already living in the countries you're considering. Go to a search engine and type in "expat resources" or "blog" along with the country name. And as I've recommended, read free e-letter services for would-be expats and retirees overseas. You can sign up to receive mine here: www.liveandinvestoverseas.com.

How to Learn a New Language

The best way to learn a new language is to acquire a boyfriend (or girlfriend) in your new home. My daughter, Kaitlin, studied French as a nearly full-time occupation during our first year in Paris. She learned to speak the language, but she didn't become fluent until she started dating a young Frenchman.

Of course, this isn't an option for everyone, as it wasn't for me when we moved to Paris. I don't think Lief would have appreciated my taking this approach to improving my French. I struggled with the language all through our first three years living in Paris. I'd studied French in college, but my university skills didn't get me far two decades later. Finally, a few months before we left Paris for Panama City, I had the opportunity to enroll in an immersion language program. After four weeks of intensive, six-hour-a-day study, I still didn't speak as well as either of my children, but I was pleased with my progress and no longer felt embarrassed conversing with French friends.

My point is that you aren't going to pick up the language of your new country by osmosis. I lived in Paris for years, frequenting the grocery store and the dry cleaner, the bank and my son's French school day after day, and managed to improve my language skills only marginally, because I wasn't making a real effort. I was working in an office with fellow Americans and running an international business in English. At home, too, we spoke English, which provided a break for the kids and ensured that young Jack didn't lose his ability to converse with his parents in their native tongue, but made it difficult for Lief and me to better our French.

In Panama, my Spanish skills improved, thanks to my Colombian maid. Olga arrived every morning at seven o'clock, and she and I spent the next thirty to forty-five minutes reviewing the plan for the day. What would we have for dinner? What special chores needed to be taken care of? How were the plants on the balcony faring? Should we change the bed linens? What time would Jack be home from school? It was basic conversation, but Olga spoke no English, so every word of it was in Spanish. My vocabulary increased day by day, and Olga patiently corrected my grammar.

In both Paris and Panama City, I took to watching the Disney Channel with Jack, in French and then in Spanish, and to watching movies in English with local-language subtitles so I could read along with the dialogue. I forced myself to read the local papers (with a dictionary on hand), and I tried to listen whenever not inappropriate to local-language conversations going on around me when walking down the street or waiting in line in a shop. A friend in Panama used to like to find the Spanish lyrics to her favorite songs online as a way of improving her vocabulary.

That same friend continues to explain, "I moved to Panama knowing *cerveza*, *casa*, and *baño*. I realized quickly that the only way I was really going to learn Spanish was to immerse myself in it. The more independent you are, the quicker you will progress."

If your goal is to learn the language of your new country, avoid other expats as much as possible at the beginning. If you want to put gas in your car, find something in the grocery store, or ask for directions, don't let yourself seek help from an English speaker. And don't be embarrassed to use sign language, pantomime, and other antics to make yourself understood. Encourage people to correct you (as I used to encourage Olga).

Making a focused effort and putting yourself in situations every day where you'll have no choice but to speak the new language, you'll find that you'll begin to understand what's going on around you within a couple of months. It will take a year or longer before you'll feel comfortable at a conversational level.

Breaking the Tourist Barrier

We lived our first two or three years in Ireland as tourists. Not intentionally, but looking back now, I see the mistakes we made. We brought with us from Baltimore the U.S. publishing business I'd been running for the previous thirteen years stateside. Our first priority, after we'd found a place to live and enrolled our daughter in school, was to establish the infrastructure required to transfer management of that publishing operation from the States to Ireland. We needed office space, office furniture, and computers. We needed to hire staff, to open a local bank account, and to engage a local attorney, local accountants, and local auditors. We needed to set up payroll, to put employee contracts in place, and to source new vendors. Between renovating our new home, managing our own relocation adjustments, and addressing these start-up business requirements, we had no time to invest in becoming Waterfordians. When family and friends from the States came to visit, we'd take them to nearby Bantry Bay for the weekend or to Dublin for a day of shopping and museums. We'd do the tourist thing. When they went home, we went back to business. We traveled internationally often. We came and went so regularly during our time in Ireland that the immigration officials at Shannon and Waterford airports came to know and greet us by name.

It's no wonder, then, that we managed to remain tourists in our adopted hometown for years. If not for our children, Kaitlin (who was nine) and Jack (born a year and a half after our move to Waterford), we might have lived our entire seven years in Ireland as visitors. Jack, though, was born Irish and welcomed at his day care and preschool as a son of the Auld Sod. Kaitlin, too, made friends, participated in activities at school, and long before the notion even occurred to Lief and me, began establishing herself as a local. Kaitlin and Jack drew us into their lives. We met their teachers and the parents of their classmates, and we gained a glimpse of real Irish living.

In Paris, we made the same mistakes at first. This time I recognized from the start that we were depriving ourselves of a true Parisian experience, but we had no choice. Again, we were relocating a business, establishing an office, hiring staff. And in Paris, we were working twelve hours a day among fellow English speakers. We were fully insulated from the French-speaking world around us. It was not until our final year as Parisians that we felt we'd begun to penetrate the tourist level of this city. We improved our French, spent more time with local French friends, and joined in neighborhood activities—the annual June street party, for example, when residents of the rue de Verneuil rope off the street, lay red carpets on the ground, and set up tables for French-style potluck—that we hadn't had time for in previous years. As my friend Rose, an American expat resident in Paris for more than ten years, points out, it can take a lifetime to penetrate the French culture.

No argument here. Still, in our final year living there, we enjoyed a clearer view beneath the surface.

In Panama, we worked hard not to repeat the errors of our past lives overseas. Within a year, we were more fully integrated in this country than we had been after seven years in Ireland or four in Paris. We arrived in Panama as full-time residents with an advantage. We'd been spending time and doing business in this country for more than a dozen years before we settled in more permanently. Again, we established a business, hired staff, etc., but we had resources already in place to help with those things, as well as local friends and contacts who made the getting-settled phase easier to navigate. A year on in Panama City, we dined and drank where the locals did, and in these places, carefully guarded secrets from the tourists, we were welcomed as regulars. We ran into friends at markets and fairs, and we were invited to help them celebrate weddings, birthdays, and anniversaries. We stood out as gringos when we walked down the street, but we did our best to blend in otherwise, and we were rewarded with a chance to experience *la vida Panamena*.

The key to assimilating is to make local friends. You want expat friends, too, of course. You want to know fellow English speakers you can call for a round of golf, a game of gin rummy, or a drink after a particularly frustrating day in the land of mañanas and fiestas. But try not to give in to the temptation to spend all your time with fellow foreigners. They won't be able to show you what local life is really like. You could live overseas for years, as we have done, without gaining that knowledge, but you're doing yourself a disservice. Why go to all the trouble of relocating to another country only to miss out on the chance to get to know what living in that place is really like?

How do you get started penetrating the tourist barrier? You understand and embrace the local customs and etiquette. This is a simple but effective first step. Much of the rest of the world is more polite and takes manners more seriously than we Americans do. In much of the world, it's impolite not to greet everyone and anyone you encounter throughout the day. In France or Panama, for example, walking in and out of a shop, getting on and off an elevator, entering and exiting a movie theater, an art gallery, or a café, you'll be thought very rude if you don't offer the appropriate greetings and farewells.

Before you arrive in your new country, therefore, make an effort to know these phrases: *bonjour, salut, au revoir, à bientôt,* and *bonne nuit . . . buenas días, buenas tardes, hola, hasta luego,* and *ciao . . .* know a handful of polite phrases and understand how and when to use them. Panamanians, for example, switch from *buenos días* to *buenas tardes* at noon and to *buenas noches* when the sun goes down. The French will think you poorly raised indeed if you do not offer a *merci* and an *au revoir* to every person you encounter when making your way out from a shop. Address every single person you pass, at least once. As you walk out the door, you might offer a final general *merci, au revoir* to the entire place. My friend John tells of an experience he had early on during his time living in Paris, when he offered but a single *merci, au revoir* to the cashier in the bakery where he stopped to buy bread on his way home. He said this "thank you, good-bye," then walked out the door. The proprietress of the shop was so appalled by my friend's lack of acceptable manners that she followed him out into the street to lecture him on proper social conduct. In France, when in doubt, it never hurts to offer one more *merci* for the road.

The point is to make an effort to show your respect for the local customs. This small thing will ingratiate and open doors for you. It's the start of penetrating the tourist barrier and becoming part of the local scene. What's polite and what's not, country to country? Two good resources for reference are www.kwintessential.co.uk/resources/guides and www.culturecross ing.net.

How to Make New Friends

Our first friends in Ireland were tradesmen. Lief and I both were working full time, departing for the office early each morning and returning home in time for dinner each evening, leaving little opportunity for socializing. Whatever free time I had during our first two years in the country I invested in renovating and then furnishing and decorating the old house in the country we'd bought to make our new home. The general contractor for the project, Noel; the crew Noel brought on board to carry out the work, including the redheaded lovable ox of an Irishman called Liam; the cabinetmaker, John, we engaged to build our new kitchen and the bookcases for the library; the architect, David, who drafted plans for converting one of the barns into a guesthouse—these people became our first and eventually our closest friends in Waterford, and we stay in contact with them still.

I like old houses the way some women like new shoes. They're a hobby for me, my preferred preoccupation. In Noel, John, and David, I found kindred souls. We enjoyed our long days together tearing out walls and building in bookcases. How do you like to spend your free time? Whatever your favorite hobby, you'll find like-minded enthusiasts in your new home, if you make the effort to seek them out. This is the best way to begin to build a new circle of friends.

In addition, worldwide, general expat organizations welcome

new members. My friend Lucy, living in the South of France, recommends the International Women's Club (known as the IWC; go to your search browser and type in "International Women's Club" plus the name of the city or country where you'll be living to find the local chapter), a group of expat women who meet monthly. Many nationalities are represented, including French, English, German, Dutch, American, and Danish. In France, where Lucy belongs to the IWC, the monthly meetings are conducted in English and French, and the annual membership fee is $38. The husbands of IWC members also go on excursions and organize regular meetings.

In addition to fellow expats living in your new hometown, you want to make an effort to get to know your local neighbors as well. To meet locals, hang out where they do. Eat at the restaurants where they eat. Learn basic phrases—for example, "It's hot out today"—as conversation starters. Even such a simple gesture will get you a smile, a friendly response, and maybe a new friend.

In France, our first local friends were the parents of Kaitlin's and Jack's classmates at school. It's true we were working full time and had little time for random socializing, but we made time for parent-teacher meetings and other school functions. As Kaitlin and Jack made friends, they were invited to birthday parties and playdates and wanted to invite their new playmates over to our apartment. We made friends with the parents of our children's friends by default, and through them were introduced to others in our neighborhood.

I have to admit, though, that our local friend-making efforts in Ireland, France, and Panama were limited. Not so the efforts of my friend Thom.

Thom, a perpetual solo traveler, made an art and a science of making friends in new places. Thom liked music and played the six-string. He carried his guitar with him wherever he went, through airports, train stations, and hotel lobbies all over the world. Before arriving in a new town, Thom would research local live-music venues on the Internet. Shortly after arrival, he'd stop in at one, sit down at the bar, strike up a conversation with the bartender, and soon enough, get himself invited to pull out his guitar and play a little. Thom kept all these music lovers' venues and contacts in his cell phone. As soon as he made the acquaintance of a barkeep, a doorman, a club proprietor, or a fellow musician anywhere in the world, he'd ask the fellow (or lady) to type in his (or her) name and phone number into his phone. Thom coded the entries in such a way that he could search them by location. Next time he arrived in town, he'd call up these local resources and friends. And this time when he showed up for open mic night at any of the venues where he'd already introduced himself, he'd be greeted, as he walked through the door, with a hearty, "Hey, Thom! You're back! Did you bring your guitar?"

Thom had cards printed with his name and cell phone number. These he handed out everywhere he went. Each time he gave someone one of his cards, he'd make a note on the back—"This is Thom, the guy who likes to play guitar," or "This is Thom, the guy you met in Club Such and Such."

Thom came to visit us in Ireland often. After his first couple of stays, when I'd accompany him for a night out, I was shamed. We'd open the door to Geoff's, for example, one of Thom's preferred pubs in Waterford, and everyone in the place, nearly in unison, would shout, "Thom!" I'd been living in the country for more than two years at this point. No one in Geoff's knew my name, but everyone knew Thom.

How to Make the Most of Your New Life

As I've explained, during our first two years in Waterford, we were all-out occupied establishing our business and renovating our house. We drove into the office early each day and spent each evening and every weekend working, either on the business or on the house. The truth is, we ignored everything else around us and managed to live in Ireland's Sunny South East a long time before seeing anything much of it.

Don't make this mistake. From the day you arrive, make a point of getting out and getting around. Go out into your new town every day. See what people do; observe how they spend their time. Even if you have a car, walk as much as possible at first until you get to know your way around. Stop in at the shops you pass, linger in the restaurants and the cafés. Expand little by little beyond your comfort zone. Take day trips. Take weekend getaways to the beach or the mountains. Try to get lost.

Wherever you go, the lifestyle you enjoy will be up to you. A friend moved to Paris several years ago. He was working for a U.S. publishing company with an office there. He rented a studio apartment near his office, and his circle of activity was restricted to the several surrounding blocks. He walked to work in the morning. He stopped at the shop on the corner on his way home for something to take away for dinner. Then he returned to his tiny apartment, where he sat on his sofa to eat alone and then to read until he fell asleep.

When I asked him how he liked Paris, he replied, "It's okay, I guess. There's not much to do, really."

Not much to do? In *Paris*? Even within the few blocks surrounding his apartment, there were restaurants and bars, a movie theater, a bookstore, and a Métro stop. My friend could have dined at a different café or bistro every night of the week or hopped on the Métro to arrive on the doorstep of any of the city's myriad attractions within a matter of minutes. My friend saw nearly nothing of Paris before he decided to leave it. He didn't return to the States; rather, he took a new position with another international publishing group, this time in Australia. I've not spoken to him since, and I wonder sometimes if he's enjoying a greater variety of diversion Down Under than he did in the City of Light.

My experience of Paris was completely contrary to that of my friend. When I realized that we were in fact going to be able to arrange to spend time in this city indefinitely, it was the realization of a dream I'd held since girlhood. I was nearly jumping-up-and-down-on-my-bed giddy as we prepared for the move. "I hope you're not disappointed," Lief remarked one day. "I hope living in Paris is everything you expect it to be."

Lief need not have worried. Nothing about Paris proved a disappointment. Part of the reason my Parisian experience was so rich and full, I realize, though, was because I made it that way. I made time nearly every day for what I came to think of as a Paris indulgence. Some mornings I'd leave the apartment earlier than usual for my walk to the office. This way I'd have time to linger as I crossed the river and then again as I traversed the Tuileries

Garden of the Louvre. This was my daily commute, and never did I come to take it for granted.

Some evenings I'd leave the office earlier than usual so I'd have time to stop for a glass of wine at my favorite brasserie, around the corner from our apartment, before returning home for dinner. I'd savor every sip as I watched the sun setting over the Seine and my fellow Parisians coming and going.

As many Sundays as possible, we'd arrange to meet friends in the park at the tip of the Île de la Cité. On this grassy, flower-fringed spot, with the River Seine flowing by on two sides, we'd spread a blanket, lay out the bread, cheese, and other picnic things we'd brought with us, open a bottle of wine, and sit back to chat away the afternoon while our children ran and played all around us.

No one took better advantage of our time in Paris than our daughter, Kaitlin. Age fourteen when we moved to the city and eighteen when she returned to the States for college, Kaitlin was at an ideal time in her life to soak up all that the French capital has to offer. She went to a museum a week, sometimes two. She and her friends frequented jazz clubs, gallery openings, and concerts of every description. She spent Saturday mornings shopping at the city's flea markets for vintage fashion and Sunday afternoons at the Shakespeare and Company bookstore browsing for secondhand classics. If we wanted to spend time with her, we had to schedule it in advance. Kaitlin was perpetually previously engaged.

That's the point, isn't it? I've been preparing you for how challenging and frustrating your new life overseas will sometimes be. Why suffer through all the challenges and all the frustrations if you don't also fully exploit all the benefits and all the advantages?

PART V

OVERCOMING CHALLENGES AND CULTURAL DIFFERENCES

Some days, once you've settled into your new home abroad, you'll be frustrated, paralyzed, maybe even driven to the point of loud screams by the paperwork, the bureaucracy, the inconsistencies, the inefficiencies, the unexpected.

Here's the key to happiness in your new life overseas: recognizing and accepting that any place you go is going to have its own ways of doing things. Those ways will be different from what you've known all your life until now. For the sake of your sanity, you must give up the notion that the "American way" is better. Sometimes, in truth, it can be. But sometimes the new ways have their own benefits. Embrace the differences. They're part of the adventure.

It can be easier to adjust to the cultural differences and challenges of your new life overseas if you have some idea what they are going to be before you get there. In this section, therefore, I introduce you to the greatest perils and pitfalls you're likely to encounter as you launch a new life in a foreign country.

Margarita Madness

Rum and real estate don't mix. You want to be sober when considering property purchase options in a foreign land. Certainly you want your wits about you when it comes time to sign on the dotted line. The trouble is, in the land of mañanas and fiestas, the rum flows, and so do the promises. The key to success navigating overseas, especially in developing-world real estate markets, is avoiding the liquor and turning a deaf ear to the assurances.

Here's how this will go. You'll arrive in the country where you're dreaming of launching your new life. In the terminal of the airport, the lobby of your hotel, and the restaurant down the street where you go for lunch, you'll be approached by friendly fellows with houses and beachfront lots to sell. Every taxi driver, every bar owner, every shopkeeper will have a piece of property for sale or a brother or a cousin in the real estate business. You won't have to seek out agents or developers to help you find your new home. They'll find you.

Once, in Granada, Nicaragua, I was early for a lunch meeting with a friend and decided to sit on a stool at the bar of the restaurant while I waited for him to arrive. Two minutes later, a fellow gringo sat down beside me.

"Hello," he offered. "Have you just gotten into town?"

"Yes," I replied.

"Well, if you'd like a tour of the city, I'd be happy to oblige. Are you having lunch? I'd love to keep you company. I could tell you about Granada. This is a beautiful town with a long and colorful history. I've been living here for five years. I know the place well. Are you thinking of moving here?"

"No," I replied.

"It's a great place to live. And real estate is a great bargain. This is the time to buy. Do you like old buildings? The old colonial haciendas of this city are a treasure. I know of two available right now for very good prices. These are the best buys in the city. Both are owned by friends. I could take you to see them after lunch if you'd like."

"I'm meeting a friend. I don't think I have time for a real estate tour today," I explained.

"Well then, maybe tomorrow. As I said, I've been in this city for five years. I know it better than anyone else you're going to find. In fact, I'm the local representative for Live and Invest Overseas. I've been working with the publisher of that organization, Kathleen Peddicord, for years. Maybe you've heard of her? Kathleen has been writing about investing and retiring in Nicaragua for a long while."

I'd never seen this man before, and clearly he'd not met me until this chance bar encounter. I didn't make an issue of these facts but let the fellow finish his pitch. Finally my friend arrived, and I was able to break away. I never ran into this particular gringo Granada property expert again, but the story of my brief exchange with him has stayed with me, because it's a good example of the absurd lengths these guys will go to to hook a buyer.

As I said, in these markets, the challenge isn't finding a real estate agent to show you around. These "experts" pick you out by the color of your skin, your dress, your gait, and your posture as you walk down the street. The challenge isn't finding one to take you shopping; it's finding one you feel comfortable doing business with. The best strategy is to speak with as many as possible and to take nothing any one of them tells you at face value.

Likewise, property developers in these kinds of emerging Wild West markets should be treated with skepticism, as should the promises they make about whatever it is they're building. When shopping with developers in an emerging market, it's important to buy only what you see, not what you're told is coming. The developer in question will drive you out to his beach. There, at the shore, he'll have erected a small clubhouse. Come in, have lunch, enjoy a drink, he'll say. The fish is fresh. My guys caught it just offshore from our beach this morning. And the rum is local.

After you've eaten your fill, the developer will take you out in his four-by-four or maybe on horseback to explore the beach and the surrounding countryside. As the sun is beginning to slip behind the horizon and the ocean's surface is glittering and dazzling, the sky behind it turning fire red and orange, the developer will begin pointing. Over there, he'll say, is where the new clubhouse will be constructed. What you see today is only temporary. Down there will be the dock, and over there, the marina. On the hills all around us will be the houses. Just look out there. Look at that sunset. This could be the view from your front porch. You could have a front-row seat for this show every evening.

Come on, he'll continue. Let's head back to the clubhouse. It's time for some Sundown Rum Punch.

You're smitten. Who wouldn't be? There's nothing wrong with appreciating what's being put on the table in front of you. The coasts of Nicaragua, Panama, Belize, and the Dominican Republic, for example, are special and extraordinarily beautiful. Seeing them for the first time can make you weak in the knees. The feeling can be something like falling in love. Don't resist it. Allow yourself to savor it. But don't so lose your balance that you marry the first beach that charms its way into your heart. Ask yourself, is this the beach you want to grow old with?

Enjoy the developer's hospitality, his fresh fish, even his rum cocktails. Let him make his pitch. Then take your leave. Go find out what the guy at the next beach has to offer. And the beach after that, all the while keeping in mind the fundamental rule of purchasing real estate in a foreign country: Buy only what you see.

The first developer who took you out showed you where the new clubhouse would be. He showed you where the dock, the marina, and all the houses would be built. If you give the guy some benefit of the doubt, you can believe that he fully intends to deliver on every promise he's suggesting. But remember, here in the land of mañanas and fiestas, things don't always go as you expect them to go. Will there be a marina? The only thing you know for certain is that there is no marina right now. That's the reality you should act on. Think about it this way: If the marina was never built, would you still be happy living here? If there was never a newer, bigger clubhouse, would your experience of the place diminish?

The what-ifs can be more critical. Sometimes the stretch of beach the developer takes you to see is nothing but a stretch of beach. No roads, no electricity, not even stakes in the ground to mark off individual lots. I've been taken to see planned private communities on stretches of the coasts of Nicaragua, Panama, Mexico, and Belize, for example, where "buy only what you see" amounted to an investment in sand, surf, and sun. Depending on your circumstances, your level of risk tolerance, and your timeline for making your move, maybe a deeply discounted, early-in purchase of a beautiful stretch of white sand, azure sea, and tropical sunshine is just what you're looking for. My point is to be clear in your purchasing objectives and to pay for only what you see when you're buying. Don't pay all-services-in prices for not-a-single-service-anywhere-in-sight real estate.

And don't buy anything on a first visit. If you were moving from Chicago, Illinois, to Santa Fe, New Mexico, would you take one trip to Santa Fe, tour around for two days, then contract to buy the first house you saw available for sale? A house offered to you by a guy you met over drinks in a bar the night before? The answer is probably no. You want to be more careful shopping for real estate in another country, where the language, the customs, the culture, the way of doing business, and the property purchase process are all foreign, than you would be back home, not more cavalier. In the unregulated markets south of the Rio Grande, you don't have the safety nets you count on back home. What if the guy offering to sell you a house isn't in fact the owner of that house? What if you don't discover this fact until after you've handed over payment? What is your recourse? In truth, you likely don't have any. There's no Better Business Bureau, Department of Housing, district attorney's office, or local congressman to contact for help, and people in the rest of the world don't sue one another the way we Americans do. You aren't going to find an attorney in Nicaragua, Belize, or most any other developing market to take your case. You must protect yourself, because no one else is standing by to protect you or to help you make things right should something go wrong.

The best way to protect yourself is to engage your own attorney to represent you through the purchase process, one who works not for the seller, the real estate agent, or the developer, but for you. You want your own independent attorney whose agenda and loyalty are clear.

Finally, you want to buy only what you see and to make sure that your vision is clear. I enjoy a local rum cocktail at sunset as much as the next girl, but I've learned to wait until the effects wear off before I begin talking business.

The Language Barrier

I've joked about our struggles understanding and being understood by the Irish when we lived among them. There's a lesson in this experience, though, that should be taken seriously. Just because a non-American in another country speaks English doesn't mean he knows what you're saying to him. There's American English, Irish English, British English, and Belize English. Then there's the English that a Panamanian kid learns by watching MTV and the English of a German national who studied it as a child in school and has spent most of her life since speaking Spanish. There's the English of a Nicaraguan architect who went to college in the States twenty years ago and the English of a Chinese shopkeeper in Buenos Aires. I didn't invent these examples. I've known people matching each of these descriptions.

With all these folks, you could carry on a conversation about what you had for dinner last night. Would you, though, be able to explain your travel plans or your ideas for your house renovation to them over the phone without worry of misunderstanding? Would you trust them to understand the details of a property purchase contract?

In Ireland, my father, in the country for a month to help with our house renovation, spent an entire morning traveling from hardware store to hardware store in Waterford in search of solder. He needed it to finish the plumbing work in the master bathroom. Only after he'd inquired at three hardware stores, where in each case the gentleman behind the counter had looked at him quizzically and insisted he'd never heard of the stuff, did he find a fourth hardware store owner able to translate from my father's American-English pronunciation of the word to the Irish-English pronunciation of the word. It's spelled the same way in both languages, but the saying of it is distinct enough one to the other that the meaning is lost in translation.

We've had countless experiences over the years when someone we're working with in another country, someone who we believe speaks English fluently, doesn't follow through as we believe we've agreed he or she would. At first we chalked the unmet expectations up to the mañana factor. Then we realized there was another factor at work. Although the person would appear to speak English fluently, he or she wasn't processing our offhand references as they were intended.

One year in Ireland, we had an au pair from France, Elizabeth, a nice young girl who maintained that she spoke English. I interviewed her in Paris over lunch. We had an easy, pleasant conversation and worked through the details of her employment with us. It wasn't until weeks later, just before her start date, that I realized she'd in fact understood very little of what I'd said to her that day over lunch in Paris. I'd explained to her that during her first weeks with us, we'd be traveling to Nicaragua and Panama for an extended business trip. We wanted to bring young Jack with us, which meant she'd be coming along as well, to mind him on the road. She had not understood these details at all and showed up to start work with no idea that a transatlantic flight was in her immediate future. Fortunately she was okay with the idea, but we could have had a big problem if she'd decided she wasn't.

Until you're certain of the level of comprehension on the other end of any conversation with a non-American anywhere in the world, keep your vocabulary simple. Avoid colloquialisms and slang. Speak literally, and especially for important and business conversations, review the key points two or three times, even asking the person you're speaking with to repeat back for you what he or she thinks has been discussed and agreed.

Also, don't assume that you can trust someone simply because he does in fact speak fluent American English. In some places in this world, a local who speaks English the way you and I speak English is the last guy you want to cultivate as a friend or business associate. How and why has he or she learned to speak so cozily with Americans? you sometimes have to wonder.

The Hassle Factor

"He's peering through a different set of lenses," my friend David remarked once. "He hasn't learned to check his expectations at the border." David was reflecting on a conversation he'd had with a colleague of his from the States who'd recently made his first trip south of the Rio Grande.

"He complained that the staff at the hotel where I suggested he stay in San José, Costa Rica, didn't speak English," David continued. "In fact, the staff at that hotel does speak English. Just not rapid-fire American English. Nor could the staff, I guess, readily understand that variety of English when it was spoken to them.

"I take a different view," David, who hails from the United Kingdom, went on. "The way I see things, I'm a guest here in this part of the world. I'm the outsider. I bend to accommodate. I don't expect staff in a Costa Rica hotel, for example, to speak Her Majesty's English. But if I speak slowly and carefully and I allow them to do the same, we understand each other fine."

The United States is the most comfortable and convenient place on earth. Nowhere else is day-to-day living as easy. In the United States, you can buy anything, do anything, engage any service you might need or want, nearly any day of the year and nearly any time of the day, simply by making a Google inquiry and sending a few emails or making a few phone calls. Living in Baltimore, I was able to find someone at eight A.M. one New Year's Day to repair my broken water heater. I'd discovered a flood in the basement the night before and had to call only three plumbers to find one who not only answered his phone early on a holiday morning, but also agreed to come right over to make the fix for me.

I promise you that, no matter where you move, even if it's to another first-world nation such as France, you will not find this same standard of easy living. Years ago, I met someone in the States who'd just returned from his first trip to Latin America. He'd spent a week in Panama. "The television channels were all in Spanish," he complained. "And the television in my hotel room was an old rabbit-eared set. Plus," he continued, appalled, "many of the police cars didn't have brake lights. Some of the fire trucks I saw were vintage World War II. And the restaurants couldn't understand that I wanted ice in my iced tea."

This fellow, like the gentleman my friend David described, hadn't checked his expectations at the border. As a result, his experience in Panama was a great big letdown, so disappointing that he abandoned his plans to relocate overseas altogether.

Another friend from the States, Andrew, decided recently to divide his time between California and Panama City. He came to Panama to outfit his new apartment, and he needed cash to buy new furniture and appliances, to pay the painter, etc. So he went to the Panama City bank where he'd held an account for more than a year to make a withdrawal. Alas, he'd forgotten his checkbook back in the States. No check, no cash, the bank teller explained.

"What do you mean?" Andrew asked incredulously. "I have money in my account. I'd like to withdraw some of it, please." After an extended back-and-forth, finally an option was offered. Go stand in that line over there, the teller suggested, and get a cashier's check. Andrew did as instructed. He stood in line for an hour and a half for the privilege of paying $10 for a cashier's check drawn on his own account. Then he stood in another line for another thirty minutes to cash it.

"Maybe you should move your account to another bank," I suggested when Andrew told me his sad tale. "Oh, no, no," he replied, "this is the best bank in the city." In other words, all banks in Panama City—indeed, all banks in this part of the world—are as inconvenient to deal with. Customer service is not a priority. Living and doing business here, you take this as a given and expect that every banking experience will be frustrating and nonsensical. You adopt this position, or you put your sanity at risk.

I remember one day, shortly after we'd moved to Panama, when Lief came bursting into the office dripping wet. "The window in my taxi was broken," he explained. "A few minutes after I got in, the skies opened. It rained buckets. I tried to close my window, but the handle was broken off. The driver reached back to hand me a pair of pliers. I tried again to close the window using the pliers, but the driver began shouting at me in Spanish, 'Not like that, not like that!' I wasn't doing it right, I guess. I never did manage to get the window to close. Rain poured in on me all the way over here."

Lief was returning to the office from our new house in Casco Viejo, where he'd gone to meet the Cable & Wireless fellow who had been promising to install Internet for us for weeks. Lief had gone from one maddening experience to another.

"The guy kept insisting that the only way for us to have Internet would be to run a cable from our neighbor's place along the sidewalk in between the two houses. I was trying to tell him that that sounded like a ridiculous strategy, when our neighbor on the other side, who happened to be sitting outside on his balcony, spoke up to say that our house was already wired for Internet. The cables for both his house and our house had been run underground at the same time, he explained. Our neighbor had a copy of the schematic. He went inside to get it to show to the Cable & Wireless guy, who was dumbfounded by what it indicated. Finally the cable guy left in a huff. Our neighbor said not to worry, though, because he has a friend at Cable & Wireless who should be able to sort us out."

Indeed—except that, when we inquired, our neighbor's friend at Cable & Wireless was away on vacation, meaning we went two weeks more without Internet at home.

So it goes in paradise.

Managing Your Expectations

It helps if you can keep some perspective, if you can remind yourself, for example, that Panama is a Spanish-speaking country in the tropics. That means the people in this country speak Spanish, and the weather is hot. Ambergris Caye, Belize, is an island in the Caribbean. That means its sandy beaches sometimes swarm with insects.

Here are other fundamental truisms it can be helpful to remember as you prepare for your adventures overseas:

Nicaragua is a third-world country. Sometimes the electricity goes out—why, nobody can explain, and for how long, nobody can predict.

The people in Nicaragua, like those throughout the developing world and in fact everyone in Europe, don't see ice in your drink as a requirement.

The French invented the word for "bureaucracy." That means that, to address any administrative task in France, you're going to have to wade through a lot of it.

In France, as in most of the world (unlike in the United States), renters are favored over landlords, and employers are assumed to be in the wrong if any employee dispute arises. If your employee is caught stealing from you on video, it's your fault.

Latinos are loud. Their parties are loud. They play their music loud. They honk their car horns . . . loud.

There are snakes in the jungle but not, typically, cell towers (your cell phone probably won't work).

Although San José, Costa Rica, is the country's capital and seat of government, there are few street signs. The Costa Ricans are not bothered by this. There are few street signs in all of Ireland. The Irish don't mind. There's no national to-your-door mail delivery service in Panama. The Panamanians don't give this a second thought. In some parts of the world, banks and other businesses close for lunch. Many countries have yet to embrace the idea of twenty-four-hour grocery and convenience stores. Almost all of non-tourist Paris shuts down for the entire month of August. For those four weeks, good luck finding a plumber who'll take your call or a *notaire* who'll schedule your apartment closing.

Unlike the United States, the rest of the world takes its holidays seriously. Latin America is a Catholic region, which means that, in addition to all other holidays, the people in this part of the world also take off Catholic feast days. And not only do the countries of Latin America and Europe have more holidays than the United States, but they also extend them. As the French put it, they *faire le pont*—that is, they "make the bridge"—between the actual holiday and the nearest weekend. In Panama, the bridge can extend through an entire week. During Carnaval and other important celebrations, the bridge can extend the full month, and the entire country crosses it. You aren't going to be able to conduct any business. I've found that the wisest strategy is to give up trying. Join the rest of the country out in the streets for the fiesta.

My friend Paul tells a great "when in the land of fiesta, join the party" story. "I wanted the four thirty P.M. bus to Mendoza," Paul begins, "and, as I boarded, my watch showed it was four twenty. I said to the driver, 'This is the four thirty bus to Mendoza, right?'"

The driver: "This is the three thirty bus to Mendoza."

Paul: "But it's already four twenty."

The driver, after a few moments of reflection: "Well, you could say this is the four thirty bus."

"Argentina," Paul continues, "had just switched to daylight saving time. Unlike in the United States, though, or in, say, France or England, in Argentina, some people go along with the new time, others don't. The way Argentines look at it, it's a matter of personal choice. You have your time. I have my time. And on that bus to Mendoza, the driver had his.

"When we arrived at our destination in Mendoza, the monitors in the terminal, like the bus driver, were on old time. However, the buses leaving that terminal ran on new time.

"The next day," Paul continues, "I was in a wine shop that was about to close for the midday siesta. I asked, 'What time do you reopen?' The owner replied, 'Six thirty.' As I was leaving, I noticed the sign on his door. It indicated he intended to reopen at five thirty.

"Last week a friend was scheduled to drop by at eleven A.M. He came at noon. 'When we scheduled the appointment,' he explained, 'we were on old time. So I figured you'd want me to show up on old time.'"

Ridiculous? Absolutely, as far as I'm concerned. I think life becomes simpler if we agree on a common time. But Argentines place no value on simple, no importance on order, efficiency, agreement, or uniformity. None.

So it never occurs to an Argentine that, for the sake of simplicity, we should agree on a common time, vocabulary, currency, handwriting, or weights and measures. Simplicity doesn't matter. Argentines value other things, like honor, friendship, and most important, individuality and personal whim.

"Several years ago," Paul goes on, "my wife, Vicki, and I spent the summer on a ranch in Uruguay with several Argentine families. In those days, Uruguayan time was an hour ahead of Argentine time, yet I heard the kids referring to Argentine time. I found the confusion intolerable and called everyone together. 'Let's decide,' I proposed. 'Should we use Uruguayan time? Or should we stay on Argentine time?' The kids unanimously chose to stay on Argentine time (that is, another country's time). Fine. We were all agreed.

"The next morning, someone proposed going to town at ten A.M. The response from the group? 'Argentine time . . . or Uruguayan time?' In only twenty-four hours, the agreement had fallen apart. I surrendered. Finally I saw the wisdom in Vicki's way of dealing with things like time in places like Argentina. When invited for dinner, Vicki cheerfully asks, 'American time [that is, roughly on time] or Argentine time [that is, an hour or so late]?' Now, with daylight saving time, she asks, 'American time or Argentine time—new or old?' My advice: When in Argentina, tell time like the Argentines."

Often it can be the things that first drew you to a place that cause you the greatest levels of frustration in the long run. A friend in Panama explains that when she told her family back in Canada she intended to make this move, her mother wanted to know why Panama. "I explained to her," Rebecca says, "that I appreciated the way Panamanians approach life. They work because they have to, and they make it a point to enjoy their time off. They don't take work as seriously as we do in North America, and they don't worry about keeping up with the Joneses."

Rebecca's position today? "In the beginning, I found this charming, but not anymore," she admits. "Today this aspect of Panamanian life drives me up the wall!"

The Mañana Factor

"Mañana" doesn't mean tomorrow. A friend living in South America for years maintains that mañana means "Relax, nobody is dying here. Slow down. Take it easy. You're going to give yourself a heart attack. Tomorrow is another day."

Another friend, Lee, has adopted a more cynical definition. "After eight years in Latin America," Lee says, "the charm of mañana has worn off. It took me a few years to reach this point. It took my wife, Julie, a few weeks. I've found that mañana is not an issue with people who respect your time and can keep their word. But in most of the world these kinds of people are few and far between. In most of the world, mañana means 'I can't keep a commitment, and I can't keep my word.'

"It means, 'Yes, I promised this morning that I'd be there today, but I didn't mean it. Maybe mañana.' Or 'I know you've changed your plans to wait for me, but it's time you realized that your time has no value, at least not to me. Maybe mañana.' And sometimes it means, 'I know I promised to pay, and the promise still stands, but let's talk about it mañana.'"

The mañana approach to living isn't restricted to Latin America. The Irish don't use the word "mañana," but they sure do embrace the concept. The punch line to a joke Irish friends once told us goes something like "Mañana? Oh, no, the Irish don't have a word to express that level of urgency." In other words, Lief and I have struggled with the mañana approach to life ever since we moved from the States, first in Waterford, more recently in Panama City. I have a greater tolerance for it than Lief. He had had enough of mañana within about twenty-four hours of arriving in Waterford, where in some ways, the syndrome was a bigger problem for us than it's been in Latin America.

The stories we could tell, about Irish plumbers who never showed up or, worse, who showed up to start a job but never returned to finish it. Sometimes we'd run into these same blokes at the local pub in the evening, on the same day when they had promised to be at our home continuing their labors but had never appeared. We've got tales of electricians, plasterers, painters, and landscapers in the Auld Sod who made appointments they didn't keep, who missed days, weeks even, of work without ever offering an explanation. These "professionals" would agree to be at our house, say, Thursday at ten A.M., then they'd show up the following Tuesday at four P.M. Every one of them was surprised that we were surprised when they turned up days late, and they seemed not to understand the question if we dared ask what had kept them away.

Everyone's tolerance for the mañana factor is different. After a while, though, it wears every expat down. Your perspective changes so that, eventually, you're surprised when someone anywhere in the world actually shows up when he says he will, returns on time, or finishes a job as scheduled. After decades of mañana in countries around the world, I find that my expectations have been reduced to zero. Today, when someone keeps his word or when some event actually transpires as expected or promised, I'm amazed and delighted.

It does happen, though. Sometimes things do work out. After a year in a condo tower in downtown Panama City, we realized that high-rise living wasn't for us. We arranged to move to Panama City's old town, Casco Viejo, with its brick-paved lanes and centuries-old French- and Spanish-colonial buildings, plazas, squares, and gardens. It wasn't an international move, just a relocation from one end of Panama City to the other. Still, we prepared ourselves for the worst.

We'd engaged the moving company to come the day before the move to pack our household contents in their entirety, so that morning we walked out the door and headed for the office, hoping for the best but fully expecting some less than optimal outcome.

That evening, Lief returned home before I did. He called to report, "There's not a fork, not a glass that hasn't been wrapped and put into a carton. And every stick of furniture is covered with plastic. Everything is in order. They even swept the floors."

The next morning, at the appointed hour, five young and energetic Panamanians, under the direction of a very on-the-ball female manager, burst enthusiastically into the apartment and set about filling their moving truck with our stuff. Once their truck was full, they navigated across town to Casco Viejo, where they parked on our narrow lane and began off-loading just as energetically and cheerfully as they'd loaded up several hours earlier.

Several pieces couldn't be made to fit up the winding first-floor staircase. That didn't slow these guys down. They carried the guest-room bed, the leather Chesterfield, and the antique armoire back out onto the street. Then they hoisted each piece of oversized furniture by rope up from the sidewalk and over the second-floor balcony railing, without even a scratch or a scrape. Our nine-year-old son, Jack, watched wide-eyed.

By the time the last cardboard box was carried inside, it was dark. Our guys had been hauling and toting since eight thirty A.M., but still cheerfully, and with no encouragement, they began unwrapping the plastic from around all the furniture, then stood for instructions from me as to where to place each piece in each room. It was nearly nine P.M. when they finished.

It was our most successful overseas move ever. After years of broken mañana promises and unfulfilled expectations, this Panamanian moving company delivered everything they'd said they would and proved themselves to be all they'd represented and more.

Not every experience living overseas is a disappointment. Enough of them are, though, that the successful experiences, like this one of moving into our new home in Casco Viejo, are remembered treats. Enjoy them. Just don't expect them often.

Handling Panic

What were you thinking? You must have taken leave of your senses. Paradise? This place is no paradise. This place is a nightmare.

Take my word for it. No matter how much due diligence you've done, no matter how ready you are for the move, at some point, probably during your first year abroad, you'll wonder what in the world ever possessed you to think this "leaving home" thing was a good idea. This isn't an adventure. This is nuts.

My best advice is to wait out the panic. It will pass.

Moving to Ireland, we thought the transition would be transparent. We Americans think we know the Irish. They're just like us, aren't they? No, they're not. Wherever you decide to chase your dreams overseas, even if it's somewhere as seemingly familiar as Ireland, you're going to discover that the people living there aren't like you either, in ways that won't be apparent at first. You're going to find that life is more difficult than it was wherever you came from. More complicated. Less predictable.

We didn't choose Waterford, Ireland, for our first international move. It was chosen for us by my employers at the time. And we didn't spend an extended time in the country before we made the leap, because we didn't have time to. My husband, my daughter, and I visited for two two-week planning trips, once in July and again in September, then we arrived as full-time residents in Waterford in November.

The first couple of months living overseas is the honeymoon period. The people, the landscape, the view from your bedroom window are all new, exotic, and interesting. Nothing is habitual or cliché. You're fully occupied and engaged with learning your way around and establishing yourself. After two or three months, though, your surroundings are more familiar. You've developed habits of day-to-day living, and you're able to relax. Suddenly your new life isn't so much exotic and interesting as it is foreign and frustrating. You begin to miss the folks back home. By now you've made new friends in your new home, but your points of common interest are limited.

So it was for us when we moved to Waterford. By February, I

was sad. Indescribably sad for no reason I could identify. We were comfortable in our rental cottage on the river. Kaitlin was doing well in school. Our office was established, and our daily commute was a pleasant fifteen-minute walk into town. All was well, but I was miserable.

Then we took a trip to Nicaragua. After we spent a few days on that country's sunny southern Pacific coast, my sadness disappeared. What was going on?

The Irish winter. Though I'd traveled in Ireland for years, I'd never lived through an Irish winter. Some days the sun rises after nine A.M. and sets before four in the afternoon. In between those hours, it's gray, drizzling, overcast, and damp. After our first long winter in Waterford, we escaped to the tropics every December and returned to the Emerald Isle in early March, in time to appreciate Irish spring and summer.

In Paris, we wondered about our sanity from the start. During our first few months, my husband and I and our two children were crammed into a six-hundred-square-foot one-bedroom apartment. Our children slept on cots in a tiny mezzanine. I stored clothes in the china hutch. Lief and I shared a single Internet connection at the single desk in the corner of the single bedroom.

Twelve hundred square feet isn't a lot of space, but it's twice as much as six hundred. Perversely, our temporary stay in super-cramped rented quarters when we first arrived in Paris made the transition from Ireland to France more palatable. Instead of going straight from 5,000 square feet and five bedrooms on seven acres in County Waterford to the 1,200 square feet and three bedrooms of the apartment we eventually bought and renovated in central Paris, we went from 5,000 square feet to the 600 square feet of our interim rental to, finally, 1,200 square feet. By the time the renovation of our little apartment on the rue de Verneuil was complete and we were able to move in, the place didn't seem so little.

I've been remarking on the panic phase of a move overseas for years. Once when I mentioned the phenomenon to a friend preparing to move overseas for the first time, suggesting that he shouldn't worry about the panic when it struck, that it'd pass, my friend smiled and nodded politely, humoring me. It can be hard to imagine during the excitement of the pre-move phase, that after maybe only a couple of months in your new home, you might find yourself questioning the move altogether. My friend insisted that it wouldn't happen to him. "I've spent months researching and making my plan," Tom explained with confidence. "I understand what I'm getting into. I've thought this through from every angle, and I'm fully prepared."

A couple of years later, over drinks one night, Tom remarked, "You know, before my move, when you talked about the panic stage that everyone goes through at some point after relocating to a new country, I laughed to myself. 'Panic,' I thought. 'Why would I panic?' The idea seemed extreme and, frankly, silly.

"But, I have to tell you, it happened to me. It was maybe a year into my move to Ecuador. I realized that I was feeling out of my element and uncertain in a fundamental way. Unsure of myself and my new situation. I was experiencing a feeling that, I had to admit, could best be described as panic."

"What did you do?" I asked.

"I remembered what you'd recommended. I waited it out. I realized that I was feeling overwhelmed by the frustrations of living in the third world. I reminded myself why I'd wanted to make the move in the first place and of all the things about Ecuador that I love. There are many. After a little while, the panic passed."

Your panic phase in your new home could be a result of the weather and the seasons, as it was for us in Ireland. It could be a reaction to the trials and frustrating tribulations of life in a developing country, as it was for my friend Tom. It could be homesickness, as for another friend, Rebecca, who often, during the first year after her move from Canada to Panama, found herself sitting home alone, missing her old life so much she almost returned to Ontario to resurrect it.

Rebecca was wise enough in the end to recognize that she wasn't going to make a new life for herself in Panama overnight or without some effort. Moving to a foreign country can be especially challenging for a woman on her own. Without a husband or partner to accompany you, you may find the idea of dinner out at the café on the corner or a weekend away exploring your new surroundings intimidating, even frightening. You consider it, maybe even plan for it, but then opt for another quiet evening or weekend at home instead. If you move to another country as a single woman, you'll have to work even harder to establish yourself. Rebecca found that the secret was making one local girlfriend. That girl introduced Rebecca to her friends and to her boyfriend's friends, and soon enough, Rebecca found herself part of a whole new circle of company. Rebecca is four years on now in her new life in Panama. Does she think today about returning to Canada? Never.

No country is perfect. Every country on my list, as we've discussed, has its pluses and its minuses. The minuses eventually are going to get to you. Living high in the mountains in Panama may provide glorious views and a gentle, springlike climate, but you won't be near a real city or an international airport. You'll be living a country life among neighbors who, in this part of Panama, speak only Spanish. Sometimes the remoteness will overwhelm you.

Ecuador may offer the most affordable cost of living in the Americas today, but Ecuador is a truly third-world country. As my friend Tom discovered, life in the third world isn't for everyone.

The key to being happy in your new home, wherever you decide to make it, is to keep your perspective and your sense of humor. When doubt and frustration creep in, as they will, remind yourself of two things. First, don't make any hasty decisions. The moment of panic will pass. Second, while you're waiting for that to subside, remember why you chose this country in the first place. Was it for the beach? Then escape to the coast for a few days of relaxation beneath the palms. Was it for the super-low cost of living? Take yourself out for a nice dinner on the cheap. What do you enjoy most in your new home—the fishing, the boating, the shopping, the neighbors? Then make time to go catch some fish or to have your new friends over for an authentic home-cooked American dinner.

Think, too, about why, specifically, you're feeling uncertain about your decision. No place is perfect. Once you identify the minuses, you can figure out ways around them. If you don't like the current season, go somewhere else until it passes. If you're missing family back home, invite them to come visit. If you're not happy in the neighborhood where you've initially settled, consider another.

My point is this: If you're considering following your daydream and moving yourself and your family to foreign shores, by all means, I say, get up and go. Take the chance. But be prepared, at some time during your first year in your new home, to wonder what in the world you've done. No, this wasn't crazy, and it wasn't a mistake. Wait it out. The panic will pass. Just on the other side is the life you came to find.

So I say this: Go now. Start your new life now. Don't let any worry hold you back.

The Argentines look at it like this: "They can't take away the dance you've already danced," they like to say. When you reach very old age, don't you want to be able to say with confidence that you've danced all the way there?

Frequently Asked (and Not So Crazy) Questions

1. *If I move overseas, could I ever return to the United States?*
   Yes, of course. Living overseas, even full time, even as a legal resident of another country, affects your ability to spend time in the United States not at all. You're still an American citizen, after all. You can come and go as you please.

2. *Living overseas, would I lose my U.S. citizenship?*
   No, your residency status abroad has no effect on your U.S. citizenship. Remember, residency and citizenship are two different things (see Part I). The only way to lose your U.S. citizenship is to renounce it formally. This is a serious step that you can't take accidentally. That is, there's no chance you'd lose your U.S. citizenship without realizing it. Renouncing it requires a formal application and at least one interview with the FBI. Once your application to renounce your citizenship has been approved, you then must appear again before federal authorities to relinquish your blue passport with the eagle on the cover. The United States doesn't want to lose you as one of its citizens, for as long as you carry American citizenship, no

matter where you roam, you are obliged to report your income and earnings to Uncle Sam.

3. *Do I need a passport to retire overseas?*
   You need a passport to travel anywhere in the world outside the United States, no matter how long you intend to stay.

4. *Do I need to let the U.S. government know that I'm leaving the country?*
   No. You can register your presence in your new country with the local U.S. embassy if you like, but you are not obligated to do so.

5. *What happens if I die in a foreign country?*
   Someone should inform the local U.S. embassy and consulate. The consulate will help organize the repatriation of your remains (if that is your wish). Note, though, that the cost of repatriation of remains is expensive. If this is your wish, be sure the expense is covered as part of your international health insurance policy.

6. *What happens if I get arrested in another country?*
   When in another country—as a tourist, a resident, a retiree, a business owner, etc.—you are subject to its laws. If you are arrested for breaking one of them, get a local lawyer quickly. The U.S. consulate likely will not be able to help much, other than perhaps making a local attorney recommendation. My best advice on this point is, don't get arrested. Know the laws of the country where you're living and respect them.

7. *Do I need any vaccinations?*
   It depends on where you're going. Some countries require you to have specific vaccinations before you'll be permitted to enter. Generally speaking, to travel from the United States to the countries I feature in these pages, you would not be required to have any vaccinations. In some cases, though, you may choose to be vaccinated nevertheless. The Centers for Disease Control and Prevention (CDC) has a good section on its website discussing the question of which vaccinations might be advisable, depending on your current state of health and

where in the world you intend to spend time. Take a look: wwwnc.cdc.gov/travel/default.aspx.

8. *Can I drink the water?*

It depends on where you're going. The tap water is potable in France, for example, of course, but it tastes funny because of the chemicals it's treated with. The tap water is generally not potable in Ireland, but it is in Panama City and other parts of Panama. The easiest strategy (the one I follow) is to drink bottled water everywhere.

9. *Is it really safe?*

Yes, every country I've recommended to you in these pages is safe. That is not to say no one ever does anything he or she shouldn't do in any of these places. Nowhere in the world is 100 percent crime-free. Use your common sense. Lock the front door to your house. Don't leave the keys in your car. Don't wear flashy jewelry on the street. But in all the places I suggest you think about living, retiring, or chasing adventure overseas, don't worry about violent crime, either.

10. *Are there bugs or snakes?*

Yes, there are mosquitoes, gnats, sand flies, cockroaches, and spiders nearly everywhere. You'll find snakes in the jungle and other rural areas, including, sometimes, poisonous ones. It's easy enough, though, to educate yourself on which varieties of creepy-crawlies you might encounter in your new home once you decide where you're moving. Note that nearly every state in the United States has snakes, too.

11. *Are there earthquakes or hurricanes?*

Yes, again, depending on where you're talking about. Panama sits outside the hurricane belt, but down here in the Hub of the Americas, sometimes the earth does quake.

12. *Can I still receive my Social Security payments?*

Yes. You can even have your monthly Social Security check direct-deposited into your account in some countries. See www.ssa.gov/foreign.

13. *Will Medicare cover me living overseas?*
No. No exceptions. You need to make another plan for covering your medical expenses overseas. See Part I.

14. *Will my computer work in another country? My cell phone?*
Your laptop computer will work anywhere, as all laptop AC adapters should be dual current, meaning they should work with 110V and 220V electrical systems. You may need a plug adapter to be able to plug your computer cord into the outlet, depending on where you're going to be spending time. Most of Central and South America use the U.S.-type plug. In Europe, Asia, and Argentina, you'll need a plug adapter. You can find adapter sets in shops in most international airports.
Your cell phone may or may not work. First, find out if your current carrier has coverage where you're traveling. Second, check with your carrier to find out if your account allows roaming in the country where you're going. In the long term, you'll want a local cell phone.

15. *Can I drive on my U.S. driver's license?*
Yes, typically for the first thirty days to one year that you're resident in a new country. After this time, most countries require you either to qualify for a local driver's license or to have your U.S. license validated locally.

16. *Do I really need to learn the local language?*
No. You could get by in most places I've written about in these pages speaking English only. I don't recommend it.

17. *Is there Burger King?*
It depends on where you're thinking about retiring. The sorry truth, however, is that, yes, fast food has gone global. You can buy Coca-Cola almost anywhere on earth, and McDonald's et al. are to be found except in the most remote regions of the planet.

18. *Can I get a job?*
Probably not. To work in a foreign country, you'll need a work visa. This is not easily obtained unless you're sponsored

for a job by an international employer and relocated to the country with their help. You can, though, start your own business in many places in the world. Easiest is a laptop-based enterprise.

19. *Can I vote in local elections?*
No, not as a foreign resident. To vote in local government elections, you'd have to become a citizen of the country. Again, remember, residency is not the same as citizenship.

20. *Will my U.S. credit and debit cards work overseas?*
Yes, they should. Before you use them, though, research what fees you'll be charged. Some credit card companies impose such onerous fees when their cards are used in foreign countries that it can be worth switching to another group before you move.

21. *How will my friends and family be able to stay in touch with me?*
Email, Skype, WhatsApp, FaceTime, etc. The Internet age has made it possible to be anywhere in the world and still communicate with friends and family elsewhere on a daily basis. Skype-to-Skype communication is free.

22. *Can I bring my car with me?*
Yes. However, as I explain in Part IV, this isn't necessarily a good idea.

23. *Can my children attend school in another country? Will it hurt their chances to gain acceptance to a U.S. university?*
Your children could attend school almost anywhere in the world, although in some cases your residency status may be an issue; that is, it may be necessary to establish legal residency to enroll your children in school. In fact, attending school overseas and, certainly, graduating with an International Baccalaureate (IB) degree is an advantage when it comes time to apply for college. An IB degree is well respected. For a list of schools around the world offering the IB course of study, take a look at this website: www.ibo.org.

24. *How much does it cost to move overseas?*

How long is a piece of string? If you pack up a couple of suit-cases and head on out, it could cost you as little as your plane ticket. If you're moving from Arizona to Mexico, the cost of your move could be tolls and a few tanks of gas. However, if you want to establish formal residency in a country, you should expect it to cost several thousand dollars per family member, between attorney and government fees. Figure $10,000 to ship your household goods, depending on how much you have and where you're shipping your stuff. The real cost of your move will be the research and travel involved if you have a long list of countries to check out.

25. *Can I continue to vote in U.S. elections from overseas? Does my vote count for less?*

Yes, you can still vote. Go to www.overseasvotefoundation.org /vote/home.htm to learn more about how to vote in U.S. elections while living overseas. And no, your vote doesn't count for any less. One vote is one vote, no matter where it's cast.

CONCLUSION

TEN THINGS LEARNED IN TWENTY YEARS AS AN AMERICAN ABROAD

The experiences of my past two decades as an American abroad have taught me two things primarily.

First, you can't spreadsheet a new life in paradise. Yes, as you consider your options, you want to review detailed budgets for the countries that interest you, as we've done in these pages. You want to understand the local tax rates and the average temperatures by season. This research and planning is important. But once you've carried it out, set it all aside. Let your heart take over.

A longtime friend, Jeff, a Brit living now in Nicaragua, says that people ask him all the time why he chose that country over Costa Rica. "There are quantifiable explanations, of course," Jeff says. "The cost of living in Nicaragua is lower than that in Costa Rica, for example. And Nicaragua has a program of special benefits, tax breaks, etc. for foreign retirees that's very competitive.

"But those aren't the reasons I recommend Nicaragua over its neighbor to the south to anyone who asks or why I chose to focus my time and attention in Nicaragua years ago, when I could as easily have based myself in Costa Rica. Nicaragua simply appealed to me more," Jeff explains, "for reasons that I have trouble explaining."

I know what Jeff means. I visited Costa Rica for the first time in the mid-1980s. I've returned dozens of times since. The country's

Pacific coast is beautiful, as is its mountainous interior. Great surfing, great bird-watching, great boating, great fishing . . . Costa Rica has all these things. When I began spending time in this country, it was also very affordable and boasted the world's premier foreign retiree program. But still, I didn't get it. I could list out the advantages and appeals of living in Costa Rica, but I couldn't make myself want to live there.

Then, a few years later, I traveled to Nicaragua. I knew within a few hours of wandering around colonial Granada that this was a place I wanted to return to. This was a place I could call home, for visiting it for the first time felt like coming home.

The two countries have many things in common, and Nicaragua has the specter of the Sandinistas hanging over it. Still, it was Nicaragua, not Costa Rica, that captured my heart. I was completely infatuated by this little country with such a troubled past, and I remain so. Every visit, I'm won over again. Everywhere I travel in Nicaragua, I find something that pleases me—the red-tile roofs and blue-and-white church steeples of colonial Granada . . . the glass-still surface of crater lake Apoyo as it appears from the deck of my little house on the mountainside . . . the barefoot children playing and laughing in Granada's central plaza . . . the sounds of the horses' hooves as they clip-clop their carriages along Granada's cobblestoned streets.

These things can't be quantified. You can't plug "classic colonial architecture" into a formula in a spreadsheet. But these can be the things that matter most. How will you know where in the world you should think about spending your time and your money? You'll just know. The French speak of the *coup de coeur*, the blow to your heart you feel at certain times in your life—when, say, shopping for a new house. It's the sudden certainty that this place is it, this place is right. I'm a big believer in the importance of the *coup de coeur* when shopping for a new country as well.

So while we've been approaching this "how to live overseas" question scientifically, making lists and drawing comparisons, in the end, the decision of where to launch your new life overseas is at least as emotional as it is intellectual or financial, for a place can make perfect sense on paper but appeal not at all in person. That's why at some point in your research process, you've got to get on a plane. Do the soul-searching to understand what you're looking for in your new life in retirement overseas. Identify the pluses and the minuses of the world's most appealing overseas havens, as we did in Part III. Identify the two or three or four countries that could be the overseas Shangri-la you seek. Then go to visit. Plan an extended stay in each country you think might work for you—if possible, through the least-agreeable time of year: the hurricane season, the rainy season, the peak tourist season, or the off-season, after all the tourists have gone home and nearly every shop, café, and restaurant in town has shut its doors until they return.

No amount of Internet research, reading, or planning can substitute for traveling around a place yourself. You've got to walk the streets, watch the sunsets, and meet the people. And when you do, listen to your gut. Sometimes you'll know within twenty-four hours of arriving in a country. If you walk out on the street in a new place and feel safe, welcome, and comfortable, then that place could be for you. If you don't, don't hesitate to move on. It's a big wonderful world full of options for a life of adventure and fun.

Here's the second most valuable thing I've learned in my years as an American abroad: You've got to show up. Woody Allen once said that this is 80 percent of life.

Do your research, make your plans, then take the leap. Don't spend your best and healthiest years analyzing and planning. These are years of your life that you'll never recover. I've met many people who've been thinking for years about living or retiring overseas. They can tell you how to get a visa, where to open a bank account, how much to budget for rent, and the per-square-foot price of buying a home in a dozen different countries. Still, they're deliberating, weighing the options, not quite sure that the time is right. To these people, every one, I've said, Just do it. Pack your bags and go for it. What's the worst thing that could happen?

Years ago at a conference in the Dominican Republic I met an American from Tennessee who explained that he had been researching opportunities in that country for two years.

"I'm convinced the Dominican Republic is a place I want to be," he told me, "but I'm just not sure the timing is right."

"Have you considered other options?" I asked.

"Well, before I started looking closely at the Dominican Republic, I researched Costa Rica for four years."

"What did you end up doing there?"

"Oh, I never did anything. After four years of looking, prices had risen so high that I figured it no longer made sense."

"Ah, well, that happens," I offered.

The truth is, it happens a lot. I have business associates who follow a strategy they refer to as "Ready, fire, aim." I think it works for life, too. That is to say, as our friend and thirty-year retiree overseas Paul puts it, "You can plan to retire overseas . . . or you can retire overseas and then make some plans."

Carry out your due diligence. But realize that, all the while you're researching, your life is passing. That gentleman from Tennessee was so worried that another, better option might come along that he could never bring himself to carry through with any one particular choice. He was a smart guy, but he continually second-guessed himself, his thinking, the timing, and the options. He kept researching and investigating and scouting, trying to identify the right time to move and the best place to go.

At another conference, this one in Panama, I met another would-be overseas retiree, Anya, who approached me to ask my thoughts on Uruguay. It's a safe, welcoming, affordable country, I replied. "Is that where you're thinking of living?" I asked. Anya wasn't sure. She and her husband were deliberating, debating, considering many options.

"My advice," I finally said, speaking frankly, "is to get on a plane. Go to Uruguay, if that's a place that has your attention, and see what you think."

I had an email from Anya recently. "When we spoke at the conference," she wrote, "you asked that I follow up with you to let you know what my husband and I finally decided to do. After more consideration, we agreed that Uruguay wasn't for us. I am happy to report, though, that we've made another plan. In fact, we've already begun following through on it. We've purchased five acres of beautiful land in Ecuador, including a house for renovation. We made the trip to see it, and it was love at first sight. We knew right away that this was the right thing for us. Not only is this place beautiful, but here, in Ecuador, we feel secure. We truly will be able to afford to live on my husband's Social Security and be comfortable indefinitely."

There is no right time, and there is no best place. But there is a place that's best for you right now. You just need to get off your derriere and go find it.

On the eve of our third international move, a friend asked, "Why Panama? Why now?" I think she was looking for a clear-cut response that would have made the case for why right now is the right time and for why Panama is the best place, and I fear I likely disappointed her. Panama makes a lot of sense for a lot of reasons, but is it the one and only best place for me or you or anyone thinking about spending time or money right now? Who could answer that question? Not even me—the expert.

Sometimes life takes you by the collar and pulls you along. Other times it waits for you to create your own momentum. I say again, there is no best opportunity and there is no right time. So here's what you do: You do something right now. If your life's circumstances aren't conspiring to pull you in the direction of new horizons, get yourself up to start chasing them.

What else have I learned after two decades as an American living, investing, and chasing adventure overseas?

1. Patience . . . the Kind of Patience You Learn Doing Time . . .

I stood recently at the counter of a small grocery shop in Panama City watching as the young man on the other side of the counter tried to tally up my purchases. One item I'd presented was missing a price tag, so the young man walked from behind the counter to the back of the shop to find a matching item that did show a price. Several minutes later he returned.

When he looked down to enter the amount into his adding machine (the shop didn't have a cash register), he noticed that it was out of paper. So he walked from behind the counter again, this time disappearing behind the door to the left. Several minutes later, he returned with a roll of adding machine paper. As he began to replace the paper in his machine, his phone rang, so he laid the roll of paper on the counter to answer it. Several minutes later, he finished his conversation and picked up the roll of paper again. Several minutes after that, he'd succeeded in getting the paper installed in the machine.

After adding up my few purchases, he reached beneath the counter for a bag to put the groceries in but found he was out of bags, so he came out from behind the counter and disappeared again behind the door to the left. Several minutes later, he returned with a single plastic bag. Four other customers stood in line behind me. I guess he was counting on their not wanting bags.

My items placed in the plastic bag, the young man looked up at me. "That's $12.65," he told me in Spanish. I handed him a ten and a five. The young man reached beneath the counter for the cigar box where he kept his change. No singles. He called out to the young woman stocking shelves, who finished what she was doing, then joined the young man behind the counter and counted out change for me from her apron pocket.

This is the kind of scene that plays out all day long every day all across the developing world. You muster the patience to take it in stride. Or you move on from the developing world.

2. To Embrace Ambiguity . . .

Will the corner grocer open his shop at nine A.M., as his sign indicates, or will he open later or at all? Will the lady behind the counter in the immigration office accept my prepared dossier or request additional paperwork not indicated in any of my four previous conversations with her? Will the banker cash my check or question the signature (as happens for me with bankers in Panama City a couple of times every month)?

Will the car in front of mine turn right from the right-hand turn lane we're both in or will he turn left across two lanes of traffic? Will the deliveryman show up on Thursday as promised? Sometime this week? Or any given Thursday next month? Will the waitress return with my order?

I've come to see these as philosophical rather than practical questions and have trained myself not to be surprised when the answer is, as it often is, contrary to expectations.

3. Not to Mind Not Understanding What's Going on Around Me . . .

Why is that work crew digging another hole in the middle of that street? They dug a hole in that same spot and then covered it over last week. Why dig another one and why do it now, during morning rush-hour traffic? Why has the government changed such and such national holiday from Friday to Monday without warning or explanation (as happened recently in Panama)? Why does the Internet go out every time it rains? Why is the electricity out again, and when will it be restored?

If you need actual answers to those kinds of questions, you'll find life in the developing world a constant challenge.

4. Not to Be Bothered by Things That Don't Matter . . .

See above.

5. To Savor the Nutella Moments . . .

The frustrations and challenges of living in a foreign country, especially in the developing world, are many, but so are the moments of extraordinary discovery and delight. Seeing the look of unadulterated pleasure on my five-year-old son's face the first time he tried a Nutella crepe in Paris was one. As were celebrating my daughter's sixteenth birthday at a café on the Left Bank of the Seine with a view of the Louvre . . . the scene of white sheep in rolling green fields outside my bedroom window in Ireland all those years . . . the view of the long line of ships awaiting their turn for passage through the Panama Canal that I saw from my bedroom window every morning in Panama City . . . and watching my children learn to ride horseback in the field behind our home in County Waterford . . .

6. To Let Go . . .

My mother helped me to pack up my house in Baltimore in advance of my move from the States to Ireland years ago. Standing on a step stool in front of an open kitchen cabinet, she asked,

"What do you want to do with all this?" I glanced over and told her to put everything in the cabinet into a box and then to take it home with her. "But all your teas and your spices!" she replied. "You can't just give all of this away!"

To make the move from Baltimore to Waterford, I had to clear out a three-bedroom house, a basement, an attic, and a two-car garage. That required a lot of letting go. At the time, it seemed hard to give so much away. Now I smile at the thought that a reluctance to part with the paraphernalia of my life to that point could have stood in the way of launching the new life I've enjoyed all these years since.

7. To Bloom Where I've Planted Myself . . .

Ireland was cold, drizzly, and gray more days than it wasn't, and Waterford, where we were based our seven years in Ireland, was a backwater, a blue-collar workingman's town. Panama City, where we lived nine years, is hot and humid every day of every year. It's also a boomtown, meaning congestion, chaos, and crazy traffic.

In Ireland I could have complained that I missed sunshine and the trappings of a bigger city, as sometimes I did, and in Panama City I could have complained about the tumult, as, I also admit, sometimes I did. Then I reminded myself of the big-picture reasons why I was where I was. Ireland was the best place for me and my family when we were there, the weather and the local economy notwithstanding. The same was true for Panama City when we were living there full time, building our Live and Invest Overseas business and raising our son. We've made all of our international moves to date for reasons that made sense at the time. When those agendas were no longer our priorities, we regrouped and made a new plan.

8. To Downsize on the Fly . . .

I began learning about letting go that afternoon with my mom in my Baltimore kitchen. My graduate lesson in downsizing came in Paris. We relocated with two children from a 5,000-square-foot house in Waterford to a 1,200-square-foot apartment in the City of Light. I stored my son's clothes in the china hutch in the tiny dining room and his toys and games under his bed. My husband and I shared a single desk when we worked at home, as we often did, and the four of us ate dinner each night at an undersized table that was like something out of *Alice's Adventures in Wonderland.*

And I wouldn't trade a single day in Paris or a single memory of our years there when both our children were young for any number of additional square feet of living space.

9. To Ask for Help . . .

I'm a resourceful, self-reliant, type-A American woman. I can take care of myself. However, living overseas all these years, I've learned that sometimes life is easier and more fun when I don't. In Panama we were able to afford a full-time maid. It was a little luxury that we aren't able to afford everywhere, but when we can, I indulge.

10. To Abandon Any Idea I Ever Had About "Normal" . . .

What's a "normal" way to celebrate a child's birthday (in Panama the piñata is key) or to shop for a Christmas tree (in Panama City ours came from a local wholesaler's refrigerated meat locker)?

More seriously, what's a normal way to raise children or to run a business? My family thought I was crazy to move my nine-year-old daughter from Baltimore to Waterford and to give birth to my second child in Ireland. They still think I'm crazy, I guess, for living and running my business in Panama. I used to worry that our lifestyle might translate down the road into years of psychotherapy for our two children. On the other hand, both of our children speak three languages fluently and have a global perspective that makes me both proud and optimistic about their future prospects. Whatever life throws at them, they'll be fine. Not normal, maybe, but fine.

"But . . . but . . . but . . ." you may be thinking. But what? What's holding you back? You're worried you can't afford it? I've shown you that you could live well in Cuenca, Ecuador, on less than $700 per month or in Chiang Mai, Thailand, on as little as $1,300 per month. Perhaps you're worried it'll be a lot of hassle and work. You're right. It will be. It's easier to stay put and do nothing. But where would that leave you at the end of the day? What stories would you have to tell? What adventures to remember? Maybe you don't like the idea of moving far from your children or grandchildren. Then don't. Try Panama or Mexico. A new life in either of these countries could put you no farther from your loved ones than a move to Oregon, say, or Southern California might. You (and they) could even drive to Mexico for visits.

Perhaps you're generally scared to death. What are you afraid of? That your new life won't work out as you hope and expect? So what? You could always return home. Or move on. Again, there's no right place, and trying different places on for size is part of the fun. For many, including Lief and me, that *is* the fun.

On the other hand, maybe you're not worried that your plans for a new life overseas might fail—maybe you're worried they'll succeed. Where would that leave you? I can't imagine. But you can.

You're not too old, and you're not too young. Your children, your parents, your family, your friends? None of them are a reason not to make the move you're dreaming about. Get up and get going right now. Your biggest regret, I promise you, will be that you didn't get going at this sooner.

STARTER BUDGETS FOR YOUR NEW LIFE OVERSEAS

How much will it cost you to live in each of the destinations I've highlighted in these pages?

I have no idea.

That's the only honest answer I have when asked about the cost of living anywhere, because in many ways, as I've tried to explain, cost of living is controllable. Your monthly expenses are a function not only of where you're living, but also, and sometimes more important, of how you're living.

That disclaimer offered, following are what I think of as starter budgets for the overseas havens I've identified as most tempting for the would-be expat, retiree, or entrepreneur. I say these are starter budgets because they include only the basic costs you'll incur. For the amount suggested in each case, you could live comfortably, but for sure, in each case, you could also spend more to live . . . well, more comfortably.

These budgets are for a couple. The cost of living for a couple is not much greater than that for a single. If you're moving on your own, reduce the costs of groceries, transportation, and entertainment accordingly. Your utility and housing costs, though, would be unchanged.

I recommend that you rent in your new home at least at first and perhaps long term; thus each budget includes a typical cost for renting a two-bedroom apartment or house (as appropriate for the destination). If you decide to buy a place of your own, address that as a separate budget.

While I continue to recommend renting as a good way to get started living wherever you decide you'd like to live, it's worth noting a current opportunity. No matter where you move, housing will likely be your biggest monthly expense. As we go to press, the U.S. dollar is relatively strong against most world currencies. This means you could buy your own apartment or home in the country where you want to live at today's strong dollar values. This way you'd not only lock in the current currency advantage but, at the same time, reduce your housing expense to a monthly HOA fee and property taxes, both typically very small amounts in the places I'm recommending.

My budget costs are referenced in the local currencies. In the first edition of this book, I converted costs from the local currency to U.S. dollars for every destination where the currency is something other than the dollar. That, I realize now, was a mistake. Currencies move, in some cases daily. If I convert today's local currency figures to U.S. dollars at today's exchange rate, what good is that to you six months from now? Plus, I figure you can use an online currency converter as well as I can. Here's the one I like best: www.xe.com.

Finally, note that your cost of living anywhere will be higher at first and decrease over time. This has been true of us everywhere we've lived. Even now, after years of experience in Paris, my husband, Lief, and I continue to find new and more affordable options for everything from a scoop of ice cream to roast chicken, dry cleaning, and a glass of champagne, all items we've purchased in the past week. Nothing makes Lief happier than finding a new, cheaper place to source something I'm in the regular market to buy.

BELIZE (in Belize dollars)

	Ambergris Caye		San Ignacio	
Rent	2,400	Median cost for an unfurnished, two-bedroom, comfortable apartment of about 750–800 square feet in a desirable part of town.	1,200	Unfurnished, two-bedroom, modern house in town. If you're willing to live in a more local-standard home, you could cut this in half. If you're renting within a gated community, you might need to spend more.
Transportation	150	Allowing for a golf cart or water taxi per day.	400	You'll need a car in San Ignacio; expect to spend this much per month on gas and maintenance.
Gas	N/A	Everything here is electric.	15	For cooking.
Electricity	300	With air-conditioning.	300	With air-conditioning (cut this figure in half if you forgo it).
Water	50		50	
Telephone	150		90	
Internet	160	Bundled with cable.	149	For 4 Mbps; if you can live with just 2 Mbps, you could spend only $89.
Cable TV	Incl.	Bundled with Internet.	46	
Groceries	600	Basic items for a couple.	420	Basic items for a couple.
Entertainment	530	Social outing: $50 per person; dinner and drinks for two: $100; drinks for two: $10.	320	Social outing: $30 per person; dinner and drinks for two: $40–$50; drinks for two: $10.
TOTAL Belize dollars, $	4,340		2,990	
Exchange Rate	2		2	
U.S. dollars	$2,170.00		$1,495.00	

COLOMBIA (in Colombian pesos)

	Medellín	
Rent	3,000,000	Unfurnished, two-bedroom, comfortable apartment in El Poblado or other expat-popular neighborhood.
Transportation	255,000	For metro and taxi use.
Gas	Incl.	Most long-term rentals would include utilities; if not, budget for about $266,000 a month.
Electricity	Incl.	
Water	Incl.	
Telephone	246,000	Bundled with Internet and cable.
Internet	Incl.	
Cable TV	Incl.	
Groceries	1,300,000	Basic items for a couple.
Entertainment	696,000	Movie tickets: $13,000 per ticket; dinner and drinks for two: $55,000–$200,000; drinks for two: $20,000.
TOTAL Colombian pesos, $	5,497,000	
Exchange Rate	3,000	
U.S. dollars	$1,832.00	

DOMINICAN REPUBLIC (in DR pesos)

	Las Terrenas	
Rent	36,500	Unfurnished, two-bedroom, comfortable apartment near the beach.
Transportation	1,375	For taxis and motos in and around town.
Gas	330	For cooking and hot water.
Electricity	5,000	With air-conditioning.
Water	230	
Telephone	2,200	Bundled with Internet and cable; highest number of cable channels.
Internet	Incl.	
Cable TV	Incl.	
Groceries	18,000	Basic items for a couple.
Entertainment	11,025	Social outing: $825 per person; dinner and drinks for two: $1,750; drinks for two: $400.
TOTAL DR pesos, $	74,660	
Exchange rate	47	
U.S. dollars	$1,588.51	

ECUADOR (in U.S. dollars)	
	Cuenca
Rent	550
Transportation	40
Gas	5
Electricity	30
Water	10
Telephone	20
Internet	35
Cable TV	25
Groceries	240
Entertainment	180
U.S. dollars	$1,135.00

FRANCE (in euros)

	Languedoc		Paris	
Rent	550	Unfurnished, two-bedroom, comfortable apartment of 750–800 square feet in a desirable part of town.	1,600	Unfurnished, two-bedroom, comfortable apartment of 750–800 square feet in a central arrondissement.
Transportation	40	For a bus pass and occasional taxis. 10-trip bus pass: €11 (Saint-Chinian to Béziers); taxi fare approx. €2/km (to Béziers would cost about €40).	130	Monthly Métro/bus pass (€65) for two. Add another €80 to account for a couple of short taxi rides per week; add €29 a year for a Vélib' bike subscription.
Gas	150	Bundled with electricity and water and garbage collection.	35	Bundled with electricity and water.
Electricity	Incl.		40	With air-conditioning.
Water	Incl.		Incl.	Included in HOA fees.
Telephone	25	Bundled with Internet and TV (240 channels; French and international programs).	30	Bundled with Internet and TV.
Internet	Incl.		Incl.	
Cable TV	Incl.		Incl.	
Groceries	350	Basic items for a couple.	600	Basic items for a couple.
Entertainment	240	Movie tickets: €7–€8 per ticket; dinner and drinks for two: €24–€60; drinks for two: €7.	300	Movie tickets: €7.20–€14.70 per ticket; dinner and drinks for two: €25–€75; drinks for two: €10.
TOTAL euros, €	1,355		2,735	
Exchange Rate	0.85		0.85	
U.S. dollars	$1,594.12		$3,217.65	

ITALY (in euros)

	Abruzzo	
Rent	600	Unfurnished, two-bedroom, comfortable house of 750–800 square feet in or near a mountain town (could go as low as €200 if you shop the countryside).
Transportation	85	€20 for public transport and taxis; a one-way, intracity bus ticket is €1.20; those age 65 or older get a discounted rate of €5 day for public transport. €65 for a tank of car fuel for the month (it's very expensive in Italy).
Gas	62	Used for cooking and heating.
Electricity	30	Air-conditioning not needed.
Water	11	For a house with no land or garden; expect to pay more if you have to irrigate.
Telephone	25	Bundled with Internet.
Internet	Incl.	
Cable TV	8	€90 annual contract.
Groceries	300	Basic items for a couple.
Entertainment	158	Movie tickets: €4–€7 per ticket; dinner and drinks for two: €25; drinks for two: €6.
TOTAL euros, €	1,279	
Exchange Rate	0.85	
U.S. dollars	$1,504.71	

MALAYSIA (in ringgit)		
	Kuala Lumpur	
Rent	3,000	Unfurnished, two-bedroom, modern apartment or house of 750–800 square feet.
Transportation	400	Monthly pass for two, plus taxi rides.
Gas	40	For cooking.
Electricity	275	With air-conditioning.
Water	40	
Telephone	96	
Internet	135	
Cable TV	155	
Groceries	1,275	Basic items for a couple.
Entertainment	870	Movie tickets: RM15 per ticket; dinner and drinks for two: RM30–RM190; drinks for two: RM50.
TOTAL ringgit, RM	6,286	
Exchange Rate	4.3	
U.S. dollars	$1,461.86	

MEXICO (in Mexican pesos)

	Mazatlán		Playa del Carmen
Rent	14,330	Unfurnished, two-bedroom, comfortable apartment of 750–800 square feet in a desirable part of town near the beach.	20,000
Transportation	1,800	For taxis and buses in and around town.	1,500
Gas	270	For cooking and hot water.	270
Electricity	1,790	With air-conditioning.	2,150
Water	90		90
Telephone	630	Bundled with Internet and TV.	630
Internet	Incl.		Incl.
Cable TV	Incl.		Incl.
Groceries	3,500	Basic items for a couple.	4,000
Entertainment	4,540	Movie tickets: $40 per person; dinner and drinks for two: $540–$1,250; drinks for two: $110.	4,540
TOTAL Mexican pesos, $	26,950		33,180
Exchange Rate	18		18
U.S. dollars	**$1,497.22**		**$1,843.33**

NICARAGUA (in Nicaraguan córdobas)		
	Granada	
Rent	40,000	Two-bedroom apartment or house with pool in historic section; difficult to find unfurnished homes here.
Transportation	2,000	For taxi use and occasional bus or car rental trips; most residents walk as much as they can.
Gas	290	For cooking.
Electricity	4,000	With air-conditioning; no pool.
Water	120	
Telephone	900	
Internet	1,300	Bundled with TV.
Cable TV	n/a	
Groceries	10,000	Basic items for a couple.
Entertainment	4,900	Social outing: C$150 per person; dinner and drinks for two: C$500–C$1,000; drinks for two: C$200.
TOTAL Nicaraguan córdobas, C$	63,510	
Exchange Rate	30	
U.S. dollars	$2,117.00	

PANAMA (in U.S. dollars)

	El Valle de Antón		Panama City
Rent	800	Unfurnished, two-bedroom, comfortable apartment of 750–800 square feet in a desirable area.	1,200
Transportation	50	Bus trips and occasional taxis.	50
Gas	5	For cooking.	Incl.
Electricity	65		150
Water	8		Incl.
Telephone	70	Bundled with Internet and TV.	70
Internet	Incl.		Incl.
Cable TV	Incl.		Incl.
Groceries	500	Basic items for a couple.	700
Entertainment	178	Social outing: $7 per ticket; dinner and drinks for two: $10–$40; drinks for two: $8.	250
U.S. dollars	$1,676.00		$2,420.00

PORTUGAL (in euros)

	Algarve		Lisbon	
Rent	850	Unfurnished, two-bedroom, comfortable apartment of 750–800 square feet in a desirable area.	1,500	Unfurnished, two-bedroom, comfortable apartment of 750–800 square feet in a desirable area.
Transportation	75	Monthly pass for two, plus occasional taxis.	100	Monthly metro/bus pass for two (€35 each), plus occasional taxis.
Gas	Incl.	Bundled with electricity and water.	Incl.	Bundled with electricity and water.
Electricity	60	With air-conditioning.	90	With air-conditioning.
Water	Incl.		30	
Telephone	50	Bundled with Internet and TV.	40	Bundled with Internet and TV.
Internet	Incl.		Incl.	
Cable TV	Incl.		Incl.	
Groceries	250	Basic items for a couple.	300	Basic items for a couple.
Entertainment	280	Movie tickets: €5 per ticket; dinner and drinks for two: €25–€50; drinks for two: €15.	322	Movie tickets: €6 per ticket; dinner and drinks for two: €25–€50; drinks for two: €20.
TOTAL euros, €	1,565		2,382	
Exchange Rate	0.85		0.85	
U.S. dollars	$1,841.18		$2,802.35	

THAILAND (in Thai baht)

	Chiang Mai	
Rent	15,000	Unfurnished, two-bedroom, modern apartment or house of 750–800 square feet in a desirable location.
Transportation	3,500	Using tuk-tuks, samlors, and taxis.
Gas	n/a	
Electricity	2,500	With air-conditioning.
Water	150	
Telephone	600	
Internet	900	
Cable TV	900	
Groceries	11,000	Basic items for a couple.
Entertainment	9,200	Movie tickets: ฿100 per ticket; dinner and drinks for two: ฿1,000–฿1,500; drinks for two: ฿500.
TOTAL baht, ฿	43,750	
Exchange Rate	33.5	
U.S. dollars	$1,305.97	

URUGUAY (in Uruguayan pesos)	
	La Barra
Rent	17,000
Transportation	1,000
Gas	1,500
Electricity	3,000
Water	300
Telephone	600
Internet	1,500
Cable TV	600
Groceries	7,500
Entertainment	5,000
TOTAL Uruguayan pesos, $U	38,000
Exchange Rate	28
U.S. dollars	$1,357.14

INDEX

Note: Page numbers in parentheses indicate noncontiguous references. Page numbers in **bold** indicate starter budget charts.